A Revolution
in Manufacturing:
The SMED System

Shigeo Shingo

A Revolution in Manufacturing: The SMED System

SHIGEO SHINGO

Translated by
Andrew P. Dillon

Preface by Norman Bodek

Productivity Press
Portland, Oregon

Originally published as *Shinguru Dandori*, copyright © 1983 by the Japan Management Association, Tokyo.

English translation copyright © 1985 by Productivity Press, a division of Productivity, Inc.

Productivity Press
P.O. Box 13390
Portland, OR 97213-0390
Telephone: (503) 235-0600
Telefax: (503) 235-0909
E-mail: service@ppress.com

Library of Congress Catalog Card Number: 84-61450
ISBN: 0-915299-03-8

Cover design by Russell Funkhauser
Printed and bound by BookCrafters
Printed in the United States of America

02 01 00 99 98 97 96   20 19 18 17 16

Contents

v

Publisher's Preface

In fifty years, when we look back on the leaders of the industrial revolution, I am certain that the name of Shigeo Shingo will rank with those of Henry Ford, Frederick Taylor, Eli Whitney, Robert Fulton, Cyrus McCormick, Thomas Edison, and others. The ideas in this book truly represent "A Revolution in Manufacturing." The essence of Mr. Shingo's message is that you *can* design a manufacturing system that is inherently responsive to change. Setup delays, EOQ's, job shop versus batch, large lots versus small lots — all these are really problems of the past. Mr. Shingo has proven that setups which formerly took days can be done in a few minutes; lead times of a month and a half can be reduced to well under a week; work-in-process inventories can be reduced by 90%. "It can't be done" is a phrase that no longer applies.

When I first met Mr. Shingo, I didn't understand the enormous power of his teaching. I thought that setup was only a small aspect of the manufacturing process. But now I realize that reducing setup time is actually the key to reducing bottlenecks, lowering costs, and improving the quality of your products. Setups are, from this perspective, the most critical element of the process.

Many people even today think that their kind of manufacturing is "different," and that Mr. Shingo's principles do not apply to them. "I don't have punch presses," says one manager. "It might apply to the auto industry, but not to the metal cutting industry." This is simply wrong thinking. Mr. Shingo's principles apply to any manufacturing context.

I recently had a conversation with an IE manager in Iowa who has one cutting machine with 300 bolts to turn between changeovers. Once he understands *why* he uses those bolts, once he understands the important difference between internal and external setup time, then *how* to make change will come to him and his company. And it will make a vital difference.

Setup is the key to changing manufacturing. It is the key to moving toward future technologies — robotics and advanced automation.

In 1981, I was leading my second industrial study mission to Japan. After an enlightening visit to Nippondenso, where we were introduced to a number of concepts on how to balance the line in a "Just-In-Time" environment, I received a small pamphlet promoting Mr. Shingo's book *Study of the 'Toyota' Production System*. One of the executives accompanying me on the trip was Jack Warne, then President of Omark Industries.

We were both excited to find something in English on the Toyota system. Jack subsequently ordered 500 copies of the book and gave one to almost every manager at Omark. Through study groups at Omark, the principles expounded by Mr. Shingo came to permeate the company. Now setups that used to take four hours are completed in less than three minutes. Lead times have dropped from forty-seven days to three. Inventory has been significantly reduced. Productivity has increased dramatically. Quality has improved, while quality costs have diminished. Vast amounts of factory floor space have been freed for new products.

The importance of the experience in Japan was to see with our own eyes the simplicity and practicality of these principles in action. After seeing a punch press changed in two minutes, we could no longer say, "But that can't be done."

Mr. Shingo teaches us that "despite a tendency to assume that something can't be done, we find an unexpectedly large number of possibilities when we give some thought to how it might be possible to do it." He helps us unlock our minds. He helps us discover *why* things are done so that we may change *how* things are done.

According to a spokesperson at one company that has adopted the SMED system, "It used to be that whenever a suggestion was made, somebody would say that it wouldn't work for such-and-such a reason, or that such-and-such a problem makes it impossible. Most of what we heard were reasons why things couldn't be done, and a lot of proposals died in the discussion stage. Since the success of SMED, though, there's a new determination to come up with ways to make them work; the emphasis is on putting ideas into practice."

Mr. Shingo also teaches us that "machines can be idle, workers must not be." In the last five years, I have visited over a hundred Japanese factories, and I can't remember seeing a single person idle watching a machine processing. In all my visits to American factories, on the other hand, I can't remember *not* seeing a person idly watching a machine. Mr. Shingo states that manpower generally costs more than machines, and this is why the Japanese don't have people idle. I believe the Toyota system embodies the idea that every worker is creatively and actively involved in the manufacturing process.

This book is going to change a lot of your thinking. Just a few of the ideas that Mr. Shingo presents should be enough to whet your appetite:

- "Managers who are responsible for production must recognize that the proper strategy is to make what can be sold . . . SMED makes it possible to respond quickly to fluctuations in demand, and it creates the necessary conditions for lead time reductions. The time has come to bid farewell to the long-standing myths of anticipatory production and large-lot production. We must also recognize that flexible production can come about only through SMED."

- "Construct a production system that can respond without wastefulness to market change and that, moreover, by its very nature reduces costs."

- "The purpose of measures resting on the twin cornerstones of 'Just-In-Time' production and automation with worker involvement is to manufacture as inexpensively as possible only goods that will sell, and to manufacture them only when they will sell quickly."

- "Like priming powder, the effects of this example touched off other improvement activities throughout the company."

- "Setup changes should allow defect-free products to be produced from the very start. It makes no sense to speed up a setup operation without knowing when quality products can be turned out."

- "After SMED improvements are completed, the next challenge is OTED (One-Touch Exchange of Die), that is, making setup changes in less than a minute."

- "The ideal setup change is no change at all. As long as setup changes are necessary, however, they should be designed to be performed with a 'one-touch' motion."

- "It is important to cut setup times, diminish lot sizes, and even loads simultaneously; no more than partial success can be expected with shortened setup times alone."

- "If you can't figure out how to do something, talk it over with your machines."

The book is filled with enough ideas to make you reconsider all the *why's* of how you manufacture. It will blow away all of the misconceptions that have prevented you from changing in the past. Once you begin to apply these principles, you will find that you can never go back to "business as usual."

This book can mark the beginning of a journey for you into a whole new world of how goods are manufactured. More importantly, it will give you, the American manager, a very quick lesson on how to catch up with the Japanese in quality. Within these pages are fundamentals that will allow you to close the gap that currently exists; the revolution in manufacturing belongs in your factory.

I would like to thank several people for making this book possible. First I must thank Shigeo Shingo himself, for selecting Productivity, Inc. as his American publisher. We are proud and honored to work with him. I would also like to thank the Japan Management Association, especially Kazuya Uchiyama, for providing us with helpful materials. Andrew P. Dillon, with the assistance of E. Yamaguchi, rendered a fine translation. Patricia Slote supervised the editorial and production staff, and designed the interior of the book. David Perlstein and Nancy Macmillan edited the manuscript, Cheryl Berling proofread the text, Russ Funkhouser designed the cover, and Rudra Press prepared the artwork and assisted in crucial stages of final production (special thanks to Julie Wright, Nanette Redmond, and Laura Santi for their help). Marie Kascus prepared the index. I thank them all. I also wish to thank Swami Chetanananda for his inspirational guidance.

Norman Bodek

Foreword

I was very impressed during a recent visit to the U.S. by the fact that many American industries are interested in Japanese production systems — in particular, Just-In-Time (JIT) and Total Quality Control (TQC) — and are attempting to integrate these systems into their operations.

It goes without saying that JIT is very effective in industrial management, but JIT is an end, not a means. Without understanding the practical methods and techniques that form its core, JIT has no meaning in and of itself.

I firmly believe that the SMED system is the most effective method for achieving Just-In-Time production.

In my experience, most people do not believe that a four-hour setup time can be reduced to only three minutes. In fact, when presented with this claim, most people will maintain that it is impossible. The SMED system, however, contains three essential components that allow the "impossible" to become possible:

- A basic way of thinking about production

- A realistic system

- A practical method

A complete understanding of all three facets of SMED will make it possible for virtually anyone to apply the SMED system, with fruitful results, to any industrial setting.

I am confident that the SMED system will be of great help in revolutionizing existing production systems, and sincerely hope that you will not only come to understand the essence of SMED, but will be able to utilize it effectively in your workplace.

Introduction

When I ask about the major difficulties encountered in the many factories I visit, the response is usually brief: diversified, low-volume production. When I dig a little deeper and inquire why diversified, low-volume production constitutes a problem, the main difficulty generally turns out to be the setup operations required — calibrations, switching of tools or dies, etc. Frequent setups are necessary to produce a variety of goods in small lots.

Even if their number cannot be reduced, however, the setup time itself can be cut down. Think of the productivity improvement that could be attained if a setup operation requiring three hours could be reduced to three minutes! This has, in fact, become possible with the implementation of single-minute setup.

Single-minute setup is popularly known as the SMED system, SMED being an acronym for Single-Minute Exchange of Die. The term refers to a theory and techniques for performing setup operations in under ten minutes, i.e., in a number of minutes expressed in a single digit. Although not every setup can literally be completed in single-digit minutes, this is the goal of the system described here, and it can be met in a surprisingly high percentage of cases. Even where it cannot, dramatic reductions in setup time are usually possible.

A host of books with such titles as *Quick Die Changes* and *The Instant Setup* has appeared recently in Japan. Japanese industrial engineers have long understood that reducing setup time is a key to developing a competitive industrial position. Most of these books, however, do not go beyond mere description of techniques. They present the know-how without explaining *why* the techniques work. These manuals are applicable as long as the examples they discuss match the situation at hand. When they do not, application is difficult.

In this book, I endeavor to present you with both practical examples and the theory behind them. Even dissimilar industries with dissimilar machines should then be able to apply the principles of SMED to their own production processes, with substantial improvements in productivity and lead time resulting.

In the following chapters, you will find:

- The conceptual stages underlying SMED

- Practical methods derived from this conceptual framework

- Illustrations of practical techniques

At this point, I would like to summarize the traditional wisdom concerning setup time improvement. It consists of three basic ideas:

- The skill required for setup changes can be acquired through practice and long-term experience.

- Large-lot production diminishes the effect of setup time and cuts down on man-hours. Combining setup operations saves setup time and leads to increased efficiency and productive capacity.

- Large-lot production brings inventory increases. Economic lots should be determined and inventory quantities regulated accordingly.

These ideas were once thought to constitute the basis for rational production policies. In fact, they conceal an important blind spot: the unspoken assumption that setup time itself cannot undergo drastic reduction. With the adoption of the SMED system, the economic-lot approach simply collapses.

Why have setup improvements not been pursued more vigorously before now? The answer is that setup procedures are usually dealt with on the spot and depend on the skills of workers on the shop floor. Managers have found refuge in the apparent rationality of the economic-lot-size concept and have not taken the trouble to pursue the matter further — chiefly, I believe, because they have been indifferent. Industrial engineers bear a special responsibility in this regard.

It has been argued forcefully in the past that diversified, low-volume production is extremely difficult and that high-volume production of fewer kinds of items is more desirable. Of course, high-volume production necessarily gives rise to inventory, which managers have traditionally regarded as a necessary evil. However, this line of thinking does not hold water. Whether production is to be diversified and low-volume, or more homogeneous and high-volume, depends on both the market (demand) and production conditions (supply).

Even when demand calls for high diversity and low volume, if several orders are combined, large lots become possible and setup frequency can be reduced. But bear in mind, this solution gives rise to excess inventory.

On the other hand, when demand calls for little diversity and high volume, the supply side can respond with numerous repetitions of small-lot production. Inventory is minimized, but the number of setup operations increases.

In this way the characteristics of demand can be separated from those of supply. Even if high-volume production is desired in order to amortize capital equipment, we must keep in mind that this is a function of demand and cannot form the basis of a theory of production (supply). Moreover, there is an unfortunate tendency to confuse high-volume production with large lot sizes, and hence to delude ourselves into thinking that because high volume is good, large lot sizes are similarly desirable. We need to recognize this problem and make clear the distinction between these two concepts.

Furthermore, while it is true that the number of setups cannot be reduced when we are engaged in diversified, small-lot production, it is still possible to reduce setup time dramatically. Consequently, even in small-lot production, the effects of setup time can be greatly diminished and inventory can be cut back significantly.

So far, we have seen that production planning as commonly practiced confuses high volume with large lots. In contrast to this approach, which assumes that excess inventory will inevitably be created, stands the concept of *confirmed production*, in which excess inventory is eliminated and small lots are produced on the basis of orders actually received.

Surely this will become the model for production planning in the future. Instead of producing goods that *ought* to sell, factories will produce only goods that have already been ordered. This idea represents a revolution in the concept of production. Indeed, I believe that the SMED system marks a turning point in the history of economic progress. What is often referred to as the Toyota Production System will be seen as the first pioneering implementation of this new concept.

It took nineteen long years to develop the SMED system. It began while I was conducting an improvement study for Toyo Industries in 1950. I realized for the first time that there are two kinds of setup operations: *internal setup* (IED, or inside exchange of die), which can be performed only when a machine is shut down, and *external setup* (OED, or outside exchange of die), which can be done while the machine is running. A new die can be attached to a press, for example, only when the press is stopped, but the bolts to attach the die can be assembled and sorted while the press is operating.

In 1957, a dramatic improvement in the setup operation for a diesel engine bed planer at Mitsubishi Heavy Industries foreshadowed an astonishing request I would receive from the Toyota Motor Company in 1969. Toyota wanted the setup time of a 1,000-ton press — which had already been reduced from four hours to an hour and a half — further reduced to three minutes! Having studied setup phenomena for many years, I was excited by this challenge and had a sudden inspiration: internal setup changes could be converted to external ones. In a flash, a whole new way of thinking dawned on me.

I mention this to illustrate a point. The SMED system is much more than a matter of technique; it is an entirely new way of thinking about production itself.

The SMED system has undergone much development in various sectors of Japanese industry, and has started to spread around the world. America's Federal-Mogul Corporation, Citrœn in France, and the H. Weidmann Company in Switzerland have all used SMED to achieve substantial productivity improvements. In any country, positive results will be obtained when the theory and techniques of SMED are understood and suitably applied.

I offer this book with the conviction that the theory, methods, and techniques of SMED, as presented herein, will contribute substantially to the world's industrial development.

Shigeo Shingo

A Revolution
in Manufacturing:
The SMED System

PART ONE
Theory and Practice
of the SMED System

Part One describes the background and theory of the SMED system, and provides concrete examples of improvement techniques. However, mere mastery of specific techniques is not enough to ensure the proper implementation of the SMED concept. Effective implementation in a wide variety of plant situations is possible only when we understand fully the whole range of theory, principles, practical methods, and concrete techniques that have evolved with SMED.

Chapter 1 explains the structure of production and the role of setup in the production process. All production is composed of *processes* and *operations*. When the basic elements of operations are analyzed, it is seen that setup operations occur at every stage in the manufacturing process.

Chapter 2 describes the nature and significance of setup operations carried out in the past and explains diversified, low-volume production. Combining diversified, small-lot production with SMED is the most effective way to achieve flexible production and maximum productivity.

Chapters 3–5 cover the center issues of this book by providing the theoretical framework and practical techniques of the SMED system. Chapter 3 shows how SMED evolved by distinguishing *internal setup*, or IED (internal exchange of die), from *external setup*, or OED (external exchange of die). The four conceptual stages of SMED are identified: first, IED and OED are not distinguished; then, IED and OED are distinguished; next, IED is converted to OED; and finally, all aspects of the setup are streamlined. In Chapter 4, practical techniques corresponding to these four stages are described. Significant improvements in setup time can be achieved at each stage of setup. Chapter 5 takes a closer look at improvements in

3

internal setup operations, stressing three areas of improvement: the implementation of parallel operations, the use of functional clamps, and the elimination of adjustments.

Chapter 6 describes the application of the SMED system to metal presses and plastic forming machines. Three types of metal presses are discussed: single-shot presses, progressive die presses, and transfer die presses. Four aspects of setup on plastic forming machines are then explored: die setup, switching resins, coolant line switching, and die preheating.

Chapter 7 completes our examination of the SMED system by looking at the effects of SMED. While shortened setup times and improved work rates are primary, other results increase a company's strategic advantage in numerous areas, including health and safety, training, costs, lead times, and inventory control.

1

The Structure of Production

A SCHEMATIC OUTLINE OF PRODUCTION

Production activities may best be understood as networks of processes and operations (*Figure 1-1*).

A *process* is a continuous flow by which raw materials are converted into finished goods. In a shaft-making operation, for example, the following sequence might be observed:

1. Store raw materials in a warehouse.
2. Transport materials to the machines.
3. Store them near the machines.
4. Process them on the machines.
5. Store the finished products near the machines.
6. Inspect the finished products.
7. Store the finished products for shipment to customers.

Although the flow would probably be more complex in a real factory, this is a valid illustration of the production process.

An *operation*, by contrast, is any action performed by man, machine, or equipment on raw materials, intermediate, or finished products. Production is a network of operations and processes, with one or more operations corresponding to each step in the process.

Upon further reflection it becomes apparent that manufacturing processes can be divided into four distinct phases:

1. *Processing*: assembly, disassembly, alteration of shape or quality.
2. *Inspection*: comparison with a standard
3. *Transportation*: change of location
4. *Storage*: a period of time during which no work, transportation, or inspection is performed on the product

5

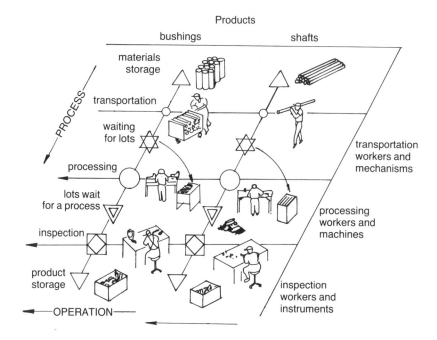

FIGURE 1-1. **Structure of Production**

The storage phase itself may be broken into four categories:

1. Storage of raw materials
2. Storage of the finished product
3. Waiting for a process: an entire lot waits because work on the previous lot has not yet been completed
4. Waiting for a lot: while the first item in a lot is being machined, the remaining items must wait to be processed in turn

The internal structure of an operation can also be analyzed as follows:

Preparation, after-adjustment. These operations are performed once, before and after each lot is processed. In this book they are referred to as setup operations.

Principal operations. Carried out for each item, these operations fall into three categories:

1. *Essential operations*: the actual machining of the material
2. *Auxiliary operations*: attaching workpieces to or removing them from machines
3. *Margin allowances*: irregularly occurring actions such as resting, drinking water, sweeping up cuttings, machinery breakdown, etc. Margin allowances can be further categorized under *fatigue, hygiene, operation* (performed only for a specific operation), and *shopwide* (performed for all operations).

Thus, there are several basic elements that combine to form operations (*Figure 1-2*).

THE RELATIONSHIP BETWEEN PROCESSES AND OPERATIONS

Each phase of the manufacturing process — work, inspection, transportation, and storage — has a corresponding operation. That is, there are work operations, inspection operations, transportation operations, and storage operations (*Figure 1-3*). Each of these operations, furthermore, has four subcategories: *setup, essential, auxiliary,* and *margin allowance*. Therefore, there are setup, essential, auxiliary, and margin allowance operations pertaining to work, inspection, transportation, and storage.

An essential operation, then, would involve, for example, the following:

- *Processing operation*: the actual cutting of a shaft

- *Inspection operation*: measuring the diameter with a micrometer

- *Transportation operation*: conveying a shaft to the next process

- *Storage operation*: storing the shaft on a rack

The same analysis applies to setup operations, whether they are processing operation setups, inspection operation setups, transportation operation setups, or storage operation setups.

Although the chief emphasis in this book will be on processing operation setups, what will be said is equally applicable to inspection, transportation and storage operations.

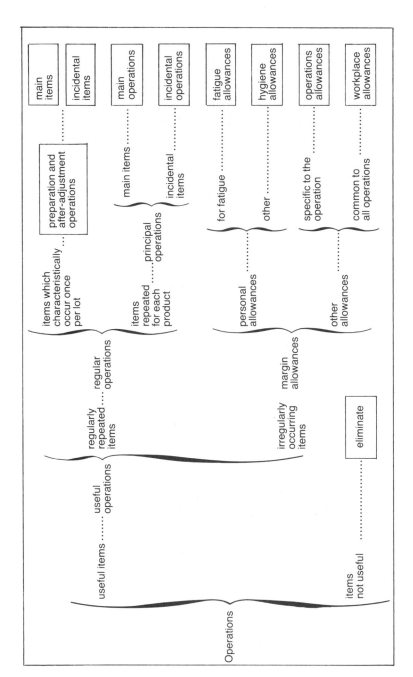

FIGURE 1-2. The Structure of Operations

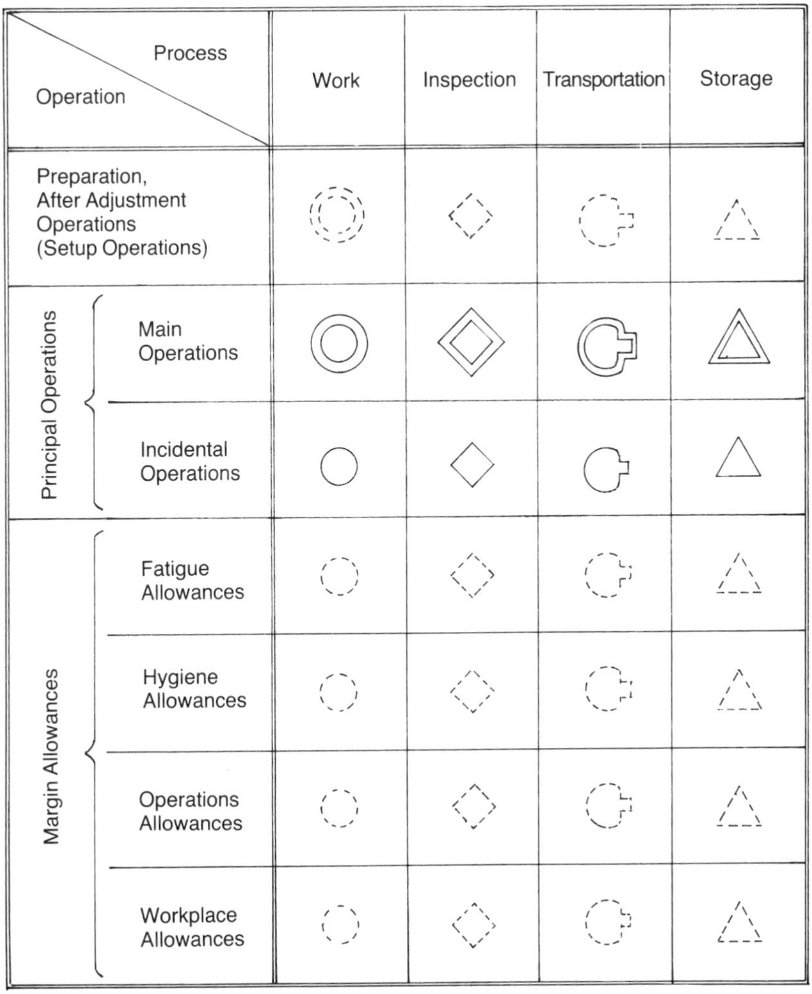

Process / Operation	Work	Inspection	Transportation	Storage
Preparation, After Adjustment Operations (Setup Operations)	⦅ ⦆	◇	⊂⊐	△
Principal Operations — Main Operations	◎	◈	⊙⊐	△△
Principal Operations — Incidental Operations	○	◇	○⊐	△
Margin Allowances — Fatigue Allowances	○	◇	○⊐	△
Margin Allowances — Hygiene Allowances	○	◇	○⊐	△
Margin Allowances — Operations Allowances	○	◇	○⊐	△
Margin Allowances — Workplace Allowances	○	◇	○⊐	△

FIGURE 1-3. The Relationship Between Processes and Operations

SUMMARY

The main point of this chapter is that production activities comprise processes and operations, and setups are included in each type of operation.

2

Setup Operations
in the Past

SOME DEFINITIONS OF TERMS

Small, Medium, and Large Lots

Although discussions of setup procedures often mention small, medium, and large lots, these terms are not precise and are, in fact, rather vague. For the sake of convenience, this book will use the following classification as a rough guide:

Small lot: 500 units or fewer
Medium lot: 501 to 5,000 units
Large lot: more than 5,000 units

Excess Inventory and Excess Anticipated Production

With a promised delivery date coming up fast, it would be awkward to find defective goods causing a shortage in the quantity ready for shipment. To avoid such a shortage, 330 items might be produced to satisfy an order for 300. If only twenty turn out, in fact, to be defective, then ten unnecessary items remain. If the order is not repeated, these leftover must be discarded; often they are kept in inventory with the hope of receiving another order for them. This stock, resulting from the production of too many goods, is called *excess inventory*.

Another type of surplus, *excess anticipated production*, results when intermediate or finished goods are produced before they are actually needed.

Everyone will agree that it is wasteful to dispose of surplus goods, and most managers do their best to avoid excess inventory.

Strangely enough, however, goods that are produced before they are needed — excess anticipated production — often are not thought of as particularly undesirable. Indeed, some relief is often felt that a deadline has not been missed.

In this book, the terms *stock* and *inventory* will usually refer to excess anticipated production. The term *excess inventory* will be used to refer to production quantities which, for one reason or another, are larger than the actual number of units needed to fill orders.

TRADITIONAL STRATEGIES FOR IMPROVING SETUP OPERATIONS

Many factory managers consider diversified, low-volume production to be their single greatest challenge. This view, however, confuses characteristics of supply with those of demand. From the standpoint of demand, diversified, low-volume production means that many kinds of products are desired, and the quantity of any given kind is low.

To overcome the problems posed by diversified production, some companies have opted simply to produce only a few kinds of products and then try to stimulate a sufficient demand for them. Volkswagen is a case in point. For a long time, Volkswagen manufactured only one type of car, the famous "bug."

In today's world of diversified demand, this strategy has met with limited success. Indeed, in recent years Volkswagen has had to develop a full line of cars. More generally, it will become increasingly difficult for the automobile industry to slow the pace of diversification as it attempts to stimulate new demand with frequent model changes. And as production diversifies, the quantity of each model will inevitably decrease.

We should, however, note one important characteristic of demand: the distinction between one-time and repeat orders. One-time orders will always pose a problem because they always require special setup changes. For repeat orders — even if each individual order is small — the number of setups can be reduced by combining several lots into one. Unfortunately, this solution gives rise to waste by producing too much too soon.

Corresponding to the demand characteristics noted above, the supply side (production) requires numerous setup operations for diversified production, and small lots.

Although numerous setup operations must be carried out in a diversified production system, several possibilities arise when we look at the problem in terms of the setup itself.

First, there may be *common setup elements*. Although the products may differ, the dimensions of the tools and parts used in processing may remain constant. On a visit to a Volkswagen plant, I remember being impressed by their use of common setup elements. Although a model change had necessitated a change in the shape of the instrument panels, the fixtures were the same as the old ones: there was no change whatsoever in production operating conditions. In situations like this, setup problems are considerably reduced.

Second, there may be *similar setup elements*. Sometimes the products differ, but the basic shape of, for example, the chuck remains constant. If it is still round, and only the diameter differs, then the only setup change required is adjusting the dimension of the chuck claws. A setup in this kind of situation is extremely simple.

By focusing on common and similar setup elements, by classifying these elements, and by choosing the right machine for each task, it is possible to reduce setup difficulties dramatically, even if the number of setups remains the same.

Small-lot production suffers from the disadvantage that as soon as one operation begins to develop momentum, production has to move on to the next one. Strategies such as the following should be considered to deal with this problem:

- Eliminate the need for guesswork as much as possible by improving operations.

- Simplify operations through division of labor and attempts to minimize the effects of shifting work rhythms.

If demand allows for anticipatory production, small lots can be combined into larger ones, thus reducing the number of setups.

At any rate, the problem facing factories is not diversified, low-volume production, but rather production involving multiple setups and small lots. We need to evaluate the problem correctly and then consider effective strategies for dealing with it.

Strategies Involving Skill

In traditional manufacturing operations, efficient setup changes require two things:

- *Knowledge* relating to the structure and function of the machinery and equipment, as well as a thorough acquaintance with tools, blades, dies, jigs, etc.

- *Skill* in mounting and removing these items, and also in measuring, centering, adjusting, and calibrating after trial runs.

As a result, efficient setups require highly skilled workers, and although a simple machine may pose no problems, the specialized knowledge of a "setup engineer" (sometimes referred to simply as a "setup man") is called for when the machinery is complex.

While the setup engineer is engaged in the setup, the machine operator normally performs miscellaneous duties as the engineer's assistant, operates another machine, or in some cases simply waits. All of these activities, however, are inefficient.

It is generally and erroneously believed that the most effective policies for dealing with setups address the problem in terms of skill. Although many companies have setup policies designed to raise the skill level of the workers, few have implemented strategies that lower the skill level required by the setup itself.

Strategies Involving Large Lots

Setup operations have traditionally demanded a great deal of time, and manufacturing companies have long suffered from the extreme inefficiency this causes. A marvelous solution was found to this problem, however: increasing lot size.

If a large order is received, large-lot production will pose no particular problems because the effect of setup time is slight when divided by the total operating time for the lot, and setup time has only a small effect on the work rate.

For diversified, low-volume orders, on the other hand, the impact of setup time is much greater. When demand takes the form of repeated diversified, low-volume orders, lot sizes can be increased by combining several orders and producing in anticipation of demand.

If lot sizes are increased, the ratio of setup time to the number of operations can be greatly reduced (*Table 2-1*).

Setup Time	Lot Size	Principal Operation Time Per Item	Operation Time	Ratio (%)	Ratio (%)
4 hrs.	100	1 min.	$1\,min. + \dfrac{4 \times 60}{100} = 3.4\,min.$	100	
4 hrs.	1,000	1 min.	$1\,min. + \dfrac{4 \times 60}{1,000} = 1.24\,min.$	36	100
4hrs.	10,000	1 min.	$1\,min. + \dfrac{4 \times 60}{10,000} = 1.024\,min.$	30	83

TABLE 2-1. Relationship Between Setup Time and Lot Size—I

As Table 2-1 shows, increasing the lot size from 100 to 1,000 units leads to a 64% reduction in production man-hours. When lot size is increased by another factor of ten, however, to 10,000 units, the related decrease in man-hours is only 17%. In other words, increasing the size of a small lot leads to a relatively large decrease in man-hours, but as size increases the rate of reduction in man-hours decreases. Similarly, the gains from increasing lot size are greater for long setup times than for shorter ones (*Table 2-2*).

Despite this law of diminishing returns, the rate of reduction rises whether the setup time is four hours or eight. The greater the setup time, the more effective are the results of increasing the lot size. Moreover, increasing lot size by a factor of ten amounts to combining ten setup operations into one. The result is a substantial increase in the work rate and in production capacity (*Table 2-3*).

Plant managers always welcome the double benefit of this con-

Setup Time	Lot Size	Principal Operation Time Per Item	Operation Time	Ratio (%)	Ratio (%)
8 hrs.	100	1 min.	$1\,min. + \dfrac{8 \times 60}{100} = 5.8\,min.$	100	
8 hrs.	1,000	1 min.	$1\,min. + \dfrac{8 \times 60}{1,000} = 1.48\,min.$	26	100
8 hrs.	10,000	1 min.	$1\,min. + \dfrac{8 \times 60}{10,000} = 1.048\,min.$	18	71

TABLE 2-2. Relationship Between Setup Time and Lot Size—II

Setup Time	Setup Time Saved	Work Day	Days Saved
4 hours	4 × 9 = 36 hours	8 hours	4.5
8 hours	8 × 9 = 72 hours	8 hours	9

TABLE 2-3. Relationship Between Setup Time and Lot Size—III

siderable increase in productive power and reduction in needed man-hours. Indeed, we might well imagine that this is the principal reason for favoring large-lot production on the shop floor. With traditional setup procedures, large-lot production seems the easiest and most effective way to minimize the undesirable effects of setup operations.

Economic-Lot Strategies

Large-lot production in response to large orders is fine, but most large-lot production in fact results from combining repeated orders for small volumes of goods, giving rise to excess anticipated production. Inventory is often called a necessary evil, since there are so many advantages associated with it. Nonetheless, we must bear in mind that no matter how "necessary" it may appear, an evil is still an evil.

Let us take another look at the pros and cons of large-lot production:

Advantages

- Since the ratio of setup time to main operation is lower, apparent operating man-hours are reduced.
- Combining setup operations reduces the number of setups, increases the work rate, and increases productivity proportionately.
- The existence of inventory facilitates load leveling.
- Inventory serves as a cushion, alleviating problems when defects show up or machinery breaks down.
- Inventories can be used to fill rush orders.

Disadvantages

- Capital turnover rates fall, increasing interest burdens.

- Inventory itself does not produce added value, so the tremendous physical space it occupies is entirely wasted.

- Inventory storage necessitates the installation of racks, pallets, and so forth, all of which increase costs. When inventories grow too large, special rack rooms or the like are installed and automated stock entry and retrieval becomes possible. Some companies pride themselves on their automated inventory control, boasting that any item can be retrieved in three minutes or so. This in turn requires managerial man-hours for taking inventory. Although all of this has been called "rationalization," in reality it is the rationalization of waste rather than its elimination.

- The transportation and storage of stock requires handling man-hours.

- Large lots entail longer lead times. As a result, discrepancies arise with respect to projected demand. This leads to internal inventories and discarded parts. Furthermore, long lead times can mean that new orders are delayed and deadlines are missed.

- Stocks must be disposed of whenever model changes take place, either by selling them at a discount or by discarding them.

- Inventory quality deteriorates over time. Rust, for example, leads to needless costs. As stocks become dated, their value diminishes.

Given these advantages and disadvantages, one can see that large-lot production generally lowers costs associated with long setup times, but raises costs by enlarging inventories. This relationship is shown graphically in *Figure 2-1*, where a curve representing setup effects (P) and a straight line representing inventory (S) intersect at point E, which scholars call the economic lot size. This is the point at which the advantages and disadvantages of setup and inventory balance out.

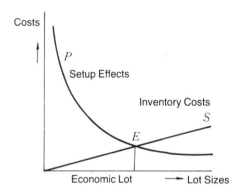

FIGURE 2-1. The Economic Lot Size

A Blind Spot in the Economic-Lot Concept

There is no doubt that the concept of economic lot size is entirely correct in theory. Yet this concept conceals an enormous blind spot: the unspoken assumption that drastic reductions in setup time are impossible.

If a four-hour setup were reduced to three minutes — and adoption of the SMED system has actually made this possible — then even without increasing lot size, the ratio of setup hours to the main operation could be made extremely small. This being so, attempts to mitigate the effects of setup time by producing in large lots would be without value.

As an example, let us examine the effect of increasing the lot size by a factor of ten on an operation whose setup time is three minutes (*Table 2-4*). In this case, the reduction in man-hours will be only 3%. Furthermore, since ten lots are combined, the savings in setup time

Setup Time	Lot Size	Principal Operation Time Per Item	Total Operation Time Per Item (Including Setup)	Ratio (%)
3 min.	100	1 min.	$1 \text{ min.} + \dfrac{3}{100} = 1.03 \text{ min.}$	100
3 min.	1,000	1 min.	$1 \text{ min.} + \dfrac{3}{1,000} = 1.003 \text{ min.}$	97

TABLE 2-4. Relationship Between Setup Time and Lot Size—IV

resulting from combining lots will be:

$$3 \text{ minutes} \times (10 - 1) = 27 \text{ minutes}$$

If we let one workday equal eight hours, the reduction is a mere 0.06 day. Suppose, however, that the setup time was previously four hours. Cutting this time to three minutes will result in a tremendous rise in both work rate and productive capacity. In addition, inventory can be kept at a minimum since there will be no obstacle to small-lot production: the question of economic lot size will not even be an issue. This is why it has been said recently that with the development of SMED, the concept of economic lots has disappeared from the profit-engineering agenda.

In fact, the very notion of economic lots was an evasive measure and in no way a positive approach to improving production. Moreover, since SMED can substantially reduce the level of skill required for setups, the need for skilled setup workers is largely eliminated. This has exploded once and for all the myth that the best way to deal with setup problems is through skill and large-lot production.

SUMMARY

The expression *diversified, low-volume production* confuses characteristics of supply and demand. By clearly differentiating between the two, we can determine what kinds of production methods will optimize productivity.

In the past, setup improvements were achieved through skill and large-lot production. The concept of economic lot size was introduced to counterbalance the effect of increasing inventories. The economic lot was considered an optimally rational approach.

In fact, there is an important blind spot in the concept of economic lot size: the assumption that drastic reductions in setup time are impossible. The economic lot lost its entire reason for being when the SMED system was developed.

3

Fundamentals of SMED

THE HISTORY OF SMED

The Birth of SMED

In the spring of 1950, I conducted an efficiency improvement survey at Toyo Kogyo's Mazda plant in Hiroshima, which at the time manufactured three-wheeled vehicles. Toyo wanted to eliminate bottlenecks caused by large body-molding presses — presses of 350, 750, and 800 tons — that were not working up to capacity. I immediately conducted an on-site inspection, and then made the following request of the section manager in charge of manufacturing: "Will you let me do a week-long production analysis with a stopwatch so I can get an idea of the work these big presses do?"

He replied that it would be a waste of time: he already knew that the presses were the cause of the bottlenecks and had assigned his most skilled and conscientious employees to work on them. He had the three presses working around the clock and felt that the only way to improve productivity further was to buy more machines, which is exactly what he hoped top management would do.

"That sounds pretty bad," I said. "But listen, let me do an analysis anyway. If it turns out that there's no other way to eliminate the bottlenecks, then I'll advise management to buy the machines." With that argument, I was finally permitted to conduct a fact-finding survey.

On the third day, there was a die change on the 800-ton press. Workers removed the old die and then started rushing about all over the place. I asked the operator what was going on. He replied, "One of the mounting bolts for the new die is missing. I was sure they were all with the die, but I can't find the last one and I've been looking all over for it."

"When you find it," I said, "you'll come back to the die, won't you? I'll wait for you here."

"All right," he replied. "Having you around here gives me the jitters, anyway."

I sat down by the machine and waited. After more than an hour, the operator rushed back, drenched with sweat and brandishing a bolt in his right hand. "Ah," I said, "You've found it!"

"No," he answered. "I didn't actually find it. I borrowed a long die bolt from the next machine over there. I cut it to make it shorter, then threaded it. That's what took so long. It wasn't easy, I can tell you!"

I said a few words of sympathetic encouragement, but a sudden thought started me worrying. "You cut it to the right length for this machine, but what are you going to do when you have to set up the machine you took it from? Does this kind of thing go on all the time?"

"No," he replied, "I wouldn't say it happens all the time. It's just something that gives us trouble now and then."

As *Figure 3-1* shows, the large press was actually engaged in the main manufacturing operation for less than 3% of that entire day.

It dawned on me at that point that setup operations were actually of two fundamentally different types:

- *Internal setup* (IED), such as mounting or removing dies, that can be performed only when a machine is stopped

- *External setup* (OED), such as transporting old dies to storage or conveying new dies to the machine, that can be conducted while a machine is in operation

Preparing the bolts was an external operation. It was senseless to stop the operation of an 800-ton press because a bolt was missing. All we had to do was establish an external setup procedure: verifying that the necessary bolts were ready for the next setup.

We established a process for thoroughly sorting all the bolts and putting the necessary ones in boxes. We also improved the entire procedure by performing all possible aspects of the setup externally. This raised efficiency by about 50%, and the bottleneck was dissipated.

Content of Operation — Machine	Setup: Preparation After-Adjustment	Main Operation: Essential Operation	Main Operation: Auxiliary Operation	Margin Allowances: Hygiene	Margin Allowances: Fatigue	Margin Allowances: Oper.	Margin Allowances: Workplace	Important Points for Reexamination: Preparation & After-Adjustment	Important Points for Reexamination: Workplace Allowances
800-ton press — Main Operator	47.0%	3.0%	24%	1.0%	5.0%	6.0%	14.0%	die transportation 869 3.5; securing die 2940 11.7; adjusting 5475 21.7; removing die 1789 7.2; miscellaneous 610 2.4 (sec / %)	material transport. 574 2.3; waiting crane 776 3.1; material cooling 902 3.6; assist adjacent press 34 0.1; miscellaneous 1162 4.6 (sec / %)
750-ton press — Main Operator	46.3	4.27	23.6	0	1.84	7.34	16.65	die transportation 1469 5.3; securing die 2033 8.2; adjusting 5968 23.5; removing die 307 1.2; misc. 1963 7.9	material transport. 2231 8.3; waiting crane 356 1.4; misc. 1599 6.4
750-ton press — Assistant	23.5	0	15.8	0	13.2	4.9	42.6	die transportation 1633 6.5; preparing and securing part 727 2.9; adjusting 1912 7.6; removing die 507 2.0; misc. 224 1.0	loading & unloading (material & products) 3711 14.8; waiting for preparation & after-adjustment 5635 22.0; waiting for main operation 701 2.8; misc. 380 1.5
300-ton press — Main Operator	40.0	9.0	27.0	0	2.0	13.0	9.0	die transportation 2000 7.9; securing die 2849 11.3; adjusting 3424 13.6; removing die 799 7.2; misc. 1699 6.7	material transport. 105 0.6; waiting crane 1220 4.8; misc. 56 0.2

FIGURE 3-1. Production Analysis of a Large Press

Ever since this episode, I have made it a policy to distinguish clearly between internal and external setup.

Thus the newly born SMED concept took its first steps at Toyo Kogyo.

The Second Encounter

In the summer of 1957, I was asked to do a study at the Mitsubishi Heavy Industries shipyard in Hiroshima. When I asked the plant manager, Matsuzo Okazaki, what the problem was, he told me that a large, open-sided planer used to machine diesel engine beds was not working up to capacity and that he wanted to streamline the operation.

After doing a production analysis, I realized that the marking-off procedure for centering and dimensioning the engine bed was being conducted on the planer table itself. This reduced the operating rate tremendously. As I discussed this with Mr. Okazaki, an idea came to me quite suddenly: *Why not install a second planer table and perform the setup operation on it separately?* That way, we could switch tables as we shifted from one lot to the next, and there would be a significant reduction in the amount of time the planing operation was interrupted for each setup. Mr. Okazaki agreed to this change on the spot.

On my next visit to the factory I found that the extra planer table had been completed. This solution resulted in a 40% increase in productivity. Mr. Okazaki and I were ecstatic and toasted one another on our accomplishment, yet even now I regret one thing. If I had grasped at the time the overwhelming importance of converting an internal setup to an external one, the SMED concept would have been perfected some dozen years sooner.

The Third Encounter

In 1969, I visited the body shop at Toyota Motor Company's main plant. Mr. Sugiura, the divisional manager, told me they had a 1,000-ton press that required four hours for each setup change. Volkswagen in Germany had been performing setups on a similar press in two hours, and management had given Mr. Sugiura clear instructions to better that time.

Together with the foreman and plant manager, I set about seeing what could be done. We took special pains to distinguish clearly between internal and external setup (IED and OED), trying to improve each separately. After six months we succeeded in cutting setup time to ninety minutes.

We were all pleased with this success, but when I revisited the body shop the following month, Mr. Sugiura had some rather startling news for me. Management had given him orders to further reduce setup time, to less than three minutes! For an instant I was dumbfounded at this request. But then an inspiration struck: *Why not convert* IED *to* OED?

A number of thoughts followed in rapid succession. On a conference-room blackboard I listed eight techniques for shortening setup times. Using this new concept, we were able to achieve the three-minute goal after three months of diligent effort. In the hope that any setup could be performed in under ten minutes, I named this concept "single-minute exchange of die," or SMED. SMED was later adopted by all Toyota plants and continued to evolve as one of the principal elements of the Toyota Production System. Its use has now spread to companies throughout Japan and the world.

Mr. Taiichi Ohno, formerly a vice president at Toyota Motor Company and now a consultant, wrote about SMED in an article entitled "Bringing Wisdom to the Factory," which appeared in the journal *Management*, published by the Japan Management Association, in June 1976:

> *Until some ten years ago, production in our firm took place as much as possible during regular working hours. Changes of cutters, drills and the like were relegated to the noon break or the evening. We had a policy of replacing the cutters after every fifty items. Yet as production has risen over the past decade or so, machine operators have often begrudged the time needed for these changes. For the multigrinder in particular, replacing the numerous cutters and drills took half a day. Since afternoon production would stop whenever a replacement was made on a weekday, workers were forced to work temporary shifts on the following Sunday.*

This was uneconomical and therefore unacceptable. Since we also wanted maintenance to be done during working hours, we began to study the question of how setup changes could be performed in a very short period of time. Shigeo Shingo, of the Japan Management Association, was advocating "single-minute setup changes" and we felt that this concept could be of great service to us. It used to be that after spending half a day on setup, the machine might be used for only ten minutes. Now, one might think that since the setup took half a day, production ought to continue for at least that long. This, however, would have left us with a lot of finished products we could never sell. We are now looking into cutting setup times down to a matter of seconds. Of course this is easier said than done. Somehow, though, we must reduce the amount of time needed for setup changes.

This passage underscores the impact of setup time reductions on the improvement of production activities as a whole.

The development of the SMED concept took nineteen years in all. It came about as the culmination of my ever-deepening insight into the practical and theoretical aspects of setup improvement. The finishing touches were stimulated by Toyota Motor Company's requirement that we reduce setup time on a 1,000-ton press from four hours to ninety minutes.

I would like to stress that SMED is based on theory and years of practical experimentation. It is a scientific approach to setup time reduction that can be applied in any factory to any machine.

BASIC STEPS IN THE SETUP PROCEDURE

Setup procedures are usually thought of as infinitely varied, depending on the type of operation and the type of equipment being used. Yet when these procedures are analyzed from a different viewpoint, it can be seen that all setup operations comprise a sequence of steps. In traditional setup changes the distribution of time is often that shown in *Table 3-1*.

Let us examine each of these in greater detail.

Operation	Proportion of time
Preparation, after-process adjustment, and checking of raw material, blades, dies, jigs, gauges, etc.	30%
Mounting and removing blades, etc.	5%
Centering, dimensioning and setting of other conditions	15%
Trial runs and adjustments	50%

TABLE 3-1. **Steps in the Setup Process**

Preparation, after-process adjustment, checking of materials, tools, etc. This step ensures that all parts and tools are where they should be and that they are functioning properly. Also included in this step is the period after processing when these items are removed and returned to storage, machinery is cleaned, etc.

Mounting and removing blades, tools, parts, etc. This includes the removal of parts and tools after completion of processing and the attachment of the parts and tools for the next lot.

Measurements, settings, and calibrations. This step refers to all of the measurements and calibrations that must be made in order to perform a production operation, such as centering, dimensioning, measuring temperature or pressure, etc.

Trial runs and adjustments. In these steps, adjustments are made after a test piece is machined. The greater the accuracy of the measurements and calibrations in the preceding step, the easier these adjustments will be.

The frequency and length of test runs and adjustment procedures depend on the skill of the setup engineer. The greatest difficulties in a setup operation lie in adjusting the equipment correctly. The large proportion of time associated with trial runs derives from these adjustment problems. If we want to make trial runs and adjustments easier, we need to understand that the most effective approach is to increase the precision of the preceding measurements and calibrations.

SETUP IMPROVEMENT: CONCEPTUAL STAGES

The conceptual stages involved in setup improvements are shown in *Figure 3-2.*

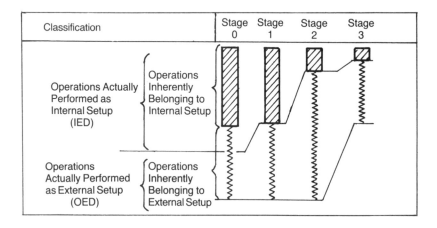

Classification		Stage 0	Stage 1	Stage 2	Stage 3
Operations Actually Performed as Internal Setup (IED)	Operations Inherently Belonging to Internal Setup				
Operations Actually Performed as External Setup (OED)	Operations Inherently Belonging to External Setup				

Setup Procedures: Basic Steps	Stage 0		Stage 1		Stage 2		Stage 3	
	IED	OED	IED	OED	IED	OED	IED	OED
Preparation and Function Checks of Raw Materials, Tools and Attachment Devices		⋀⋀⋀⋀		⋀⋀⋀⋀	⋀⋀⋀⋀		⋀⋀⋀	
Attachment & Removal of Dies, Blades, etc.	▮		▮		▮⋀		▮	
Centering, Dimensioning, Setting Operating Conditions	▮		▮		▮⋀		▮⋀	
Trial Processing, Adjustments	▬▬		▬▬		▮		▮	
Total	▬▬⋀⋀⋀		▬▬⋀⋀⋀		▬⋀⋀⋀⋀⋀⋀		▬⋀⋀⋀	

FIGURE 3-2. Conceptual Stages for Setup Improvement

Preliminary Stage: Internal and External Setup Conditions Are Not Distinguished

In traditional setup operations, internal and external setup are confused; what *could* be done externally is done as internal setup, and machines therefore remain idle for extended periods. In planning how to implement SMED, one must study actual shop floor conditions in great detail.

A *continuous production analysis* performed with a stopwatch is probably the best approach. Such an analysis, however, takes a great deal of time and requires great skill.

Another possibility is to use a *work sampling study*. The problem with this option is that work samples are precise only where there is a great deal of repetition. Such a study may not be suitable where few actions are repeated.

A third useful approach is to study actual conditions on the shop floor by *interviewing workers*.

An even better method is to *videotape* the entire setup operation. This is extremely effective if the tape is shown to the workers immediately after the setup has been completed. Giving workers the opportunity to air their views often leads to surprisingly astute and useful insights. In many instances these insights can be applied on the spot.

At any rate, even though some consultants advocate in-depth continuous production analyses for the purpose of improving setup, the truth is that informal observation and discussion with the workers often suffice.

Stage 1: Separating Internal and External Setup

The most important step in implementing SMED is distinguishing between internal and external setup. Everyone will agree that preparation of parts, maintenance and so forth should not be done while the machines are stopped. Nonetheless, it is absolutely astounding to observe how often this is the case.

If instead we make a scientific effort to treat as much of the setup operation as possible as external setup, then the time needed for internal setup — performed while the machine is off — can usually be cut some 30%–50%. Mastering the distinction between internal and external setup is thus the passport to achieving SMED.

Stage 2: Converting Internal to External Setup

I have just explained that normal setup times can be reduced 30%–50% by separating internal and external setup procedures. But even this tremendous reduction is insufficient to achieve the SMED objective. The second stage — converting internal setup to external setup — involves two important notions:

- Re-examining operations to see whether any steps are wrongly assumed to be internal
- Finding ways to convert these steps to external setup

Examples might include preheating elements that have previously been heated only after setup has begun, and converting centering to an external procedure by doing it before production starts.

Operations that are now performed as internal setup can often be converted to external setup by re-examining their true function. It is extremely important to adopt new perspectives that are not bound by old habits.

Stage 3: Streamlining All Aspects of the Setup Operation

Although the single-minute range can occasionally be reached by converting to external setup, this is not true in the majority of cases. This is why we must make a concerted effort to streamline each elemental internal and external setup operation. Thus stage 3 calls for a detailed analysis of each elemental operation. The following examples are drawn from successful applications of stages 1, 2, and 3.

- At Toyota Motor Company, the internal setup time of a bolt-maker — which had previously required eight hours — was cut to fifty-eight seconds.

- At Mitsubishi Heavy Industries, the internal setup time for a six-arbor boring machine — which had previously required twenty-four hours — was reduced to two minutes and forty seconds.

Stages 2 and 3 do not need to be performed sequentially; they may be nearly simultaneous. I have separated them here to show that they nonetheless involve two distinct notions: analysis, then implementation.

SUMMARY

SMED was born over a period of nineteen years as a result of examining closely the theoretical and practical aspects of setup improvement. Both analysis and implementation are thus fundamental to the SMED system and must be part of any improvement program.

There are two types of setup, internal and external (or IED and OED). The four conceptual stages of setup improvement involve the distinguishing of these two types of setup, and the converting of internal setup to external setup. Once that is done, all aspects of setup can be streamlined. At every stage, however, setup improvements can be realized.

4

Techniques for Applying SMED

Now that you know the concepts involved in setup improvement, let us take a look at some practical techniques corresponding to the conceptual stages.

PRELIMINARY STAGE: INTERNAL AND EXTERNAL SETUP ARE NOT DISTINGUISHED

In traditional setup operations, several kinds of waste recur:

- Finished goods are transported to storage or the next batch of raw materials is moved from stock after the previous lot has been completed and the machine has been turned off. Since the machine is off during transportation, valuable time is lost.

- Blades, dies, etc., are delivered after internal setup has begun, or a defective part is discovered only after mounting and test runs. As a result, time is lost removing the part from the machine and starting over again. As with the transportation of raw materials or finished goods, waste can occur *after* processing. Parts that are no longer needed are transported to the tool room while the machine is still turned off.

- With jigs and gauges, a jig may be replaced because it is not accurate enough and repairs have not been made; bolts cannot be found; a bolt is no good because the nut is too tight; or no blocks of the appropriate thickness can be found.

You can probably think of many other instances where shortages, mistakes, inadequate verification of equipment, or similar problems have occurred and led to delays in setup operations.

33

Traditionally, managers and manufacturing engineers have failed to devote their full abilities to the analysis of setup operations. More often than not, they assign setup to the workers, and assume that because their workers are conscientious, they will do their best to perform setups as quickly as possible. In other words, the problem of setup time is left to be resolved on the shop floor. Surely this attitude is one of the main reasons why, until recently, no great progress has been made in improving setup operations.

STAGE 1: SEPARATING INTERNAL AND EXTERNAL SETUP

The following techniques are effective in ensuring that operations that can be conducted as external setup are, in fact, performed while the machine is running.

Using a Checklist

Make a checklist of all the parts and steps required in an operation. This list will include:

- Names
- Specifications
- Numbers of blades, dies, and other items
- Pressure, temperature, and other settings
- Numeric values for all measurements and dimensions

On the basis of this list, double-check that there are no mistakes in operating conditions. By doing this beforehand, you can avoid many time-consuming errors and test runs.

The use of a so-called *check table* is also very handy. A check table is a table on which drawings have been made of all the parts and tools required for a setup. The corresponding parts are simply placed over the appropriate drawings before the internal setup is begun. Since a single glance at the table will tell the operator whether any parts are missing, this is an extremely effective visual control technique. The only limitation on the usefulness of the check table is that it cannot be used to verify the operating conditions themselves. Nonetheless, it remains a valuable adjunct to the checklist.

It is very important to establish a specific checklist and table for each machine. Avoid the use of general checklists for an entire shop: they can be confusing, they tend to get lost, and because they are confusing they are too frequently ignored.

Performing Function Checks

A checklist is useful for determining whether all the parts are where they should be, but it does not tell whether they are in perfect working order. Consequently, it is necessary to perform function checks in the course of external setup.

Failure to do this will lead inevitably to delays in internal setup when it is suddenly discovered that a gauge does not work right or a jig is not accurate. In particular, inadequate repairs to presses and plastic molds are sometimes discovered only after test runs have been completed. In this event, molds that one has already taken the trouble to mount on a machine must be removed and repaired, thus increasing setup time substantially.

One frequent problem is repairs that are anticipated, but take longer than expected. The operation is begun before repairs are completed. When defective goods show up as a result, the die is hurriedly removed, and further repairs are made, interrupting production. It is always important to finish repairs before internal setup is begun.

Improving Transportation of Dies and Other Parts

Parts have to be moved from storage to the machines, and then returned to storage once a lot is finished. This must be done as an external setup procedure, in which either the operator moves the parts himself while the machine is running automatically, or another worker is assigned to the task of transportation.

One factory I worked with conducted setup operations on a large press by extracting the die on a moving bolster. A cable was attached to the die, which a crane then lifted and conveyed to the storage area. I suggested a number of changes to the shop foreman:

- Have the crane move the new die to the machine beforehand.

- Next, lower the old die from the moving bolster to the side of the machine.

- Attach the new die to the moving bolster, insert it in the machine, and begin the new operation.

- After that, hook a cable to the old die and transport it to the storage area.

"That's no good," the foreman argued. "Cables would have to be attached twice, and that's inefficient."

"But," I replied, "it takes four minutes and twenty seconds to transport the old and new dies to and from the machine. If the press were put into operation that much earlier, you could manufacture about five extra units in the time you would save. Which is preferable, attaching the cables only once or producing five extra products?" The foreman agreed right away that he had been looking at the setup operation the wrong way, and the new system was implemented immediately.

This example illustrates a tendency of people on the shop floor to be distracted by small efficiencies while overlooking bigger ones. Considered on a deeper level, it shows the need for front-line managers to understand internal and external setup thoroughly.

STAGE 2: CONVERTING INTERNAL TO EXTERNAL SETUP

Preparing Operating Conditions in Advance

The first step in converting setup operations is to prepare operating conditions beforehand. We will illustrate this method with a number of examples.

Trial Shots on Die-Casting Machines

Trial shots are usually performed as part of the internal setup of die-casting machines. Cold dies are attached to the machine and gradually heated to the appropriate temperature by injecting molten metal. The first casting is then made. Since the material injected during the heating process will produce defective castings, items from the first casting must be remolded.

If gas or electric heat were used to preheat the mold, however, good castings would result from the first injections into the mounted and preheated die. Generally speaking, this method can cut internal setup time by about thirty minutes. In addition to increasing productivity, it will reduce the number of poor castings that must be re-melted.

At one die-casting facility, a special rack was built on top of a holding oven installed at the side of a die-casting machine. Dies to be used in the following operation were preheated by heat dissipated from the holding oven.

Using recycled heat to preheat the dies killed two birds with one stone. The only expense the company incurred was the cost of building a special rack strong enough to hold the dies (*Plate 4-1*).

PLATE 4-1. Preheating of Dies

Die Preheating on a Large Plastic-Molding Machine

As in the previous example, dies had been preheated by injecting molten resin. Preheating the mold with an electric heater before attaching it to the machine made it possible to produce quality goods right from the beginning of each lot. Setup time decreased, and the number of trial shots was reduced.

With resins, as with metals, defective items can sometimes be crushed and reused, but this is not satisfactory, because it leads to a deterioration in quality. It is always preferable to manufacture quality goods from the start and to avoid producing substandard goods altogether.

In another case, molds for a mid-sized plastic molding machine were preheated simply by passing warm water through a coolant hose. A mobile steam generator was moved next to the molds to generate the warm water. This improvement was extremely efficient because of its simplicity and the fact that capital investment was less than ¥ 200,000 [about $826].*

Thread Dyeing

At a fabric manufacturing plant, dyeing operations had been conducted by immersing a rack holding a number of threads in a dyeing vat and then heating the vat with steam. This was a very time-consuming operation, because it took quite a while for the vat to reach the right temperature.

The solution to this problem involved setting up a second vat. The auxiliary vat was filled with dye and preheated while the previous lot was being processed. When the first lot was completed, a valve was opened in the auxiliary vat and the preheated dye was allowed to flow into the dyeing vat. It thus became possible to eliminate the delay caused by heating the dye. This solution also had the effect of improving product quality by producing crisper colors.

Previously, there had been only one thread rack for each vat. When a lot was finished, the thread was removed from the rack, and a second lot of thread was installed on it. We were able to further reduce setup time by installing a second rack that was preloaded and switched with the first as soon as processing of the first lot was completed.

By combining this new procedure with the improvement in dye heating, we were able to more than double the operating rate of the dyeing operation.

---

* EDITOR'S NOTE: The exchange rate at the time of publication was ¥ 242 to the dollar. All figures have been rounded off for simplicity.

The improved operation thus took place as follows:

- Prepare a rack by placing new thread on it.
- After dyeing, remove the rack bearing the dyed thread and clean the vat.
- Fill the vat with preheated dye from the auxiliary vat and begin the dyeing process.
- While the dyeing operation is in process, remove the thread which has already been dyed in the previous lot.

Plastic Vacuum Molding

Plastic vacuum molding is normally carried out in four steps:

- Join a movable mold with a fixed mold.
- Pump out air to form a vacuum in the mold.
- Inject resin.
- Open the mold and remove the finished product.

Vacuum molding is successful only when a nearly complete vacuum has been created in the mold; this means that a great deal of time is spent on the second step. A combined system, as described in *Figure 4-1*, helps solve this problem:

1. Install a vacuum tank with a capacity roughly 1,000 times the volume of the mold.
2. Connect the mold to the vacuum tank and open the escape valve. This will cause the pressure in the mold to drop by a factor of about 1,000 within one second.
3. Close the valve connecting the mold to the vacuum tank and turn on the pump to suck out any remaining air.
4. Begin the next injection. When it is completed, close the valve between the mold and the pump.
5. Simultaneously connect the vacuum tank to the pump and remove the air that has entered the tank.
6. Continue expelling the air from the tank until the injection is completed, open the mold to remove the finished product, and close the mold again.

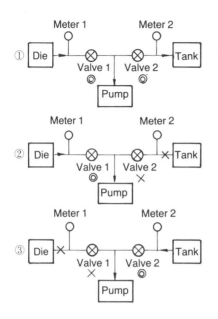

① Valves 1 and 2 are opened simultaneously after die is closed; air in die moves to tank
• Close valve 2 when valves 1 and 2 read the same; pressure inside die will fall to 1/1001

② • Expel air remaining in die with pump at 1/1001 atm.
• After injection, close valve 1

③ • Open valve 2 to connect tank and pump
• Expel air from tank in external operation
• Since vacuum pumps aspirate by volume, tank interior should be compressed as much as possible. After aspiration, volume should be enlarged again.

FIGURE 4-1. A Combined System

This combined system offers many advantages. Air inside the mold is not simply sucked out during internal setup. Once it moves to the vacuum tank, it is expelled during external setup. This efficient method of creating a vacuum in the mold clearly distinguishes between internal and external setup.

Setting Centers for Press-Die Processing

When press dies are tooled, they are attached to a planer bed and centered by marking off the center of the die on the surface plate. This center-marking operation was eliminated by cutting centering grooves on a cast pattern, thereby indicating the item's correct position in advance.

The Continuous Materials Method

In a spring manufacturing plant, a spool-changing operation had been performed when the end of each roll of spring stock was reached. As shown in *Figure 4-2*, it was possible to eliminate the internal setup operation in changing spools by joining the spring stock

The end of A₁ is welded to the start of A₂

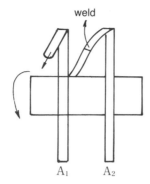

FIGURE 4-2. Continuous Materials Method

at the end of one lot, A_1, to the next spool, A_2. Thus, a new spool would automatically begin when the end of the old spool was reached.

When the spring stock is narrow and thin, long lengths can be wound onto wide spools, since kinks will not occur even when up to ten bands of stock are welded together.

A Temporary Spring Stock Holder

In this example of a progressive type press, a forklift brought each roll of spring stock and positioned it when the end of the previous roll was reached. An insufficient number of forklifts, however, meant frequent delays while waiting for raw materials to arrive.

The solution here was to build a spool holder (*Figure 4-3*) on which the next roll of stock was held ready for processing. At the end of one processing run, a worker would simply push the roll into position from its temporary holder. No time was wasted waiting for materials.

Function Standardization

Anyone can appreciate the appeal of standardizing setup operations. One way this can be done is by standardizing the sizes and dimensions of all machine parts and tools, but this method, called *shape*

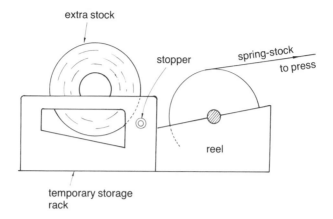

extra stock

stopper

spring-stock
to press

reel

temporary storage
rack

FIGURE 4-3. Temporary Spring Stock Holder

standardization, is wasteful: dies become larger to accommodate the largest size needed, and costs rise because of unnecessary "fat."

In contrast, *function standardization* calls for standardizing only those parts whose functions are necessary from the standpoint of setup operations. With this approach, dies need not be made larger or more elaborate, and costs rise only moderately.

To implement function standardization, individual functions are analyzed and then considered one by one. That is, general operations are broken down into their basic elements, for example clamping, centering, dimensioning, expelling, grasping, and maintaining loads. The engineer must decide which of these operations, if any, need to be standardized. He must then distinguish between parts that can be standardized and parts that necessitate setting changes.

Although there are many ways to replace a mechanical arm — from the shoulder, elbow, wrist, fingertip, or only the fingernail — the most cost-efficient procedure is to replace the smallest part that includes the part needing replacement.

The quickest way to replace something, of course, is to replace nothing. For example, a transfer die press feed bar performs three operations:

- Gripping the object

- Sending the object to the next process

- Returning the feed bar to its original position

In this case, only the gripping function should change according to the shape, dimensions, and quality of the object being handled: there is no need to replace the entire feed bar.

Similarly, the workpiece-removal mechanism of a large press may require changes involving both the design of the chuck, which grips the workpiece, and the length of the plucking bar, which removes the workpiece.

To summarize, efficient function standardization requires that we analyze the functions of each piece of apparatus, element by element, and replace the fewest possible parts. The examples below illustrate the principle of function standardization.

Function Standardization of a Press Die

In the setup procedure for a press, adjusting shut height requires a great degree of skill. It is widely believed, furthermore, that this operation must be performed as part of internal setup. Yet given two die heights of 320 mm (die A) and 270 mm (die B), shut height adjustments would be unnecessary in changing from die A to die B if shims or blocks 50 mm thick were placed under die B to raise it to a height of 320 mm (*Figure 4-4*). Once this has been done, the height of the attachment edges on die A will be 30 mm, while those on die B will be 80 mm.

Thus if $30 \times 30 \times 50$ mm shims are welded to the attachment edges of die A, the same clamping bolts can be used for both dies. Since the equalizing blocks are standardized, handling can be simplified by welding the blocks to the clamp. This also eliminates

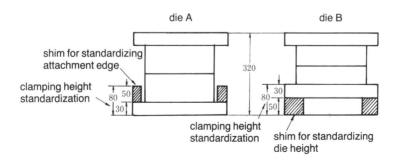

FIGURE 4-4. **Standardized Height of Die and Attachment Edge**

the trouble of having to search for a block of the proper height or having to store blocks of varying dimensions. The dies can be attached to the machine with only a special clamp and bolts. Both setup and management of the dies are made easier (*Plate 4-2*).

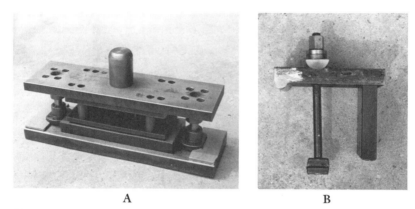

A   B

PLATE 4-2. **Standardized Attachment Edges and Die Heights**

Bottom Centering Jig

In another setup, the shanks found on some small press dies give rise to a troublesome operation. To align the ram hole and shank, the worker inches the ram downward and adjusts the position of the die by sight. Suppose that a centering jig is mounted on the far side of the machine (*Plate 4-3*), and the distance from the center of the shank hole to the centering jig is 350 mm. If the distance from the center of the die shank to the far edge of the die is 230 mm, then a 120-mm centering jig will be attached to the far side of the die (*Plate 4-4*). A V-shaped projection is made in the middle of the fixed centering jig and a corresponding V-shaped depression is cut in the movable jig. If the top jig is made to fit snugly in the bottom one, the holes in the ram and the shank will align automatically. There will be no need to inch the ram downward and the shank can be engaged very simply.

PLATE 4-3. Bottom Centering Jig   PLATE 4-4. Top Centering Jig

Centering Jig

In this example, only the essential function of centering the shank was standardized (*Figure 4-5* and *Plate 4-5*). The diameter of the bolts securing the shank was 22 mm, while the die's clamping bolts measured 19 mm. Special bolts were made for clamping the die. The heads of these 19-mm bolts were made to correspond exactly to the heads of the 22-mm bolts. This simplified the operation considerably by making it possible to tighten both sets of bolts with a single wrench.

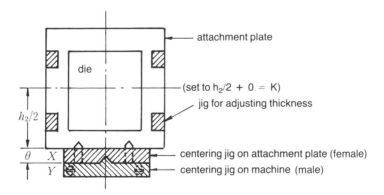

FIGURE 4-5. Bottom Centering Jig Engaged

PLATE 4-5. Bottom Centering Jig Engaged

Multipurpose Die Sets

Dies are used for two general purposes: to make objects of various shapes, and to bear loads. By standardizing the external part of a die and designing it so that the metal die set can be inserted and withdrawn like a cassette, manufacturers have achieved setup times as short as twenty seconds. This approach is particularly useful with small press dies.

Machining Camera Bodies

A die-cast camera body is defective if there is so much as a pinhole in the film plate. In one factory I worked with, the first fifty plates produced used to be trial-cut on an endmill, then inspected. This procedure, which took about fifteen minutes, had to be completed as quickly as possible so as not to delay the main operation. It also required a high level of skill because:

- The plate's thickness was controlled to a high degree of precision.

- Shapes and dimensions varied according to the type of camera body being produced.

- Each cutting jig was different, so the height of the cutting surface had to be set with a high degree of accuracy.

- The body had to be set to the center of the machine.

Several improvements were made:

- The height of the milling machine table was fixed and the distance to the endmill blade was set at 120 mm.

- The dimensions of the various bodies and jigs were determined. Contact jigs compensating for height were mounted and set on the table so that the cutting surface would be 120 mm.

- The horizontal and vertical dimensions of the contact jigs were standardized. By pushing them up against stoppers set into the table, workers could easily center the body.

These improvements made it possible for even an ordinary machine operator to take charge of the setup. They also reduced setup time to about thirty seconds. There had been some concern that improvement would be hampered by the large number of body types. In fact, only two functions had to be standardized: the height of the cutting surface, and centering the attachment of the camera body (*Figure 4-6*).

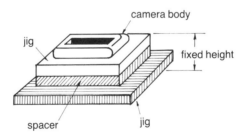

FIGURE 4-6. **Camera-Body Machining**

Attaching Instrument Panels

I have already mentioned being impressed by the cleverness of Volkswagen engineers. Although the exterior of the instrument panel for a new model had been redesigned, the new instrument panel was attached in precisely the same way as the old one. The operation itself had not changed. This, too, is a good example of function standardization.

Using Intermediary Jigs

In the processing of many items, two standardized jig plates of the appropriate size and shape can be made. While the workpiece attached to one of the plates is being processed, the next workpiece is centered and attached to the other jig as an external setup procedure. When the first workpiece is finished, this second jig, together with the attached workpiece, is mounted on the machine. This standardized jig plate is called an "intermediary jig."*

Setup on a Profile Milling Machine

Form blocks for television picture tubes are machined on a profile milling machine. Marking off was done on this machine when centering and setting heights for the template and the material to be processed. This required both tremendous accuracy and considerable time because of the many curved shapes involved. The machine was turned off during this period, and the loss of time was considered an unavoidable consequence of the setup operation.

We made two standardized intermediary jigs that were slightly smaller than the milling table. While one item was being machined, a template and the next workpiece were attached to the other intermediary jig on the table surface. They were then centered and set for the proper height.

When one operation was over, the intermediary jig with the template and attached workpiece was mounted on the milling machine table. Since the intermediary jig was standardized, centering and positioning were now performed very easily. Mounting simply required clamping the jig to a fixed place on the table (*Plate 4-6*). As a result, idle time on the milling machine was reduced considerably and productivity rose substantially.

Setting Bits on a Lathe

Previously, lathe bits had been attached directly to the tool post while various operations, such as setting blade protrusion and aligning cutting height, were carried out. This situation was improved by making a standardized rectangular holder to which a bit could be attached in external setup.

---

* EDITOR'S NOTE: Companies may have different names for this, e.g. "master shoe."

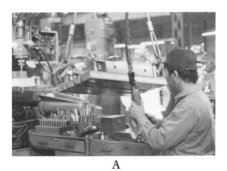
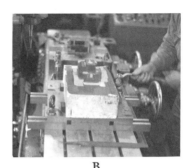

A B

PLATE 4-6. Profile Milling and Intermediary Jig

With the use of a dial gauge, the center height can be set accurately and correct blade protrusion measurements can be made. When a new operation is begun, centering and dimensioning are performed in one step by pushing the rectangular holder against the surface of the tool post. Setting the bit is now a simple operation and setup can be completed in a short time (*Plate 4-7*).

B

A

PLATE 4-7. Setting Lathe Bit

Countersinking a Hole in Bearing Metal

This operation involved countersinking the upper surface of an oil hole in bearing metal. Previously a drill had been attached to a drill press at a predetermined angle, then pressed against the bearing metal to start cutting. Since the countersinking depth had to be precise, once the drill had started cutting into the metal, measurements were made with a micrometer and the degree of drill protrusion was often adjusted.

We improved this operation by making an additional standardized drill holder. The drill attached to the holder was clamped in place after the precise degree of protrusion was gauged. Whenever it was necessary to replace drills, the setup was completed merely by pushing the holder into the taper hole of the drill press. As a result, even an inexperienced worker could replace drills, and do it quickly (*Figure 4-7*).

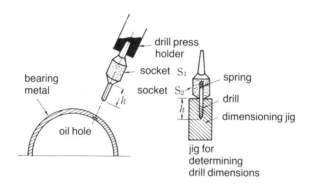

FIGURE 4-7. **Countersinking a Hole in Bearing Metal**

Multiple Dies on a Large Press

Attaching multiple dies to a large press was another troublesome operation, because the dies were of many sizes and heights. Previously this operation had been conducted directly on top of the press bed. The press had to be turned off, resulting in a highly negative impact on productivity.

To improve the operation, two thick plates — intermediary jigs — were made with nearly the same areas as the bed. Setup for the next operation was then carried out on the plates. With this improvement, the press had to be turned off only while a forklift switched the dies and the intermediary jigs.

In this example, a deep drawing operation was carried out with long, slow strokes. Since this was the only large press, it held back the rest of the operation, which always went into overtime. Setup was reduced to about three minutes, and productivity for the entire operation more than doubled (*Figure 4-8*).

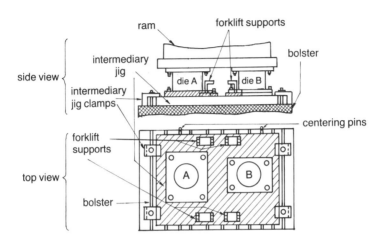

FIGURE 4-8. **Multiple Dies and Intermediary Jig**

STAGE 3: STREAMLINING ALL ASPECTS OF THE SETUP OPERATION

After going through stage 1 (separating internal and external setup) and stage 2 (converting internal to external setup), you can proceed to make sweeping improvements in elemental setup operations.

Radical Improvements in External Setup Operations

Improvements in the storage and transportation of parts and tools (including blades, dies, jigs, and gauges) can contribute to streamlining operations, although by themselves they will not be enough.

In the case of medium-sized press dies, advanced equipment is available for storing and moving parts and tools. The rack room is one such arrangement, in which dies are stored on three-dimensional racks, and automated equipment is used to store the dies and send them off on conveyors to the appropriate machines. This kind of automated storage system reduces the number of man-hours needed for external setup, but does not represent an improvement in internal setup. Consequently, it does not directly help us achieve the SMED objective, and should be used only when control of a large number of unwieldy dies is very difficult.

Radical Improvements in Internal Setup Operations

The techniques described in the following chapter can lead to sweeping improvements in internal setup.

SUMMARY

The full benefits of SMED can be achieved only after an analysis of setup operations has been made and the four conceptual stages of setup identified. However, effective techniques can be applied at every stage, leading to impressive reductions in setup time and dramatic improvements in productivity even early on in your efforts.

5

Applying SMED to
Internal Operations

IMPLEMENTATION OF PARALLEL OPERATIONS

Operations on plastic molding machines, die-casting machines and large presses invariably involve work both at the front and at the back of the machine. When a single person performs these operations, movement is continually being wasted as he walks around the machine.

Parallel operations involving more than one worker are very helpful in speeding up this kind of work. With two people, an operation that took twelve minutes will be completed not in six minutes, but perhaps in four, thanks to the economies of movement that are obtained.

When a parallel operation is being performed, special attention must be given to avoiding unnecessary waiting. Indeed, a poorly conceived parallel operation may result in no time savings at all (*Table 5-1*).

The most important issue in conducting parallel operations is safety. Each time one of the workers has completed an elemental operation, he must signal the other worker or workers. Sometimes this can be done by shouting, but in a noisy place like a factory shouts are often inaudible and confusing. It is preferable to signal with a buzzer or whistle, having agreed in advance on signals for "go ahead" and "wait."

In another variation, a worker at the back of the machine presses a button when his operation is completed. This lights a "confirmation board" at the front of the machine. After checking it, the worker in front is free to start the machine.

Better safety can also be achieved by using an interlock mechanism that prevents operation of the machine from the front unless the worker at the back has tripped a release switch.

Task	Time (sec)	Worker 1	Worker 2	Buzzer
1	15	Lower ram (to bottom dead point).	Prepare to remove rear bolts.	
2	20	Remove front mounting bolts securing upper die.	Remove rear mounting bolts securing upper die.	Yes
3	30	Raise ram (to top dead point).	Turn press switch off.	Yes
4	20	Remove bolster setting pins.	Prepare to remove mounting bolts securing lower die.	
5	60	Move bolsters.	Remove mounting bolts securing lower die.	
6	20	Attach cable to transport metal die.	Attach cable to transport metal die.	
7	20	Hoist.	Move metal die for mounting.	
8	30	Position metal die.	Position metal die.	
9	20	Tighten front bolts securing lower die.	Tighten rear bolts securing lower die.	
10	50	Move bolster.		Yes
11	30	Set pins for bolsters.	Move crane.	
12	30	Set ram at bottom dead point.	Adjust ram stroke.	Yes
13	50	Tighten front mounting bolts securing upper die.	Prepare to tighten rear bolts securing upper die.	
14	20	Raise ram (to top dead point).	Tighten rear bolts securing upper die.	Yes
15	15	Test die action of empty press.	Check switches and meters. Set pressing lever.	Yes
16	40	Insert material and process.	Check for safety and quality, etc.	
	Total time 470 sec. (7 min. 50 sec.)	Problems to watch for: (1) Twisted or severed cables or strands. (2) Vertical movement of dies while they are being exchanged. (3) Presence of any hazard on floor.	Actions to be confirmed: (1) Tightening of bolts. (2) Switch (on or off). (3) Bolster pin setting. (4) Meter. (5) Quality check.	OK On

TABLE 5-1. Procedural Chart for Parallel Operations

Managers often say that insufficient manpower prevents them from conducting parallel operations. With the SMED system this problem is eliminated because only a few minutes' assistance will be needed, and even unskilled workers can help, since the operations are simple ones. Assistance might be given by the operator of an automatic machine, by someone taking advantage of a lull between operations, or by a shift supervisor. With a little ingenuity, any number of methods can be found.

Even when the number of man-hours needed for setup operations is unchanged, parallel operations will cut elapsed time in half. This is a powerful tool for bringing setup times down to the single-minute range.

THE USE OF FUNCTIONAL CLAMPS

A functional clamp is an attachment device serving to hold objects in place with minimal effort. For example, the *direct attachment method* is used to secure a die to a press (*Figure 5-1*). A bolt is passed through a hole in the die and attached to the press bed. If the nut has fifteen threads on it, it cannot be tightened unless the bolt is turned fifteen times. In reality, though, it is the last turn that tightens the bolt and the first one that loosens it. The remaining fourteen turns are wasted. In traditional setups, even more turns are wasted because the length of the bolt exceeds that of the part to be attached. Moreover, fifteen threads on the bolt mean that fifteen threads' worth of friction will be required to oppose the clamping resistance when the nut is fastened.

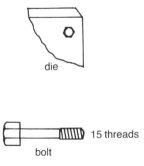

FIGURE 5-1. Direct Attachment Method and Bolt

If the purpose of a bolt is simply to fasten or unfasten, its length should be determined so that only one turn will be needed. The bolt will then be a functional clamp.

One-Turn Attachments

The following are examples of functional clamps that can fasten or unfasten objects with only one turn.* I have frequently challenged plant managers to adopt this technique. I like to tell them that they will be allowed one turn per screw during setup, but that they will be fined ¥100,000 ($413) for every additional turn.

The Pear-Shaped Hole Method

The problem here involved a large vulcanizing pan. Products were packed into the pan. The lid was then closed and secured with sixteen bolts, using a direct attachment method. The large number of bolts was needed to withstand considerable pressure. The operation took quite a long time because tightening required turning each bolt about thirty times. Opening the lid took a long time as well, and similarly required thirty turns for each of sixteen nuts. The movements needed to find and pick up loose nuts set down by the side of the pan made this a bothersome operation. Even though a few minutes had been saved by the use of an air-driven nut runner, the operation was still a nuisance.

To improve this setup, the bolt holes in the lid were made into pear-shaped holes (*Figure 5-2*) so that each nut could be loosened in one turn.

When all sixteen bolts had been loosened, the lid was turned counterclockwise by one bolt diameter. This brought the nuts to the large ends of the holes. The lid could now be removed immediately by a crane. To fasten the lid, the reverse process was carried out, and a single turn was sufficient to tighten the nuts. It was no longer necessary to remove the nuts from the bolts, so the process of searching for nuts was eliminated. In the old method, bolt and nut combinations changed with each setup; the new method solved this problem as well.

---

* EDITOR'S NOTE: Some people find that one turn of a standard thread bolt is insufficient and that specially designed threads are needed for this purpose.

clamping holes

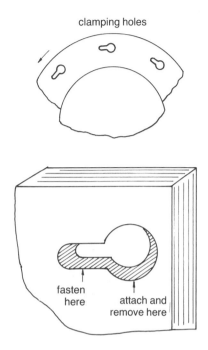

fasten
here

attach and
remove here

FIGURE 5-2. Pear-Shaped Holes for Clamping

The U-Shaped Washer Method

In this operation, wire was wound around the core of a motor.

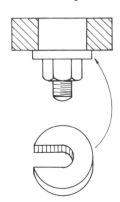

When winding was completed, the operation was carried out in the following sequence:

1. Loosen and remove clamping nut.
2. Remove washer.
3. Remove finished core.
4. Attach washer.
5. Turn nut and clamp.
6. Begin next winding operation.

FIGURE 5-3. The U-Shaped Washer

This operation was streamlined by replacing the washer with a U-shaped one (*Figure 5-3*).

The resulting sequence was as follows:

1. When winding is finished, stop the machine and loosen nut by one turn.
2. Slide off U-shaped washer.
3. Remove core with the nut in place (this is possible because the inside diameter of the core exceeds the outside diameter of the nut).
4. Slide U-shaped washer back on.
5. Fasten with one turn of the nut.
6. Begin next winding operation.

Using a U-shaped washer thus simplified the operation considerably. This example provides further evidence that fastening and unfastening can be readily performed with a single turn.

The U-shaped washer method was also very successful when applied to the attachment and removal of replacement gears on a gear-cutting machine.

The Split Thread Method

While doing some consulting work in the U.S. for Federal-Mogul Corporation, I commented that screws could be fastened or unfastened with a single turn. "Since one turn is all that is needed," I said, "let's agree that on my next visit you'll pay me a $1,000 penalty for each additional turn you use." Having extracted this promise, I returned to Japan.

When I revisited the plant six months later, a single-turn method had been implemented successfully. This is how it worked (*Figure 5-4*):

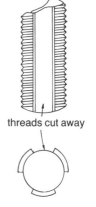

threads cut away

1. Grooves were cut along the length of the bolt to divide it into three sections.
2. Corresponding grooves were cut in the threads of the female screw.
3. In the attachment process, insertion was accomplished by aligning the ridges of the bolt with the grooves of the female screw. The bolt was then simply slipped all the way into position.

FIGURE 5-4. The Split Thread Method

4. The bolt was then tightened by a one-third turn.

In this particular case, the area of effective friction was preserved by lengthening the female screw.

The U-Slot Method

A U-shaped slot was cut in the attachment edge of a die. By inserting the head of the bolt into a dovetail groove on the machine bed, then sliding the bolt into the U-slot of the die, it became possible to fasten the die with one turn of the nut. This method guarantees a very strong attachment (*Figure 5-5*).

In one instance, problems were caused by washers slipping off and falling. This was solved by spot-welding the washers and nuts together. This U-slot method can often be used to improve setups where direct clamping has been used previously. It must be pointed out, though, that a single screw turn is not sufficient for fastening when the U-slot pieces are not of uniform thickness.

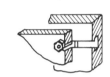

FIGURE 5-5. The U-Slot Method

The Clamp Method

As we have already pointed out, direct attachment methods often require many screw turns. One widely used alternative is the clamp method. In this technique, the die is secured by tightening the bolt on a clamp that presses down on the die (*Figure 5-6*).

This method, like the U-slot method, is useful only if all the items to be fastened are of uniform thickness. If thicknesses vary, the engineer will first have to standardize the parts to be attached.

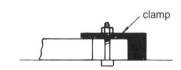

FIGURE 5-6. The Clamp Method

We have now seen various methods that make it possible for a screw to attach or release a die with a single turn. The key to developing attachment techniques lies in recognizing that the role of engaged threads is to maintain friction corresponding to the clamping pressure.

In the past, whenever an object needed to be secured, it was immediately assumed that it would be attached with screws, yet no thought whatsoever was given to the number of times the screws would have to be turned. Surely this point needs to be reconsidered. It is also important to recognize that screws and bolts are by no means the only way to attach objects.

One-Motion Methods

The concept of securing an object with a single motion lies behind a number of devices, including:

- Cams and clamps

- Wedges, tapered pins, and knock pins

- Springs

The elasticity in springs can be used to secure objects. Springs are usually used in pincer-type or expansion mechanisms. One company, however, applied spring elasticity in a simple operation to secure the replacement gears on a gear-cutting machine (*Figure 5-7*). In this application:

- A semicircular groove was cut along the length of the gear-shaft.

- Spring-mounted check pins with semicircular heads were installed at three points around the inside circumference of a clamping device.

- Where screws had been used in the past, the check pins of the new clamping device gripped the shaft from the side. When the correct position was reached, the check pins engaged the groove and clamping action was achieved.

This extremely simple clamping device made it possible to attach and remove replacement gears more quickly and easily. At the time I worried that the gears, which had previously been attached with

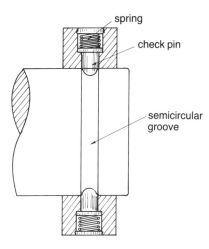

FIGURE 5-7. Spring Stops

screws, might come off if held in place only by springs. In fact, this has never happened. This method is also effective with helical gears, where the gear teeth are tapered. In this case, however, the number of check pins is increased to four.

Magnetism and Vacuum Suction

Magnetism and vacuums are very convenient when the entire surface of the workpiece is to be machined and there is no room for attachment devices. When suction is used, care must be taken that the surfaces are smooth and no air can leak out.

Interlocking Methods

We tend to assume that some sort of fastener is needed whenever an object is to be secured. On the contrary, in many circumstances it is enough to simply fit and join two parts together.

Securing Molds on a Plastic Forming Machine

At T Synthetics, handles are molded on a 500-ton plastic forming machine. Not a single screw is used to attach the molds. The procedure is as follows (*Figure 5-8*):

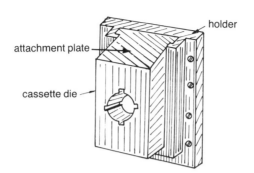

FIGURE 5-8. An Interlocking Method for Securing Plastic Dies

- The sizes and thicknesses of holding plates for both fixed and movable dies are standardized.

- "Cradles" corresponding to these plates are installed on the machine.

- Holding plates and the lower parts of the cradles are tapered so as to allow precise centering.

- Setup is conducted using two cranes. First, one crane hoists simultaneously the two molds used in the operation just completed and moves them away horizontally. At the same time, the two dies needed for the next operation are brought over by the second crane and fitted into the cradle. Engagement of the tapered sections ensures that the molds are set in the correct position.

- Since the same resin is used in both operations, and molds are always preheated, quality goods are produced from the first injection.

Only twenty-eight seconds are needed to complete this setup.

When we say that the capacity of the molding machine is 500 tons, we mean that the pressure of the injected resin is 500 tons, and that the mold is closed with a force of 500 tons. By no means does this mean that a 500-ton force is needed to open the mold. Only a small amount of force is needed to peel away the finished product. Consequently, sufficient strength is obtained by engaging the holding plate and machine. Maintaining a load on the mold itself is also required, and engagement alone is adequate to achieve this.

Thus, it is possible to secure the molds without using a single screw, and to reduce setup time substantially. The two molds are centered easily with the use of tapered pins on one and tapered projections on the other that serve as guides for engagement.

An Interlocking Method for Press Dies

The following work is performed by a metal press:

1. The upper die is lowered from the top dead point until it touches the raw material.
2. From contact with the raw material until it reaches the bottom dead point, the upper die punctures, bends, compresses, etc. by downward pressure.
3. For puncturing, pressure is needed only during the instant when the hole is actually opened. After the hole has been made, the only resistance remaining is friction between the punch and raw material, so no great force is needed.
4. For bending or compressing, the material separates as the upper die rises from the bottom dead point. With puncturing, too, the punch leaves the raw material as it passes through the hole.
5. After separating from the raw material, the upper die is raised to the top dead point.

From this perspective, the only time a machine needs its full capacity is during active processing in step 2. It is fair to say that the machine is "loafing" during the other steps (1, 3, 4, and 5), and that it is working only about one-tenth of the time.

On an ordinary press, the upper die is attached to the machine ram, the lower die is attached to the machine bed, and the accuracy of the machine guarantees the accuracy of alignment between the dies. In general, we need to question why the same number and diameter of bolts are used to attach both dies. The reason for this is that the attachment of the upper die must support the weight of the die and prevent horizontal movement. But because the weight of the lower die is supported by the machine bed, the lower die need only be attached so as to prevent horizontal movement. In addition, the capacities of the clamping bolts are more or less irrelevant when the mold is being made, for the strength of the ram and the bed, and of the dies themselves, is sufficient to withstand the casting load. Consequently, no screws at all are needed. All one has to do is:

- Standardize the sizes and thicknesses of the holding plates.

- Install cradles for these holding plates on the ram bed.

- To align the dies, either maintain a high degree of accuracy in mounting each die, or, where this is inadequate, install tapered holes and pins as alignment guides.

If the die set method is used, moreover, the function of aligning the dies will be accomplished by the die set itself.

In any event, analysis of the function of various presses will more or less eliminate the need for screw fastening. The interlocking method alone will perform this function adequately. The adoption of this method makes substantial reductions in setup time possible.

As explained above, the actual processing time of a press is extremely short. You must therefore consider techniques for using its energy efficiently. When a press is rising, for example, its capacity can be used to:

- Activate devices to extract items

- Activate devices to clear away scrap

- Activate devices to carry items away

- Power the raising of upper dies for die set presses

- Power conveyors transporting items to the next process

To sum up, one should not assume that screws are necessary every time something needs to be secured. It is extremely important to analyze basic functions and devise the least costly and troublesome securing method.

Direction and Magnitude of Forces

Very effective methods of securing objects can be found by considering the directions in which forces are needed and the magnitude of force needed in each direction.

For instance, in one operation, six stoppers were screwed to each of the six spindles of a boring machine. The operation was a nuisance because the screws had to be turned in extremely cramped conditions. After completing an on-site inspection of the operation, I asked the section chief what the function of the stoppers was.

"We need them," he replied, "for setting positions during processing."

"Look," I told him, "there are three directions in space: left-to-right, front-to-back, and up-and-down. Since the stopper is engaging the opposite spindle, left-to-right and up-and-down movement are both prevented, aren't they?"

"The problem is front-to-back movement," he said.

"The stopper obviously bears a force from the opposite direction," I replied. "Since it is engaged, it will be supported by the end of the spindle. The remaining difficulty is determining how much force is required to remove it." I suggested that pulling off the stopper should involve, at most, enough force for the head of the workpiece to catch on the stopper face when covered with oil. In that case, there would be no need to use screws. We improved the operation as follows (*Figure 5-9*):

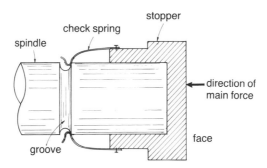

FIGURE 5-9. **Securing a Stopper**

- Threads were removed to make cylindrical fits.

- Circumferential semicircular check grooves were cut near the ends of the spindles.

- Springs were attached at three places around the edge of each stopper. When a stopper was fitted on a spindle, the springs and groove would engage and the spring tension would prevent the stopper from coming off.

The stoppers were attached merely by fitting them onto the spindles, thereby greatly simplifying the operation. An analysis of the directions and magnitudes of the necessary forces had led to the adoption of this simple method.

Analysis of the forces involved in attaching press dies also made it possible to improve setup by switching from threaded clamps to an interlocking method.

In short, effective improvements can be made by studying actual clamping functions rather than by assuming that threaded fasteners will suffice for everything.

ELIMINATION OF ADJUSTMENTS

As already explained, adjustments and test runs normally account for as much as 50% of setup time. Eliminating them, therefore, will always lead to tremendous time savings. Note that elimination of adjustments means just that — *elimination* — not just a reduction in the time given over to them.

Test runs and adjustments are necessitated by inaccurate centering, dimensioning, etc., earlier in the internal setup procedure. It is extremely important to recognize that adjustments are not an independent operation. To eliminate them, we must move back a step and improve the earlier stages of internal setup.

Fixing Numerical Settings

Eliminating adjustments requires, above all, abandoning reliance on intuition in setting machines for production. Intuitive judgments may have some sort of statistical validity, but they remain inexact and do not have the same precision as constant value settings.

In my frequent visits to factories, I often tell the foremen: "Since you are so convinced of the value of determining settings by intuition, do it three times on the same machine. If you get the same results each time, then there's no problem. If you get good results only twice, then the method has to be abandoned."

"Why," I am asked, "is three times all right, but not twice?" To this I reply that although three plums on a slot machine is a winning combination, two plums alone are worthless. This gets a laugh, but it also underscores an important point: as long as settings are made on the basis of intuition, there is no way to avoid test runs.

The initial step in doing away with adjustments is to make calibrations. When intuition prevails, there is no way for fixed amounts to be represented. Calibrations overcome that problem. Everyone knows what it means to "set the dial at five," and the same value can be set the next time. It is possible, moreover, for other people to set the machine to the same value.

Although graduated scales in themselves have a positive impact, they by no means eliminate adjustments completely. Still, the use of graduated scales will lead to significant improvements in setups involving a wide range of possible settings.

Visual calibration readings generally yield accuracies to 0.5 mm. When greater accuracy is required, calipers will permit another magnitude of precision. Installing a dial gauge makes it possible to take readings on the order of 0.01 mm, and even greater accuracy can be obtained with numerical control devices. The use of the digital method is also satisfactory in this respect. Measurement devices for numerical settings have been greatly refined in recent years, so improvements can often be secured simply by installing a sufficiently accurate measurement tool for the task at hand.

In one application, a magnescale was used for dimensioning on a woodworking double sizer. This dramatically increased accuracy and allowed faster setup time than the previous method, in which parallels were set by sight.

When measurements require fixed numerical values, gauges can be used for extremely rapid settings for dimensioning and centering. As the types of measurements to be set increase, however, the number of gauges grows and the operation becomes cumbersome. In this situation, it is possible to reduce the variety of gauges considerably by using combinations of a limited number of instruments. This combination is determined by a mathematical technique based on powers of two. Consider this series:

$$1, 2, 4, 8, 16 \ldots 2^n$$

In combination, the first four terms can represent any number up to fifteen. This result is obtained as follows:

a

a + 1 = b

a + b + 1 = c

a + b + c + 1 = d

The number of values can be increased by continuing this series. For reference purposes, *Figure 5-10* gives the values from one to thirty-five expressed in terms of these powers. When these values are multiplied by a power of ten — 10, 100, 1,000, etc. — they can be applied to a considerable range of common gauge settings.

Imaginary Center Lines and Reference Planes

When setup is actually being performed on a machine, no center lines or reference planes are visible. They must be found by trial and error, which can be a lengthy process. A number of techniques can alleviate this problem.

Lathe Operations and Taper Cutting

In this example, a section of each shaft had to be tapered. The taper was cut on a lathe by offsetting the tailstock toward the front. Setting the amount by which the tailstock was to be offset was a very difficult task. The following method arrived at the correct setting by repeated trial and error and test runs:

- The shaft was suitably offset, then cut. The product was measured and further adjustments in the degree of offset were made.

- Another shaft was cut, the taper was measured, and adjustments were made.

This had become an operation requiring considerable time and skill. The difficulty was increased because it was impossible to know in advance how much to offset the tailstock, since a taper had already been cut in the previous one.

We were able to make several improvements in this operation:

- A reference scale was installed on the machine bed near the tailstock and parallel to the machine's center line.

Prime Nos \ Totals	1	2	3	4	5	6	7	8	9	10	11	12	13	14	15	16	17	18	19	20	21	22	23	24	25	26	27	28	29	30	31	32	33	34	35
1	◎		◁		◁				◁	◁																									
2		◎	◁		◁				◁	◁																									
4				◎	◁				◁	◁			◁		◁								◁	◁											
※6						◎							◁		◁						◁		◁	◁											
※7							◎		◁				◁		◁				◁	◁			◁		◁			◁	◁						
8								◎								◎										◁	◁	◁		◁					
11											◎														◁	◁	◁				◁	◁	◁		
12												◎		◎					◁	◁								◁		◁					
14																					◁				◁	◁	◁				◁				
※16																◎	◎						◁				◁	◁				◁	◁	◁	
※17																	◎						◁					◁			◁	◁	◁	◁	◁
18																		◎						◁	◁				◁	◁	◁	◁		◁	◁

1. ◎ Only one gauge necessary
2. ◁ Combination of two gauges
3.   Other combinations are possible
4. ※ May be omitted from the series if three-gauge combinations are permitted

FIGURE 5-10. Powers of Two and the Number of Gauges

- A gauge was set on this scale. The side of the tailstock was pushed against it. This brought the tailstock parallel to the center line and positioned the center of the tailstock above the center line.

- Standard calibration marks were made in a section of the tailstock and a dial gauge was placed against them. The degree of offset corresponding to the taper indicated on the calibrated scale was then set.

With this method, it became possible to produce correctly machined products after the initial setting.

The distinction between *setting* and *adjusting* is not fully appreciated in most factories. Many people are under the impression that adjustments are a necessary evil in setup procedures. Workers pride themselves on how frequently, cleverly, and quickly they can make adjustments. This is indeed a skill — an important one — but we must not lose sight of improvements that can make the adjustments unnecessary. We must recognize clearly that setting and adjusting are completely different functions. Our goal should be to design measures based on settings, not adjustments. A highly effective approach is to substitute visible center lines and reference planes for imaginary ones. This approach is applicable to drill presses, milling machines, and all other machine tools.

Setting Centers on a Milling Machine

At D Plastics, making a plastic mold involves aligning the center of the milling machine cutter with the center of the workpiece. In the usual operation, which is tedious and requires a certain degree of skill, the cutter was pushed up against the material. Measurement depended on markings made on the workpiece. We improved this operation considerably (*Figure 5-11*):

1. Two V-blocks were installed on the machine parallel to the table's center line to function as centering jigs.
2. Two more V-blocks parallel to this center line were installed on the table itself.
3. Cylindrical standard blocks were made. By pressing them against the table so that they were held between the V-

blocks, we were able to align the center of the table with the center of the cutter.

4. When the workpiece was attached to the center of the table, it was in alignment with the cutter. Trial cutting thus became unnecessary.

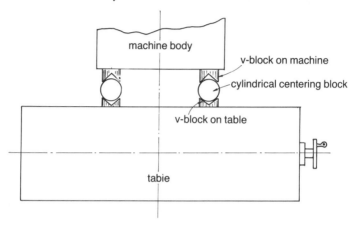

FIGURE 5-11.   Centering on a Milling Machine (Top View)

The cutter's center line was imaginary. Since processing on the milling machine involved constant back-and-forth movement of the table, no reference line had previously existed.

Our basic improvement consisted of using V-blocks and cylindrical blocks to return the table to a reference line, and then making settings from that position.

Another problem soon emerged. Even though the workpiece was easily centered, it shifted about 0.05 mm while being secured by clamps and fastened with bolts. This was annoying because it meant fastening the workpiece temporarily, measuring it with a dial gauge, making adjustments, and then securing the adjusted workpiece without disturbing anything.

After studying the operation, I asked the section manager: "Do you know why putting on two pairs of socks keeps you from getting blisters from golf shoes that are too tight?"

"I'm afraid I don't," he said, so I gave him the following explanation (*Figure 5-12*):

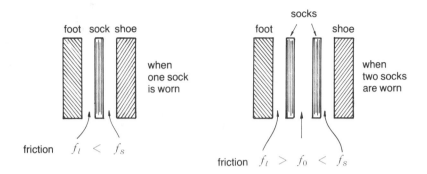

FIGURE 5-12. Socks and Chafing Action

"Suppose f_s is the coefficient of friction between your socks and your shoes. When you wear one layer of socks, f_s is greater than the coefficient of friction between the socks and your foot (f_t), so the socks adhere to your shoes and rub freely against your skin, giving you blisters. If you wear another layer of socks, though, the outer socks adhere to your shoes, and the inner socks adhere to your foot; friction occurs only between the inner and outer socks. You don't get blisters because your feet aren't rubbed.

"Similarly, if you use only one washer in attaching the workpiece to the milling machine, then friction will gradually increase between the bottom of the washer and the top of the clamp as you tighten it. The force of friction on the lower surface of the clamp will cause the workpiece to shift. Why don't we try attaching it with two washers?"

We then fastened the workpiece by putting two washers on the clamp, with a drop of oil between the washers. The lower washer no longer moved at all and the workpiece did not slip. We were able to do away with the pointless operation of temporary fastening, adjusting, and then securing.

Setting Drill Positions on a Multishaft Drill Press

At H Optics, a multishaft drill press was used to drill six holes of equal pitch in flanges. An operation was conducted to determine the proper positions of the drills. Workers were often unable to determine the correct drill positions, so I was called in to observe the setup operation.

The position of each drill holder was set by attaching the workpiece to the bed and then using markings to align it with the drill head. Since the six positions could not be determined simultaneously, repeated adjustments had to be made. This required quite a long time.

At this point, I made a simple suggestion: "The center line of this drill press passes through the socket supporting the drill head, but this is an imaginary line and there is no corresponding reference line on the bed to which the workpieces are attached. How about transferring the line corresponding to the center of the machine to the bed?"

We made a tapered hole in the center of the bed that was aligned exactly with the center of the machine. The shaft of a jig was then engaged in this tapered hole. Above it, we installed a jig that determined the position of the hole's center. The drill holder was pressed against this. In this way it was possible to set drill positions at one stroke.

This example, in which the imaginary center of a machine is made visible, demonstrates the principle of making settings but not adjustments.

Setting Blanks on a Hobbing Machine

At Z Enterprises, a cutter was mounted on a hobbing machine and a gear blank was inserted so that it could be cut into a helical gear. This operation involved adjusting the alignment of the blank holder according to variations in the sizes of the hob cutters and blanks. Previously, the hob cutter had been set in the center, rotated and gradually made to approach the blank on the blank holder. At the instant contact was made, the blank holder was stopped and secured. Judging the precise moment of contact required a great deal of skill.

This setup was improved as shown in *Figure 5-13*. First the equipment was modified as follows:

- A reference shaft for the cutter was installed in a location corresponding to the center of the cutter spindle on the fixed bed of the machine.

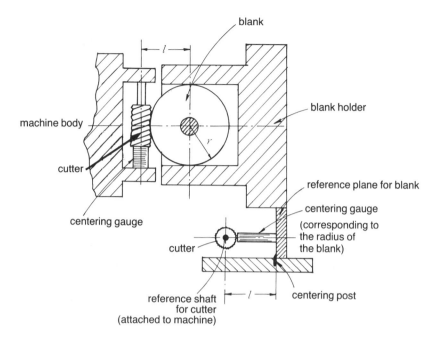

FIGURE 5-13. **Setting the Position of a Blank**

• A reference plane was installed on part of the blank holder.

The new setup took place in four steps:

1. The cutter to be used on the reference shaft was attached.
2. A gauge corresponding to the radius of the blank was inserted between the cutter and the reference plane. The blank holder was then brought into contact with the cutter.
3. This position was marked with a centering post.
4. The cutter was attached to the cutter shaft and rotated. The blank was mounted on the blank holder. Then, the blank holder was secured to the position indicated by the centering post.

This eliminated the demanding task of determining the position of the blank holder while rotating the cutter.

In this operation, it was necessary to align the centers of the hob cutter and the machine. This step, too, was simplified and alignment made easier: a reference plane was installed on the part that joined the cutter shaft, and various saddle-shaped gauges were used to set the center of each cutter, depending on the cutter's length.

Height Gauges and Center Settings

F Precision Instruments is a manufacturer of metal dies for die casting and plastic molding machines. While drawings often showed measurements from a center line, they did not show measurements from a reference plane used in processing. For this reason, it was necessary to place the raw material on the surface plate and then mark off the locations of holes or parts to be cut.

- The material was first leveled with a spirit level, and then supported with a jack.

- The height of the upper surface was measured with a height gauge.

- Drawing values were consulted, the distance to the center position calculated, and the center marked off with a height gauge. Allowance was made, of course, for the top and bottom cutting margins.

- With this center line as a reference, the positions of holes and sections to be cut were marked off successively. By using the drawings, it was then possible to calculate the values for setting the center line.

This was all quite a nuisance and led to lost operating time. Furthermore, occasional miscalculations led to quality defects. The following improvements were made:

- A specially designed height scale was developed by attaching an auxiliary scale, or vernier, to the back of a regular height gauge. A center point was marked on the vernier, with graduations above and below it.

- With the workpiece held level, the dimensions of its upper face were measured with the height gauge. Then the center of the main scale was set and secured at the height of this surface.

- With the drawing as a reference, the indicator needle on the main scale was lowered by an amount corresponding to the distance from the center line to the upper surface plus an estimated value for the cutting margins.

- The center of the vernier was then aligned with the needle on the main scale. The vernier needle now indicated the center point, so measurements above and below the center line could be marked by moving the needle on the vernier.

This did away with the need to make calculations based on drawings and virtually eliminated subsequent errors. Although it seems trivial, the workers had often made errors in subtraction, and this in turn had necessitated repeated checks of their arithmetic. With the improved procedure, anyone could mark off divisions easily by using the specially-made height gauge.

The Least Common Multiple System

The Least Common Multiple (LCM) System may be thought of as a technique for eliminating adjustments. It is a powerful method based upon a simple concept of arithmetic. The name refers to the notion of providing a number of mechanisms corresponding to the least common multiple of various operating conditions. The workers then perform only the functions required for a given operation. This can greatly enhance the speed of setup operations.

A slogan arising from this method is: *Leave the mechanism alone, and modify only the function.*

One-Touch Exchange of Plastic Forming Molds

This example comes from an operation for molding television dials. Notable features of the production process included the following:

- It was necessary to change molds because two parts being made, A and B, required different types of resins.

- The large orders for these parts required the use of one machine for a solid month.

- To avoid excess inventory of one part or the other, lots were alternated daily. This led to an enormous amount of setup time.

The improvements described below successfully dealt with this situation.

- As shown in *Figure 5-14*, four dies — A_1, A_2, B_1, B_2 — were cut in a single die block.

- The flow of resin was directed into A_1 and A_2 when part A was produced, and into B_1 and B_2 when part B was produced, simply by rotating the central resin channels 90°.

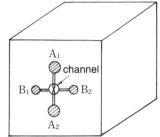

FIGURE 5-14. A One-Touch Exchange Die

This made it possible for setup changes and resin switches to be performed in five minutes or so. By raising productivity and drastically reducing inventories, this method succeeded in killing two birds with one stone.

Inspecting Steering Wheels for Wobble

Toyota used a special device for inspecting molded steering wheels. A jig fitting the steering wheel of each car model — Crown, Corolla, Corona, and Celica — was mounted in the center of this device. Setting the central jig required great accuracy.

Since this was beyond the abilities of the part-time workers charged with inspection, a shift supervisor handled the setup. He turned it back to the workers only after repeated centering and adjusting had allowed him to align the jig. In addition to requiring a high level of skill, this operation kept workers idle during the centering procedure. A quality control (QC) circle assigned to study the problem came up with the following suggestions (*Figure 5-15*):

- Build a box-shaped inspection bench.

- On its four faces mount the special center jigs for each car model, one to each surface, making sure that the jigs do not wobble at all.

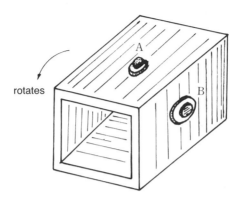

FIGURE 5-15. Rotating Jig for Wobble Inspection

- In the actual operation for, say, the Corona, turn up the appropriate face of the inspection bench and hold it in place with a stopper.

With this procedure, there was no need to center each jig every time an operation changed. Furthermore, the setup operation could be performed easily, quickly and independently by a part-time worker.

Countersink Boring of Motor Core Shafts

This operation involved using a drill to countersink a hole for a stationary screw in a motor core shaft. Since the cores were of eight different lengths, stoppers had to be repositioned each time the operation changed. This required repeated test runs and adjustments, following this procedure:

- The stopper was loosened and repositioned.

- Measurements were made and a preliminary setting was established.

- A test run was conducted. If unsuccessful, it was followed by further adjustment.

- When the correct measurements had been made, the stopper was tightened and the operation began.

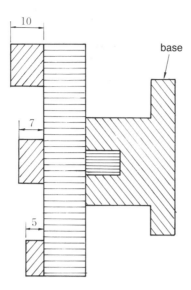

FIGURE 5-16. A Rotary Stopper

With the improvement shown in *Figure 5-16*, the entire operation was vastly simplified:

- Stopper plugs of eight heights were made and mounted on a single plate.

- When the operation changed, all that had to be done was to rotate the plate to set the stopper at the desired height. The plate was then secured.

This arrangement eliminated the need for adjustment or test runs. While the old method had produced three or four substandard products each time, this new technique reduced that number to zero.

Changing Bits on an Automatic Lathe

At T Industries, machining two types of camshaft necessitated changing four bits on an automatic lathe at every setup. The operation was originally performed in the following manner:

- Remove the four bits for the previous operation.

- Mount the four new bits and use gauges to adjust them.

- Conduct test runs, measure product and make adjustments.

- After repeated adjustments have yielded the correct measurements, begin cutting.

We made two significant improvements in this setup (*Figure 5-17*):

- A rotating toolpost was constructed. Four bits were mounted on the front and four on the back.

- Setup consisted merely of rotating the toolpost 180 degrees to place the appropriate set of bits in position. The subsequent operation could then begin.

(A) for large workpieces

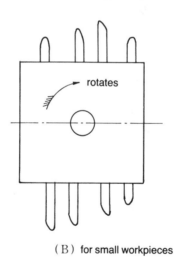

(B) for small workpieces

FIGURE 5-17. A Rotating Toolpost

Exchanging Profile Templates

Cutting shafts on a copying lathe at H Optics involved a troublesome exchange of profile templates. The procedure was time consuming because it called for great skill, precision, and repeated adjustments. All of this resulted in a bottleneck in the manufacturing process.

While on a visit to the plant, I saw that the template was spindle-shaped and cut around its circumference. I remarked that the copying function called for a linear template rather than a circular one. By sinking six flat templates into a shaft, one could obtain the required copying function by rotating the shaft. This improvement made it possible to perform setup changes with a one-sixth rotation of the template shaft (*Figure 5-18*).

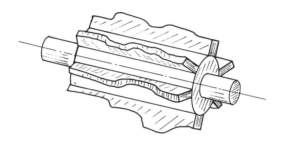

FIGURE 5-18. **Rotating Profile Templates**

Since spindle-shaped templates had always been used in the past, it had been assumed that templates had to be removed to be changed. The key to this improvement was the realization that we only needed a linear template to perform this function. The improved procedure also led to a significant reduction in time and in the skill required to perform the task.

Setting Intervals on a Grinding Machine

H Iron Works manufactures shafts of varying shapes and sizes. Since the pitch of surfaces ground on shafts varies according to the size of the outer shaft involved, every setup change required several steps:

- Remove the outer grinding wheel.
- Extract a spacer.
- Insert a thin spacer of the next width.
- Remount the grinding wheel.

We made several changes to improve this setup (*Figure 5-19*):

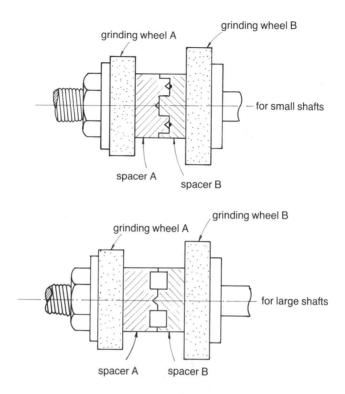

FIGURE 5-19. Setting Intervals on Grinding Surfaces

- Notches of equal pitch were made at four locations around the circumference of each of the two ring-shaped spacers.

- For processing the larger shafts, the peaks of the notches cut into the two spacers were placed together, leaving open spaces between them.

- For the smaller shafts, the peaks and valleys of the two spacers were fitted together.

This eliminated the bothersome task of constantly removing grinding wheels and replacing spacers.

One-Touch Exchange of Press Dies

In this case, setup was performed on a 500-ton press used to make washing machines at M Electric Company. The firm produced several types of machines, including left-handed and right-handed models, and plain and deluxe models. In addition, two styles of control knob placement were available. Even though all the bodies were the same, eight types of setup were required for the various notches and holes. The results of mechanical improvements in this instance were that:

- One press combined functions for all eight types of molds.

- A spacer could be inserted and removed for lowering the ram and punches.

- The spacer could be controlled electrically.

By flipping switches on a control panel, a worker could make instantaneous changes so that, for example, two standard models could be followed by one deluxe, five right-handed, and three left-handed models. This alternating production led to a considerable reduction in inventories and a dramatic drop in setup time.

Setup on a Multishaft Drill Press

In this operation holes were made in clutch parts at either four or six points. Because every change in the type of workpiece required a new drill holder setting, the setup time was considerable.

Two holders were added so that a total of eight holders permitted both four-drill and six-drill configurations (*Figure 5-20*). When four holes were to be drilled, drills were mounted in the holders for the four-hole configuration and the other four holders were left empty. When six holes were to be drilled, drills were mounted in the holders for the six-hole configuration and the remaining two holders were left empty. This made it possible to shift between the two combinations merely by inserting or removing drills.

The result was the elimination of setup change adjustments and a setup which could be performed in about two minutes.

Two-Story Bender Dies

K Industries is a manufacturer of filing cabinets, desks, and other office equipment. At its factory, two bending operations, L-shaped and U-shaped, were needed to form the side plates for filing cabinets. These operations had previously been carried out separately on a single bender. Side plates that had been bent once would thus

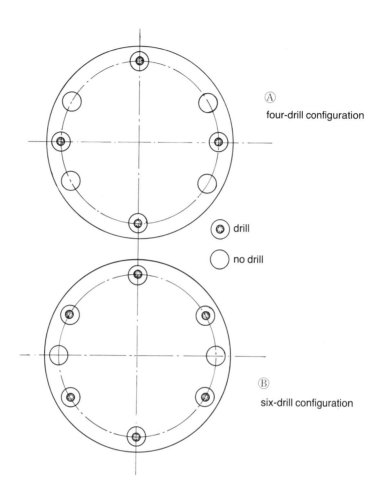

A
four-drill configuration

drill

no drill

B
six-drill configuration

FIGURE 5-20. **Setup on a Multishaft Drill Press**

tend to accumulate around the machine. Not only did they take up a great deal of space, but they were often damaged in handling.

The operation was improved by the development of a "two-story" bender: the first bending operation was performed on the "upper-story" die, and the second bend was made on the lower die. This made it possible to process the products continuously in an assembly-line procedure. Goods no longer piled up next to the machine, and a continuous flow could be conveyed to the next operation. Handling operations were greatly reduced, man-hours were cut, and productivity rose about 20%.

Positioning Washing Machines

Automatic mounting is an intermediate process in washing machine assembly. In this process, positioning stoppers are installed on a pallet where the machine is to be set. In this example, there were four models, and each change required replacing the stoppers.

This operation was modified by placing in the corners of the pallet four stoppers that were made to rotate automatically just before the assembly began (*Figure 5-21*). The widths and depths of the washing machine models varied, and the rotating stoppers were made with notches corresponding to these differences. They could be turned easily to the proper position.

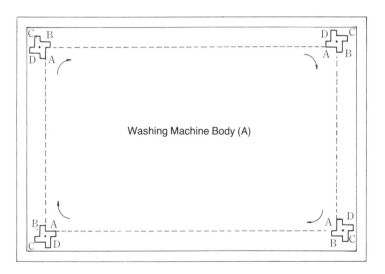

FIGURE 5-21. Positioning Washing Machine Bodies

This change made setup quite simple and eliminated the need for human labor. Small-lot production was adopted, and no problems arose in spite of the increased number of setups.

Changing Limit Switches

This example concerns an operation in which a limit switch controlled the end point of machining for making shafts. Since there were five types of shafts involved, the switch needed to be moved among five locations. Every time a position was changed, a number of steps were followed. First, the switch was moved. Test runs were then conducted to verify that the switch was at the proper location. When it was not, adjustments were made. Its position was then rechecked. With this system, as many as four readjustments had to be made.

The operation was improved as follows (*Figure 5-22*):

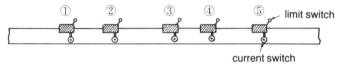

FIGURE 5-22. **Changing Limit Switches**

- Five switches were installed — one at each of the five sites.

- An electric switch was provided to supply current to each of the five limit switches.

- To activate, for example, the third limit switch, only the third electric switch was turned on; no current flowed to the other switches, which remained off. This system functioned similarly for all the other limit switches.

This arrangement made it possible to perform setup changes simply by flipping a switch. It demonstrates the successful application of the "one-touch" concept. Using this technique, it became possible to change limit switches in less than one second.

The large number of examples of the Least Common Multiple system has been presented for two reasons. The first is that with this system, extremely easy, yet extraordinarily effective improvements are possible. The second is that these examples can be applied in a variety of situations if the engineer will only take the trouble to modify them according to the conditions in his plant.

It is important to recognize that the LCM system rests on two fundamental principles:

- Make settings, not adjustments.

- Change only functions; leave mechanisms as they are.

Undoubtedly many improvements can be made by examining your own operations in the light of this concept. I fervently hope that many important improvements in production will result from using this approach.

Mechanization

Only after every attempt has been made to improve setups using the methods we have already described should mechanization be considered. Bear in mind that the many basic techniques we have covered so far will often serve to reduce a two-hour setup to one requiring about three minutes. Mechanization may then further reduce the time by another minute or so.

Avoid the mistake of jumping into mechanization from the start, however. There is a simple reason for this. Mechanizing an inefficient setup operation will achieve time reductions, but it will do little to remedy the basic faults of a poorly designed setup process. It is much more effective to mechanize setups that have already been streamlined.

Mechanization of Die Movement

Although small blades, jigs, dies, and gauges do not pose much of a problem, mechanization is essential for moving large press dies, die-casting dies, and plastic molds. The following methods deal with this type of mechanization.

Using forklifts for insertion in machines. Using forklists to align dies and insert items in machines is both simple and widely practiced. It requires the conducting of simultaneous operations as well as a certain degree of ingenuity.

Moving bolsters. This method is convenient for moving the heavy dies used on large presses. It is even more convenient when two bolsters are made to move in parallel. Due consideration should be given, however, to the fairly high investment required for equipment.

The roller conveyor method. Medium-sized dies can be inserted into machines by a roller conveyor. A single roller cart can deliver one set of dies and pick up the dies from the previous operation.

In a variation on this method, two carts are used. The old dies are removed from the machine, and the new dies, which have been brought over on one cart, are installed. At the same time, the old dies are loaded on the second cart and carried away. This method is often employed where human power is used instead of machinery.

The circuit method. Where small dies are involved, a roller conveyor is sometimes set up around the sides and back of a machine. The dies to be used for a given operation are lined up on the conveyor. Setup consists of moving from right to left, inserting and removing dies in order. This is certainly a possible approach, though perhaps it does not merit an overly enthusiastic recommendation.

Some plants perform successive setups with the help of parking elevator-type racks constructed on either side of the machine.

Revolving die holders. One common and fairly convenient method for dealing with medium-sized and smaller dies makes use of a revolving holder equipped with a roller conveyor. After picking up the old die, the holder is rotated so that the new die can be inserted in the machine.

The rubber cushion method. A rubber cushion apparatus to insert in the dovetail grooves of a press can be quite useful. This device works as follows:

- Roller bearings or needle bearings are installed on the upper side of the cushion.

- Fairly rigid urethane rubber is glued to the bottom half.

- When a die is being inserted, the elasticity of the rubber allows the heads of the bearings to project onto the bed. The new die can now be inserted with a light push.

- When the die is attached and tightened with bolts, the rubber contracts and the bearings sink below the level of the bed.

- Die removal is performed in the reverse order.

This apparatus is widely used because it can be manufactured inexpensively.

The air cushion method. Some devices on the market use air pressure to the same effect as the rubber cushion just described. This method also permits simple and inexpensive transportation of dies (*Figure 5-23*).

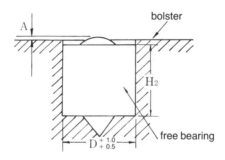

FIGURE 5-23. Air Cushion

The air cushion uses a simple attachment method:

- As shown at the right in the figure, free bearings are inserted in holes made in the bolster of a press or similar machine.

- With care given to the depth of the hole, A is set at 2 mm (+ 0/ − 0.5), as shown at the left.

In another method, balls are buried in the bed of a large press. When the balls sink under the weight of a die, air is released that supports the die. Although this method enables a worker to insert fairly large dies easily, the apparatus is more expensive than the air cushion.

Various other improvement devices that depend on mechanizing die movement are also available. In choosing among them, one must weigh the advantages against the cost of the necessary equipment.

Mechanization of Die Tightening and Loosening

Dies can be tightened or loosened by remote control by using oil or air pressure. This approach is extremely convenient, but it is only cost effective on fairly large machines.

Automated Shut Height Adjustment

Electrical devices exist that may be used to adjust shut heights automatically. However, bear in mind that priority should always be given to eliminating these adjustments altogether by standardizing die heights.

Using Energy From Presses

Many methods have been developed for moving dies onto presses. I find it strange, however, that the energy of the press itself is rarely used to power die insertion. The power of a press is more than adequate, and can be applied either with wheel-and-axle and gear mechanisms or by simply repeating the up-and-down motion of the die three or four times.

As already mentioned, mechanization may be of great importance in itself, but it is only incidental to SMED. Furthermore, though mechanization can often produce dramatic improvements, costs can be excessive, and they must always be weighed carefully against the desired benefits.

SUMMARY

Chapter 5 completes the description of techniques that can be used to implement SMED by focusing on the improvement of internal setup operations. The most powerful techniques involve the implementation of parallel operations, the use of several types of functional clamps, and the elimination of adjustments.

Chapters 3–5 have covered the central issues of this book. If one is simply going to imitate SMED, then it is probably enough to understand the concrete techniques presented in these chapters.

Techniques alone are of help, however, only in circumstances that precisely match those cited.

Broader and more varied applications and developments can be found for other industries and other machines if the following aspects of SMED are understood (*Figure 5-24*):

- Conceptual stages

- Practical methods

- Concrete techniques

As you will soon appreciate, success in a variety of manufacturing situations ultimately depends more on knowing *why* than on merely knowing *how*.

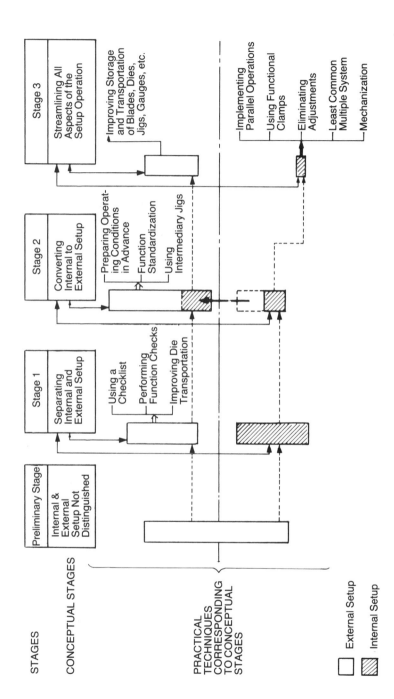

FIGURE 5-24. The Single-Minute Setup (SMED): Conceptual Stages and Practical Techniques

6

Basic Examples of SMED

The SMED system can be applied to many types of machines. Following are examples involving metal presses and plastic forming machines.

METAL PRESSES

Single-Shot Presses

On single-shot presses, the following operations must be improved to decrease setup time:

- Shut height adjustments

- Die centering

- Die mounting

- Moving dies within machines

- Transporting dies from storage to machines

Adjusting Shut Height

Shut height adjustment is one of the most critical and demanding aspects of setup on a press. Punching allows a small margin of error, but if a shut height adjustment for bending or pressing results in an insufficient stroke, perfect moldings will be impossible. If the stroke is too large, on the other hand, the mold will be destroyed. For this reason, small strokes are generally used at first. The proper measurements are then found by making a series of slight adjustments. This is a tedious operation requiring considerable skill.

93

The reason that shut height adjustments are necessary in the first place is that die heights differ. In other words, the entire problem of shut height adjustment can be eliminated by standardizing die heights. Die heights should be made uniform according to the capacity of the machine in question. In general, die heights are standardized by attaching shims or blocks of appropriate thicknesses on shorter dies so that they match taller ones, or shaving off sections that are too high where necessary.

In actual practice a single die may be used for operations on both a 60- and a 100-ton press. In such a situation, it would be desirable for die heights on the two presses to be the same, but this is not really necessary. It is sufficient to use spacers attached during external setup.

If die heights are standardized, then once the shut height is set, no subsequent resetting will be necessary. Tedious and demanding operations will have been eliminated and setup time reduced substantially.

As mentioned above, however, setting shut heights demands a high degree of precision. Consequently, it is important to make corresponding die settings accurately. Otherwise, shut height adjustments will be unavoidable in spite of the effort devoted to die height standardization.

A further question often arises concerning dies that must be reground. Spacers must be inserted and die heights reset. One method used in this situation is replacing the block with one that is thicker by the amount that has been ground off. Blocks used in such die height adjustments are usually attached to the bottom of the lower die. In some situations they may be attached to the top of the upper die (*Figure 6-1* and *Plate 6-1*).

This approach may be thought of as an application of the external function standardization concept described in Chapter 4.

Centering the Die

When setting up a press, the die must be positioned in the center of the bolster. With small presses in particular, the shank attachment hole in the center of the ram must fit onto the die shank and then be secured with screws. This method requires centering the die precisely. In the past, the ram would be inched downward, aligned by

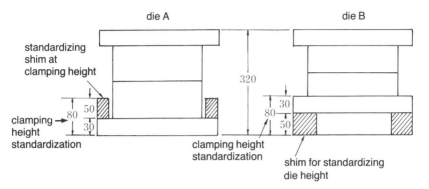

FIGURE 6-1. Die Height Standardization (Block on Bottom)

PLATE 6-1. Die Height Standardization (Block on Top)

sight with the die's shank, then joined. Since the die could be destroyed if the ram had not been correctly aligned, this alignment procedure was carried out with extreme caution. The entire operation was both time-consuming and difficult.

This operation can be improved as shown in *Figure 6-2*. A centering jig is fixed on the machine at a spot 200 mm from the center of the bolster. V-shaped projections are provided on both sides of the center of this jig. If the distance from the center of the shank to the far edge of the die is, for example, 140 mm, a jig 60 mm wide is spot-welded to the other side of the die. (If the distance from the center were 160 mm, the jig would be 40 mm.) V-shaped depressions are then made at the centers of the right and left ends of the jig.

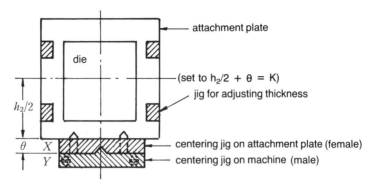

FIGURE 6-2. Upper and Lower Jigs for Centering

During setup, both front-to-back and right-to-left alignment are set automatically when the upper jig comes into contact with the centering jig. This way, the shank and shank hole engage easily even when the die is lowered at normal speed. Thus, the need to inch the ram downward and perform the alignment by hand is eliminated. Marking the top of the shank is helpful in this situation.

Using this technique, setting a die to center position becomes an extremely simple operation and setup time can be reduced considerably. This is another improvement based on external function standardization as discussed in Chapter 4.

Mounting the Die

The dimensions of the clamping points on upper and lower dies should first be determined. Then the thicknesses of the clamping points of all dies should be standardized to the dimensions of the thickest one. In doing this, one must take into consideration those cases in which blocks or shims have been attached to standardize die heights (see *Figure 6-1*).

Thus, die heights must be standardized prior to standardization of clamping points. If clamping points are standardized first, further adjustments will be required when die heights are standardized. Since this additional work is completely unnecessary, it is essential to observe the correct sequence of standardization operations. Moreover, blocks used for clamping point standardization must be fashioned so that they are mounted on the inside of the attachment plate (*Figures 6-1, 6-2*).

When an attachment surface is too high because of excessively dissimilar die heights, the die height adjustment shim should not be a single block. Rather, a number of blocks should be mounted on the attachment plate. A die is then attached using the plate on which the blocks are mounted. Following this method, the clamping point need not be raised very much, and mounting bolts do not have to be particularly long (*Figure 6-3*).

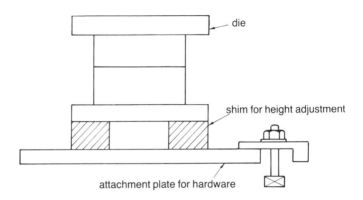

FIGURE 6-3. Blocks and Attachment Plate for Die Height Adjustment

In any case, when the thicknesses of die clamping points are standardized, uniform mounting bolts, clamps, and equalizing blocks can be dedicated to specific uses. This makes the entire attachment operation extremely simple. In addition, standardization:

- Reduces setup times substantially
- Simplifies organization
- Eliminates the need to search for appropriate bolts and blocks
- Eliminates the need to adjust blocks to suitable heights
- Eliminates the need to regulate bolt-clamping heights

This technique can be considered an application of function standardization, discussed above in Chapter 4.

Moving Dies Within Machines

Small dies can be inserted and removed by hand, but air cushions or rollers should be used for heavier dies. The use of moving bolsters or the like should be considered for dies that are even larger. For more information, see the section in Chapter 5 on mechanization.

Where large dies are involved, one possibility is to prepare two forklifts. One of the forklifts removes the die which has finished operations. The other — which has been waiting with the next die — immediately places the new die in the machine. This extremely effective method eliminates setup time wasted by using a single forklift to store the old die and fetch the new one.

Transporting Dies from Storage to Machines

Operations in which old dies are transported to storage and new dies are transported to machines should be performed as part of external setup. As already explained, including transportation in internal setup invariably increases the number of times crane cables need to be attached or removed.

Progressive Die Presses

We shall now explore several examples on progressive die presses. These setup improvements are basically the same as for single-shot presses. Certain aspects, however, need special consideration.

Shut Height Adjustments

Just as for single-shot presses, attention here must be given to standardizing die heights and eliminating shut height adjustments. In the case of progressive die presses, however, the line along which the stock passes must always be constant. Therefore, the plates used to standardize die heights should be attached only to the upper die so that this "pass line" does not vary.

Setting Die Alignment

Die alignment should be approached exactly as in the case of single-shot presses.

Die Attachment

This, too, is the same as for single-shot presses.

Setting Feed Volumes for Progressive Die Operations

With progressive dies, it is necessary to set stock feed volumes to correspond to the pitches of individual dies. We will discuss two methods, the crank method and the air-feed method.

The crank method. In general, the feed volume should equal the amount by which the crank directly connected to the press shaft is offset. For this purpose, a worker climbs up and makes the setting by turning a knob that determines the crank plate offset. Once the knob is suitably set, the stock is run through and measured. Depending on the result, it may be necessary to climb up and readjust the knob. Measurements and readjustments are frequently performed three or four times in succession. Although this is tolerable if the operation is being carried out jointly by two people, it is quite troublesome when a single worker is constantly climbing up and down.

As shown in *Figure 6-4*, however, the offset can be gauged to a fixed value for each product. Then a reference plane can be built on the edge of the screw framework that moves the knob. A saddle gauge is fit onto this plane. When the knob is attached to it, setting is completed in a single movement. (This approach applies some of the techniques for eliminating adjustments that were presented in Chapter 5.)

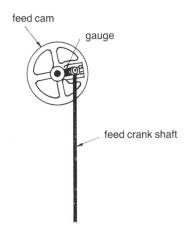

FIGURE 6-4. Setting Stock Feed Volumes (Crank Method)

The air-feed method. The air-feed method shown in *Plate 6-2* is another technique for feeding stock. In this method, the rear stopper, B, is advanced and retracted. The clamp, C, clamps onto the stock and travels back and forth between the front stopper, F, and the rear stopper, B. The volume of stock fed is determined by the distance the clamp travels. Consequently, the amount of stock fed is measured out by advancing the rear stopper. As a result, the position of the rear stopper must be adjusted again and again.

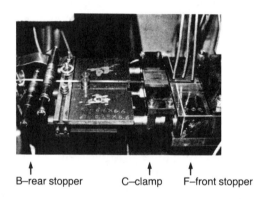

↑   ↑   ↑
B–rear stopper   C–clamp   F–front stopper

PLATE 6-2. Setting Stock Feed Volume (The Gauge Plate Method)

The operations department at M Electric improved this operation in the following way:

- The rear stopper was opened wide and secured in the hindmost position.

- A gauge plate wide enough to compensate for the feed volume was constructed. When this gauge plate was set between the front stopper, F, and the rear stopper, B, backward movement of the clamp was restricted and the required stroke was produced. This regulated the feed amount and made it possible to set the feed volume in a single operation.

Fourteen gauge plates of this type were manufactured. Setting the amount of feed stock became merely a matter of changing gauge plates, an extremely simple operation that anyone could perform quickly (*Plate 6-3*).

PLATE 6-3. **Stock Feed Volume Gauge Plates**

Performing Preliminary Setup for Stock

The preliminary setup stage for progressive dies involves setting by hand the leading edge of the stock for each die. After processing has been completed, the stock is sent by hand to the next die. This movement is both troublesome and dangerous, since the operator's hands must enter the machine. It is also quite time-consuming.

The following measures are effective in dealing with this situation:

- At the end of one operation, partially-made products are cut off and saved.

- When setting up for a subsequent operation involving the same products, the tail end of a partially-made product is joined to the leading edge of the new stock. This eliminates the need for successive hand settings at each setup.

This approach represents a great improvement in both time and safety.

Moving and Transporting Dies

This situation should be approached exactly as in the case of single-shot dies.

In 1971, early in the development of the SMED concept, the system was tried out on a 150-ton progressive die press at K Electric, a plant operating in collaboration with M Electric. On a visit to the plant, I spoke with the company's president, Mr. Suekane. I explained to him in concrete terms what I wanted done. On leaving, I urged him to get to work on the problem, as I would be visiting again in a month.

When I returned, I was told that the difficulties had been resolved and that a test would be taking place right away. Indeed, as Mr. Suekane had told me, where previously the setup had taken ninety minutes, the first product could now be completed in a mere eight minutes and twenty-six seconds. I shook his hand and congratulated him. Then I said I wanted to discuss the test further, and asked that all those concerned be assembled in the conference room on the second floor. After describing additional improvements I wanted to see made, I was leaving the room when a foreman came up to me, hung his head and apologized.

"What for?" I asked him in surprise.

"Well," he said, "the president told us about the SMED system last month. The setup for that 150-ton progressive die press now takes less than nine minutes. Before we started, I would have believed that you could cut the time down to an hour, but when the president said it had to be less than nine minutes, I told him that was ridiculous. I've been working with these presses for forty years, and working hard, too. Nobody was going to tell me that something that used to take an hour and a half could be done in nine minutes. Anyway, I told him I would bet my job that it couldn't be done."

"I see," I said.

"The president told me," the foreman continued, "that I had better get everything ready as you were coming back in a month, and...."

"And?"

"Well, I gave my section boss the gist of my conversation with the president. My section boss would occasionally ask me what we had to do, because the president was asking him about our progress. I always answered that I was busy and that we ought to put the matter off. I never did a thing, and before long I forgot all about it.

"A week ago, though, the president came by and asked me directly how the setup was coming along because you were due to show up pretty soon. When I told him that actually I hadn't done anything, he said that was awful. He took charge of things and work started on the project.

"Naturally, we were short on time and I had to work all last night to meet today's deadline. We didn't even have time for a trial run, so we went into today's test cold....

"I wouldn't have thought it possible, but we really have done this setup in less than nine minutes. I'm amazed, because I've always believed that it had to take an hour and a half. In fact, that's how long it has always taken. Anyway, while you were speaking, I was just thinking, 'It worked.'

"When you finished your talk and we all got up, the president came over to me and said, 'Well, you did it in less than nine minutes — what should we do about your job?' I begged him to let me keep it and he told me to come over here to apologize to you for my lack of confidence. So that's why I'm telling you I'm sorry...."

With this, the foreman ended his long story.

"I see," I said. "But I can't blame you for thinking the way you did. Nobody would believe that something that had always taken an hour and a half could be done in less than nine minutes. But, in fact, you've done it in eight minutes and twenty-six seconds. Your job now is to reduce setup time on all your dies to less than ten minutes."

With this appeal, I took my leave. In a very short time, this foreman's efforts made SMED a reality throughout M Electric.

Many people are skeptical that a setup operation that used to take considerably more than an hour can be carried out in less than ten minutes. Indeed, resistance can be greatest among those with long years of practical experience. Yet, SMED can always be achieved if the fundamental concepts and techniques are correctly applied.

In short, it is important to believe in the inevitable success of SMED and to persevere in following procedures that will put it into effect.

Transfer Die Presses

Setups on transfer die presses should be approached in exactly the same way as for single-shot presses in terms of:

- Adjusting shut heights
- Aligning dies
- Attaching dies

- Moving dies into machines

- Transporting dies between storage areas and machines

The problem here is how to handle setup for the feed bar that carries the products. The feed bar's functions can be divided into two categories:

- Main body of the feed bar (for example: transporting goods and returning to the original position)

- "Fingers" (functions analogous to those of human fingers: grasping, holding, and releasing items)

As product types change, problems will arise concerning the grasping of different shapes, and how to change the bar's length to respond to items of different size. Both of these issues relate to the "fingers" function. Thus, although feed bars and fingers are generally specialized and changed as a unit, why not merely change the fingers?

At O Industries, the bases of the fingers are fixed, and switching between two products is handled by attaching and removing finger "caps." Changes to accommodate two further kinds of goods are made by using L-shaped fingers. Since the main body of the feed bar is fairly large, expensive, and demanding of accuracy, it seemed that the wisest approach was to change only the fingers.

Another difficulty is that dies generally have to be pulled out sideways during die changes, since the feedbar gets in the way otherwise. An example of an extremely simple solution to this problem may be to divide the dies into three sections — right, left, and center — hoisting only the center sections with cables.

PLASTIC FORMING MACHINES

Plastic molding machines differ from metal presses only in the way the dies are joined. In the molding machine, the dies are joined laterally, while metal dies are joined vertically. Consequently, strategies for dealing with plastic molds are much the same as those for dealing with metal press dies.

Setting Up Dies

In this section we will discuss standardizing die heights, setting die alignment, and standardizing clamping point thicknesses.

Standardizing Die Heights

A toggle switch method is used on many pressurized adhesion devices for plastic forming machines. When die heights vary, changing settings with this method is an extraordinary nuisance demanding considerable time and labor. Standardizing die heights is an effective way to eliminate the need to touch the toggle switch mechanism (*Figure 6-5*). For this purpose, blocks are attached to the rear surface of the die. Since this requires changes in the dimensions of the knockout pins, suitable coupling devices must be devised to lengthen them.

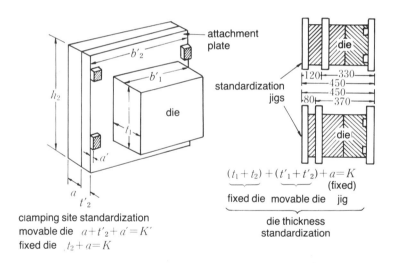

FIGURE 6-5. Die Height Standardization

Setting Die Alignment

To set die alignment, a male centering jig is attached at an appropriate place below a hole used as a locating ring on the machine (*Figure 6-6* and *Plate 6-4*).

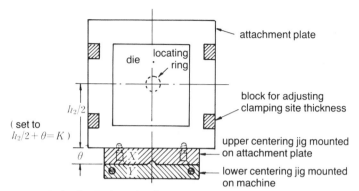

centering jigs for lateral and vertical alignment (fixed die)

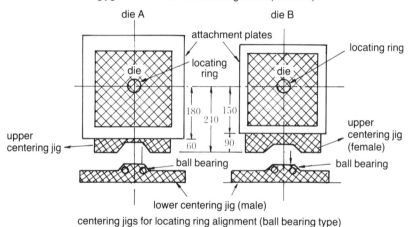

centering jigs for locating ring alignment (ball bearing type)

FIGURE 6-6. Centering Jig

PLATE 6-4. Centering Jig

A female centering jig of corresponding dimensions is fastened to the bottom of the die. By fitting the protrusion on the male centering jig onto the female centering jig, the locating ring on the die can be engaged perfectly with the locating ring on the machine. The centering jig is usually provided with a sloped section for this purpose.

Since such locating rings are often convex, the male centering jig needs to be large enough to bear the load of the descending die.

At D Industries, centering jigs were used to align the tip of the injection nozzle with injection holes, thus eliminating locating rings completely. This is perfectly justifiable.

Although centering jigs are usually attached only to fixed dies, it is more effective to attach them to movable dies as well. That way they can bear most of the load of the dies.

Standardizing Clamping Point Thicknesses

Die clamping surfaces should be standardized just as they are for metal dies. With plastic dies, however, the direct attachment method — in which fasteners are passed through holes — is used with surprising frequency. Since this method demands quite a lot of time, consideration should be given to the adoption of clamping methods (*Figure 6-7* and *Plate 6-5*).

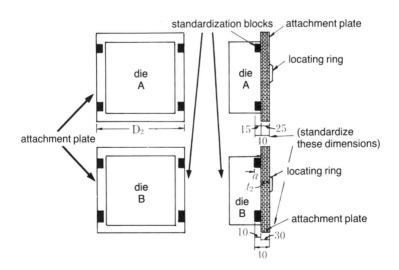

FIGURE 6-7. **Standardization of Clamping Point Thicknesses**

PLATE 6-5. Standardization of Clamping Point Thicknesses

In clamping procedures, the entire weight of the die is typically supported by the friction derived from clamping pressures. When a centering jig is provided, however, the jig bears the greater part of the load and all the clamp has to do is keep the die from falling over. Used this way, a centering jig can greatly facilitate clamping procedures (*Figure 6-8* and *Plate 6-6*).

Each of the three examples described above exemplifies function standardization as discussed in Chapter 4.

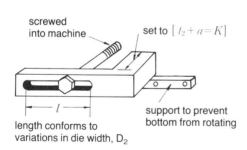

FIGURE 6-8. A Clamping Method for Attaching Dies

PLATE 6-6. A Clamping Method for Attaching Dies

Switching Resins

In this section, we will consider the related activities of switching resins, changing hoppers, and cleaning out nozzles.

Switching Resins

When changing from resin A to resin B, the volume of resin A in the hopper just prior to completing the first operation is proportional to the number of shots remaining. Any excess is removed. Resin B is then introduced. This ensures that when the change is made, most of the resin in the nozzle will be resin B. The changeover is thus streamlined and little of resin A is wasted (*Figure 6-9*). A daily plan of operations is drawn up so that work proceeds from lighter to darker colored resins. When changing resins, it is necessary to follow this order, for example:

- Transparent
- White
- Yellow
- Red
- Black

This simple approach minimizes the effects of dye contamination.

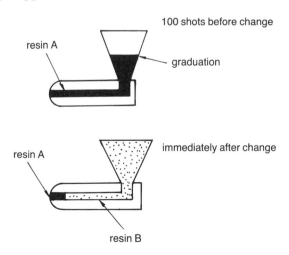

FIGURE 6-9. Changing Resins

Changing Hoppers

Cleaning the interiors of hoppers for resin or dye changes is quite a chore. This is especially so on large hoppers that have dryers attached. One effective technique here is to devise hopper liners. This way, instead of cleaning the hoppers, one simply changes the liner.

Preferable to this, however, is the "floating dryer" I developed for one company. By suspending and drying resin in a stream of hot air, it is possible to dry in five minutes items that used to take an hour to heat and dry.

Since only one shot's worth of resin needs to be dried per cycle, only five to ten shots of resin need to be kept in the hopper. As long as a regular supply is made from the raw materials vat, a very small hopper will suffice and cleaning is simplified. The operation becomes even simpler when the hopper is switched with a new spare hopper.

At the S Pen Company, hopper cleaning and changing operations are carried out in a very simple way. A small dual hopper is spun around and a new hopper is used. This way hoppers can be specialized for use with individual resins and dyes. The handling operations are simple because the small hoppers have capacities of only about 100 mm × 200 mm.

Cleaning Out Nozzles

Cleaning out nozzles is the most annoying problem in changing resins. Resins adhering to the nozzles' inner walls and to screw surfaces remain there and mix in with the next batch of resin, thus contaminating the colors. Eventually, the old resin is flushed away, but when this takes too long, a suitable purging agent must be used. How to speed up this operation is a problem requiring further study.

Coolant Line Switching

Coolant lines should be connected with clasps that snap open and shut with a single motion. In addition, one manifold-like fitting provided with multiple channels should be connected to the coolant line from the machine. Another one should be connected to the line from the die. When these two fittings are connected to one another, all the coolant lines become linked, leading to a considerable improvement. This is another example of an intermediary jig, as discussed in Chapter 4.

Die Preheating

When a die needs to be preheated, one extremely effective method is to use a steam generator and circulate hot water through the coolant channels to actually heat the die. Another common method is to use electric heaters.

In a case similar to that of die preheating, a considerable amount of internal setup time used to be spent making forty electrical connections on a hot runner die after the die was mounted on the machine. By preparing another connecting jig, connecting it in advance to the next die and plugging it in, substantial reductions in internal setup time were secured. Here again is an example of the use of an intermediary jig.

To a great extent, the setup of plastic forming machines may be approached in exactly the same way as the setup for die casting machines; I refer you to appropriate paragraphs in that section for further information.

The examples presented so far can also be applied to other machine tools, forging machines, casting machines, painting and woodworking machines, etc. My experience has led me to the firm conviction that SMED can be achieved in all cases by applying the conceptual framework and corresponding practical techniques.

SUMMARY

Through studying actual examples of the SMED system in operation, it is possible to gain further insight into the concept and the principles behind it. This insight, in turn, will be helpful in applying the concept and the associated techniques to diverse production operations.

7

Effects of SMED

In this chapter we discuss time savings achieved and other effects of applying the SMED system.

TIME SAVED BY APPLYING SMED TECHNIQUES

Table 7-1 shows time reductions achieved by around 1975, when the SMED system was beginning to gain ground. In the last ten years reductions have been even greater; the average setup now takes one-fortieth (2½%) of the time originally required.

OTHER EFFECTS OF SMED

Stockless Production

It is true, of course, that inventories disappear when high-diversity, low-volume orders are dealt with by means of high-diversity, small-lot production. Yet the multiplicative effects of the high-diversity component, on the one hand, and the small-lot component, on the other, lead inevitably to a substantial increase in the number of setup operations that must be performed. Cutting setups that used to take two hours to three minutes with SMED, however, changes the situation considerably. The SMED system offers the only path to both high-diversity, small-lot production and minimal inventory levels.

Moreover, when a system of production that minimizes inventories is adopted, the following collateral effects can be expected:

- Capital turnover rates increase.

No.	Company	Capacity (in tons)	Before Improvement	After Improvement	1/n
Presses (single-shot dies)					
1	K Auto	500 t-3 machines	1 hr 30 min	4 min 51 sec	1/19
2	S Auto	300 t-3 machines	1 hr 40 min	7 min 36 sec	1/13
3	D Auto	150 t	1 hr 30 min	8 min 24 sec	1/11
4	M Electric	"	2 hr 10 min	7 min 25 sec	1/18
5	S Electric	"	1 hr 20 min	5 min 45 sec	1/14
6	M Industries	"	1 hr 30 min	6 min 36 sec	1/14
7	A Auto Body	"	1 hr 40 min	7 min 46 sec	1/13
8	K Industries	100 t	1 hr 30 min	3 min 20 sec	1/27
9	S Metals	"	40 min	2 min 26 sec	1/16
10	A Steel	"	30 min	2 min 41 sec	1/11
11	K Press	"	40 min	2 min 48 sec	1/14
12	M Metals	"	1 hr 30 min	5 min 30 sec	1/16
13	K Metals	"	1 hr 10 min	4 min 33 sec	1/15
14	T Manufacturing	80 t	4 hr 0 min	4 min 18 sec	1/56
	(dies for springs)				
15	M Ironworks	"	50 min	3 min 16 sec	1/15
16	H Engineering	50 t	40 min	2 min 40 sec	1/15
17	M Electric	"	40 min	1 min 30 sec	1/27
18	M Electric	"	50 min	2 min 45 sec	1/18
19	H Press	30 t	50 min	48 sec	1/63
20	K Metals	"	40 min	2 min 40 sec	1/15
21	Y Industries	"	30 min	2 min 27 sec	1/12
22	I Metals	"	50 min	2 min 48 sec	1/18
	(multiple dies)				
23	S Industries	150 t	1 hr 40 min	4 min 36 sec	1/22
	(progressive dies)				
24	K Metals	100 t	1 hr 50 min	6 min 36 sec	1/17
25	M Electric	100 t	1 hr 30 min	6 min 28 sec	1/14
				Average	1/18

TABLE 7-1. Time Reductions Achieved by Using SMED

Plastic Forming Machines					
26	M Manufacturing	140 ounces	6 hr 40 min	7 min 36 sec	1/53
27	TM Manufacturing	100 ounces	2 hr 30 min	8 min 14 sec	1/18
28	Y Manufacturing	"	1 hr 50 min	4 min 36 sec	1/24
29	N Rubber	"	2 hr 30 min	6 min 28 sec	1/23
30	N Rubber	50 ounces	2 hr 0 min	4 min 18 sec	1/28
31	T Industries	"	1 hr 20 min	6 min 46 sec	1/12
32	TT Industries	"	1 hr 10 min	7 min 36 sec	1/9
33	N Chemicals	20 ounces	40 min	3 min 45 sec	1/11
34	D Plastics	10 ounces	50 min	2 min 26 sec	1/19
35	GA Electric	"	50 min	6 min 45 sec	1/7
36	S Lighting	"	40 min	3 min 38 sec	1/11
37	Y Synthetics	"	40 min	2 min 48 sec	1/14
38	W Company (Switzerland)	50 ounces	2 hr 30 min	6 min 0 sec	1/25
				Average	1/20
Die-cast Molding Machines					
39	M Metals	250 t	50 min	6 min 24 sec	1/8
40	T Die Casting	"	1 hr 20 min	7 min 46 sec	1/10
41	S Manufacturing	"	1 hr 10 min	5 min 36 sec	1/13
				Average	1/10
				Overall Average	1/18

TABLE 7-1. Time Reductions Achieved by Using SMED (continued)

- Stock reductions lead to more efficient use of plant space. (For example, the manager of a Citroën factory told me that twenty-two days' worth of inventory had been reduced to eight days' worth after SMED was adopted. He said this made the planned construction of a new building unnecessary.)

- Productivity rises as stock handling operations are eliminated. (Production in the Citroën plant cited above rose 20%.)

- Unusable stock arising from model changeovers or mistaken estimates of demand is eliminated.

- Goods are no longer lost through deterioration.

- The ability to mix production of various types of goods leads to further inventory reductions.

Increased Machine Work Rates and Productive Capacity

If setup times are drastically reduced, then the work rates of machines will increase and productivity will rise in spite of an increased number of setup operations.

Elimination of Setup Errors

Setup errors are reduced, and the elimination of trial runs lowers the incidence of defects.

Improved Quality

Quality also improves, since operating conditions are fully regulated in advance.

Increased Safety

Simpler setups result in safer operations.

Simplified Housekeeping

Standardization reduces the number of tools required, and those that are still needed are organized more functionally.

			Setup time (min)		Ratio
Die Exchange 120 min (27 min) 5:1	External Setup 60 min (19 min) 3:1	Transporting die to press	5	} (10)	1:1
		Transporting die to maintenance area	5		
		Organizing maintenance area	15	} (4)	4:1
		Exchanging die block	35	} (5)	7:1
	Internal Setup 60 min (8 min) 7:1	Removing die	10		
		Disposing scrap material in machine	5	} (5)	6:1
		Attaching die	15		
		Positioning die	15	} (3)	10:1
		Various adjustments	15		

FIGURE 7-1. Reduction in Total Setup Time

Decreased Setup Time

The total amount of setup time — including both internal and external setup — is reduced, with a consequent drop in man-hours (see *Figure 7-1*).

Lower Expense

Implementing SMED increases investment efficiency by making possible dramatic increases in productivity at relatively little cost. The cost of setups for small, single-shot metal press dies runs about ¥ 30,000–¥ 50,000 ($124–$206) in Japan and is about the same for plastic molding machine dies (*Figure 7-2*).

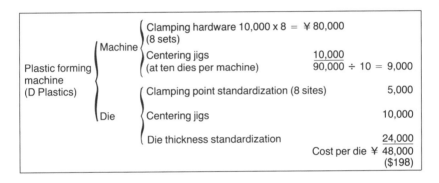

FIGURE 7-2. **Cost of Implementing SMED**

Operator Preference

Since adoption of SMED means that tooling changes are simple and quick, there is no longer any reason to avoid them.

Lower Skill Level Requirements

The ease of tooling changes eliminates the need for skilled workers.

I once observed a setup operation for helical gears on a gear-cutting machine at a Citroen plant in France. By using SMED, an unskilled worker in charge of the machine was able to complete in seven minutes and thirty-eight seconds an operation which previously had taken a skilled specialist about an hour and a half to perform.

As the plant manager and I returned to the office after observing this operation, he said to me, "You know, I saw something odd recently. A worker was wiping his machine with oil. This setup used to be handled by a specialist, so that while the setup was going on the regular machine operator would go off to some other machine and do something else. Since workers would take turns handling various machines, no one felt that any particular machine was his own. That's why up until now you would never see a worker taking care of the machine he was handling.

"Lately, though, machine operators have been able to perform setup changes themselves and they spend a month at a time concentrating on the operation of a single machine. This gives them a feeling of responsibility for their machines. I'm sure that's why they're now oiling and taking care of the equipment."

When I heard this, I realized that consideration for the feelings of workers was just as important in France — or anywhere else — as it is in Japan.

At Y Metals in Kyushu, a foreman used to perform each setup change on a 30-ton press. Only after he completed a setup were part-time female workers allowed to take charge of operations. SMED, however, made it possible for the part-timers to do in three minutes what used to take the foreman about an hour. As Mr. Koga, the company's president, says, "Part-timers can do it in part of the time."

Reduced Production Time

Production periods can be shortened drastically. Generally speaking, the following three strategies have proven effective.

Eliminate waiting for processes. The greatest delays in production are caused not by inspection or transportation, but by time spent waiting for the processing of one lot to be completed before another lot can be processed.

The ratio of time devoted to processing and to waiting for processes is frequently of the following order:

Waiting for processes	:	Processing
60	:	40
80	:	20

If the waiting periods could be eliminated, production time could be cut by as much as two-fifths. This can be accomplished by standardizing both processing quantities and processing times — that is, by equalizing the number of units processed in each operation, and by making the processing time in each operation the same.

Standardizing processing quantities can be accomplished fairly easily; the real problem lies in standardizing processing times. This is because machines used for individual operations are not necessarily of equal capacities. Processing time standardization seems to be impossible, for example, when the daily production capacity of machine A, used in Process 1, is 3,000 items, while that of B, the machine used in Process 2, is only 2,500 items. In a situation like this, there is a tendency to try to balance things out by installing another B machine.

Another important concept is applicable here, however: *The quantities produced should be the quantities needed.* If the required daily output is 2,000 items, there is no need to bring the capacity of machine B into line with that of machine A, since one B machine has sufficient capacity to process the daily amount needed. Consequently, the capacities of machines A and B should both be brought into line with required daily output. This still leaves a disparity between the capacities of machines A and B, however — a disparity that can be handled by adopting a *full work control system.*

A full work control system would fulfill the following functions in the given example:

- It sets up a buffer before machine B.

- It halts operation of machine A (the previous process) when twenty products accumulate in the buffer.

- It resumes operation of machine A when there are five products in the buffer.

In this way, process flows can be standardized using minimum cushion amounts. It is important to bear in mind, however, that while machines can be idle, workers must not be, because the cost of manpower is generally far higher than the cost of amortizing machines. Thus, it can be extremely effective to have several machines engaged in waiting operations so that workers will always have machines to take charge of.

Eliminate waiting for lots. Much time is lost when intermediary and raw materials must wait for processing of an entire lot to be completed. These delays can be eliminated only by establishing "transport lots" of one item each, so that each item moves to the subsequent process as soon as it has undergone processing. It is necessary, in other words, to adopt what might be termed "single-item-flow" operations. As shown in *Figure 7-3*, all the intervals between processes will now take the time needed to process one item. If single-item-flow operations are established for, say, ten processes, overall lot processing time can be cut by 90%.

On the other hand, processing a lot of 1,000 items will require 1,000 transport operations. Various strategies must be devised to deal with this, such as improving plant layout so as to simplify transportation, and finding convenient transportation procedures, for example, using conveyors.

Produce in small lots. Production time can be cut 90% by engaging in small-lot production, for example, by dividing lots of 1,000 into lots of 100, and by using standardized processing times and single-item-flow operations.

This leads, however, to a tenfold increase in the number of setup operations that must be performed. Through the use of SMED, production times can be shortened considerably even when the number of setups increases, since, for example, if a setup time that used to take two hours is cut to three minutes, ten repetitions of the setup will still take only thirty minutes.

Combining the savings in production time attainable by employing the three strategies described above leads to dramatic results (*Figure 7-3, bottom*).

At the washing machine division of M Electric, the completion of everything from blanking a washing machine body on a press to press forming, welding, painting, and assembling is carried out in a mere two hours by means of standardized processing times and single-item-flow operations. This achievement is based on the approach outlined above.

For the first time, moreover, SMED makes it possible to perform the several daily changeovers required by the adoption of a "di-

(A) Improvement of Process Delays

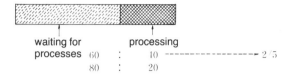

waiting for processes	:	processing	
60	:	10	----------------→ 2/5
80	:	20	

(B) Improvement of Lot Delays

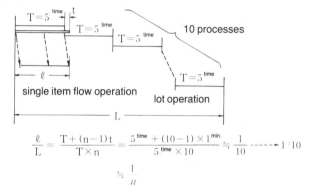

$$\frac{\ell}{L} = \frac{T + (n-1)t}{T \times n} = \frac{5^{\text{time}} + (10-1) \times 1^{\text{min.}}}{5^{\text{time}} \times 10} \approx \frac{1}{10} \quad ----→ 1/10$$

$$\approx \frac{1}{n}$$

(C) Small Lot Production

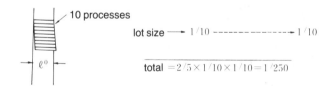

lot size ──→ 1/10 ---------------→ 1/10

$$\text{total} = 2/5 \times 1/10 \times 1/10 = 1/250$$

Strategy	Proportion of Previous Time	Percentage of Previous Time
Waiting for processing	2/5	40%
Waiting for lots	1/10	10%
Small lot production	1/10	10%
Total production time	1/250	.4%

FIGURE 7-3. **Reducing Production Time**

vided production scheme," in which the same items are produced every day in small lots.

Production lead times are drastically cut by the use of methods such as this. As a result:

- Production can take place after orders are received, rather than before.

- Even before orders are confirmed, production can begin on the basis of reliable information about incoming orders.

- Rush orders can be dealt with promptly.

- It is easy to meet delivery dates.

In this instance, SMED has not only reduced production times dramatically, it has also reduced both work in process and stocks of finished products.

Increased Production Flexibility

In addition to shortening production times, the adoption of SMED facilitates product changeovers, thereby making it possible to respond rapidly to changes in demand and substantially increasing manufacturing flexibility.

Elimination of Conceptual Blind Spots

I once heard the following from Ashton Marcus, Vice President of Omark Industries of Portland, Oregon:

> Omark has always wanted to reduce inventories, but little ever came of the idea because smaller lots and more setup changes meant lowered productivity. We had always assumed that a setup change had to be performed by a specially skilled worker and that it had to take several hours. It wasn't just that we had resigned ourselves to several-hour setups; we never even questioned them.
>
> Even though it sounded logical, I had my doubts when I read in your book, Study of the 'Toyota' Production System, that our setup changes could be completed in less than ten minutes. Nevertheless, several of our operations accepted the challenge, and they separated internal setup and external setup,

shifted internal setup to external setup and eliminated adjustments.

As a result, one operation was able to reduce to one minute and thirty seconds a setup operation which had previously taken two hours.

The results were similar in other pilot programs, and improved setup times gained momentum in other operations. Reductions of as much as 98% of previous times in some locations allowed them to move to small-lot production. In half a year total company inventory was reduced over 25%, and productivity in those locations rose 30%.

I keep thinking of how our biggest problem had been the presence of a conceptual blind spot which kept us resigned to the idea that the setup change was a long operation requiring a skilled worker.

Conceptual blind spots of this sort may surely be found in other companies as well.

New Attitudes

A revolution in thinking makes the impossible possible. At a SMED seminar, participants from Hitachi, Ltd. and Bridgestone Tire made observations of the following sort:

In putting SMED into practice, the thing I was most keenly aware of was making the impossible possible.

Frankly, I didn't believe that setups that used to take two or three hours could be completed within nine minutes. After actually trying it, though, I found that it was indeed possible. I figured that it was no good just to keep telling myself that it couldn't be done. Instead, I tried to think of ways to make it work. The important thing, I kept telling myself, was to take up the challenge. Gradually I realized that what I had always thought to be impossible could, in fact, be done.

Nowadays, when someone in our company makes a suggestion, expressions such as "that can never work" or "that's impossible" are taboo. When reminded that SMED had in fact proved to be possible, we think again and find that a surprising number of things can be accomplished when we accept chal-

lenges in a positive way. At any rate, despite a tendency to as-sume that something can't be done, we find an unexpectedly large number of possibilities when we give some thought to how it might be possible to do it.

In addition, I heard the following from Xavier Carcher, Vice President of Citroen, when I visited his firm in 1982:

The atmosphere within the company has changed com-pletely since you came to give us advice. There was a "pre-Shingo" attitude and now we have a "post-Shingo" attitude. It used to be that whenever a suggestion was made, somebody would say that it wouldn't work for such-and-such a reason, or that such-and-such a problem made it impossible. Most of what we heard were reasons why things couldn't be done, and a lot of proposals died in the discussion stage.

Since the success of SMED, though, there's a new determi-nation to come up with ways to make them work; the emphasis is on putting ideas into practice. What's more, when someone who comes up with a suggestion is told why his idea won't work, he changes his tack and makes other suggestions. This has speeded up conferences, and a number of problems have been re-solved by putting suggestions into practice. With so many im-provements, productivity has recently risen substantially.

The thing I have been most grateful for has been the revo-lution in everyone's attitudes toward improvement.

Here, as before, we see that the major cause of success has been the change in peoples' perceptions after they witnessed the effects of SMED first-hand.

Revolutionized Production Methods

In the past, many people believed that mass production was a good thing. Since large orders are a good thing, it was reasoned, large-lot production is also a good thing. This belief, however, de-rives from a confusion of the terms involved.

It is true, indeed, that large orders are advantageous in many ways. They hasten the amortization of machinery and dies and simplify management, thereby lowering management costs. Yet large orders constitute an area in which the buyer has the power to decide and the producer is without the authority to make choices. The only choice left to the producer is whether to conduct large-lot or small-lot production.

Of course, since producers prefer large-lot production, they can combine small orders into larger ones. These larger orders, however, will be apparent orders, not real ones. What we think of as a large order — say, an order for 30,000 cars in the space of ten days — is really nothing more than a real demand for 30,000 cars in thirty days which, for the sake of convenience, we have compressed into ten days. When the 30,000 cars produced in ten days are delivered, either the client or the dealers will have to keep them as inventory.

Even with such a large order, inventories would be greatly reduced if production were spread over thirty days. Managers have always assumed, however, that anticipatory production was the right way to go. They have thought, unconsciously, that anticipatory production was the *only* kind of production. In the end, anticipatory production — which we euphemistically refer to as "planned production" — is essentially nothing more than production based on guesswork. Of course, we do our utmost to improve the reliability of our guesswork by conducting large-scale market surveys and seeking the counsel of experts, but guesswork will always be guesswork. We cannot expect it to coincide 100% with actual demand. A cool summer, for example, will tend to result in unsold summer clothing, and stocks of winter goods rise during a warm winter. Moreover, long-range forecasting will always be necessary to plan for future materials, equipment and manpower needs.

When production is linked directly to actual demand, however, it becomes possible to use small-lot production to produce the minimum necessary, cut lead times to a minimum, and respond immediately to changes in demand. These benefits will surely eliminate the motivation to cling to traditional large-lot production.

It is true that large-lot production has some undeniable advantages:

- Efficiency rises and skills improve quickly, since the same operation is performed repeatedly.

- Work rates rise because few setups are needed.

The impact of these advantages is lessened considerably, however, when the SMED system is employed: needed levels of skill are reduced by means of improved and simplified operations, setups are simplified, and setup times are cut drastically.

In any case, the belief used to be widely held that mass production is good and inventory is a necessary evil. Now, with the realization that large orders and large-lot production are separate phenomena with separate advantages, we should recognize that large orders are indeed desirable, but they should be met by small-lot production. Managers who are responsible for production must recognize that the proper strategy is to make only what can be sold.

The single indispensable condition for making this strategy succeed is the adoption of SMED, for two reasons: SMED makes it possible to respond quickly to fluctuations in demand, and it creates the necessary conditions for lead time reductions.

The time has come to bid farewell to the long-standing myths of anticipatory production and large-lot production. We must also recognize that flexible production can come about only through SMED.

In this sense, it is a great pleasure to see recognition of the need for the SMED concept reflected in recent machine advertisements. They now treat as a selling point the fact that changes on such-and-such a machine can be made in three minutes or so. I believe that the theory and practice of SMED constitute a key that is about to open the door to a new concept of production.

SUMMARY

The results of SMED go beyond shortened setup times and improved work rates. Producers who adopt the SMED system can obtain fundamental strategic advantages by eliminating inventories and revolutionizing their basic concept of production.

A Revolution
in Manufacturing:
The SMED System

Chapter	Cutting	Presswork	Plastic	Die Casting	Forging	Casting	Welding	Discharge Process	Stitching	Painting	Rubber	Assembly
8 Implementing SMED *Matsushita Electric Industrial Co., Ltd.* *Washing Machine Division* *(Mikuni Plant)*	O	O				O				O		O
9 Setup Improvements Based on the Toyota Production System *Toyoda Gosei Co., Ltd.*	O				O							
10 A Quick-Setting ("Q-S") Campaign *Nippon Kogaku K.K. (Oi Plant)*	O											
11 Using SMED on a Farm Machinery Processing Line *Kubota, Ltd. (Sakai Plant)*	O											
12 Setup Improvements Based on Shop Circle Activities *Toyota Auto Body Co., Ltd.*		O										
13 Comprehensive Development of the SMED Concept to Include Affiliated Plants *Arakawa Auto Body Industries K.K.*		O						O				
14 SMED Developments in Producing Slide Bearings—*T.H. Kogyo K.K.*	O					O		O				
15 Examples and Effects of the SMED System *Glory Industries K.K.*	O						O					
16 Achievement of SMED Through Company-Wide Activities *Kyoei Kogyo K.K.*	O											
17 SMED in Tire Manufacturing Processes *Bridgestone Tire Co., Ltd.*	O	O										
18 Using SMED for Aluminum Die Casting Dies *Tsuta Machine and Metals Co., Ltd.*											O	
19 The Shingo One-Touch Die Exchange System: The Boltless Method				O								

Summary of Case Studies

PART TWO
The SMED System—
Case Studies

Through case studies drawn from twelve companies, this section presents examples of how the SMED System has actually been applied (see table on facing page). You will no doubt be able to implement many of these ideas directly.

Study of these examples in the light of the concepts and principles that have been presented in Part One, moreover, should suggest a variety of other applications.

Note that examples from various companies are ordered so as to group together processes carried out on similar machines.

8

Implementing SMED
Matsushita Electric Industrial Co., Ltd.,
Washing Machine Division (Mikuni Plant)

THE COMPANY

This division of Matsushita Electric was established in 1956 to produce "National" brand washing machines. It currently produces dishwashers and twin-tub washing machines on a 1,000-meter conveyor line at a rate of approximately one machine every six seconds.

Backed by a policy of "perfect quality, consistent production, and respect for the human factor," cumulative unit sales reached 18 million in 1980. National washing machines are in regular use not only domestically, but in over sixty-eight countries throughout the world.

The plant lot size is 30,000 square meters, with a total building area of 39,500 square meters.

APPLICATIONS OF SMED

Changing Blades on a Six-Spindle Lathe

A six-spindle lathe is used to machine the diameter of shafts used for the revolving blades in washing machines.

Delicate adjustments had been carried out to set dimensions in changing blades and tips, but cramped conditions made these adjustments difficult and time-consuming. Adjustment errors, moreover, gave rise to size defects.

To eliminate these problems, we needed to shorten blade-changing times and eradicate defects. A period of five months (June – October 1982) was allowed for these improvements.

131

Before the improvement program began, tips were changed inside the machine and many fine dimensioning adjustments were made (*Figure 8-1*).

In the new process, holders are removed from the lathe and tips are changed outside the machine. Fine dimensioning adjustments are performed with the aid of a gauge (*Figure 8-2* and *Plate 8-1*). This new procedure has led to dramatic improvements in two key areas: adjustment and tip-changing times have been reduced from fifteen to five minutes, and size defects went from thirty per month to zero.

The entire investment for required materials was approximately ¥15,000 ($62).

—(*Reported by Shigeru Kita, Parts Manufacturing Section*)

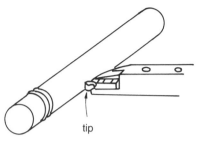

FIGURE 8-1. Changing Tips on a Six-Spindle Lathe

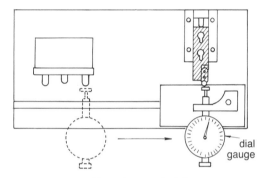

FIGURE 8-2. Changing Lathe Tips Outside of Machine

PLATE 8-1. Changing Lathe Tips Outside of Machine

Grease Application Changeovers

Grease application is one of many operations performed on the washing machine assembly line. Where grease had previously been applied by hand to parts needing it, machines now apply it automatically (*Figure 8-3*).

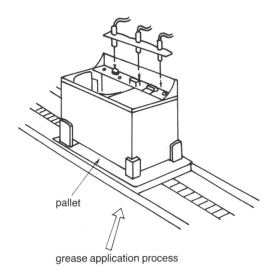

pallet

grease application process

FIGURE 8-3. **Automatic Application of Grease**

Both the number and location of places to be greased vary by machine model. For this reason, nozzles used to be switched every time machine types changed (*Figure 8-4*). This took longer than other processes, so bottlenecks developed on the assembly line.

Ways of dealing with this situation were discussed in small group meetings and the following approach was agreed upon. These improvements were implemented in the four months from June to September 1980.

Rotary mounting hardware was made that adapts immediately to the specific machine models ordered by rotating 180° (*Figure 8-5*). Two kinds of machines can be handled by this arrangement. Where more than two kinds are involved, nozzles should be changed during external setup operations.

As a result of this improvement, what previously took twelve minutes was cut to thirty seconds. Since this was a minor improve-

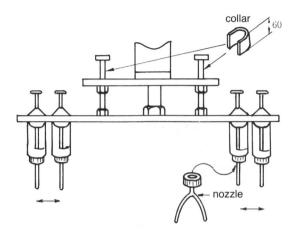

FIGURE 8-4. Changing Nozzles to Apply Grease

ment performed largely by the workers on the site, the only expenses were for materials: costs were approximately ¥ 40,000 – ¥ 50,000 ($165 – $205). In addition, everyone involved felt a sense of accomplishment in having managed to achieve SMED through self-reliance and the active application of appropriate techniques.

Product-type changes had been disliked up to this point, but these improvements fostered the attitude that diversification is natural and normal.

— *(Reported by Tateo Matsumoto, Assembly and Manufacturing Section)*

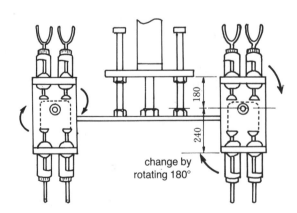

FIGURE 8-5. Rotary Mounting Hardware

Changing Pallet Guides Automatically

Positioning guides are attached to pallets used on the washing machine assembly line conveyor (*Figure 8-6*).

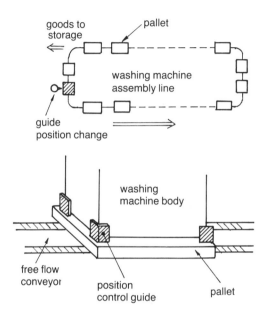

FIGURE 8-6. Pallet Guides

Body sizes differ according to the items being manufactured, so the positions of these guides must be changed whenever a product switch is made. Repositioning the guides by hand created several problems:

- Workers had to be in constant attendance to change guide positions one after another on approximately 100 pallets at the top of the line.

- Some machine bodies were dented or gashed because of guide repositioning errors.

- The repositioning operation posed a safety hazard.

The development and manufacturing section was asked to reduce setup time to the single minutes range and to mechanize the positioning of the guides. This was accomplished in the six months between May and October 1981.

Before improvement, a worker removed the guides from each pallet and remounted them in fixed positions. Thus, four guides were changed on each pallet (*Figure 8-7*).

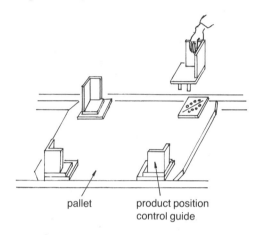

FIGURE 8-7. **Changing Pallet Guides Manually**

After improvement, a machine lifted all four guides simultaneously with suction pads and then reset them in predetermined positions (*Figure 8-8*).

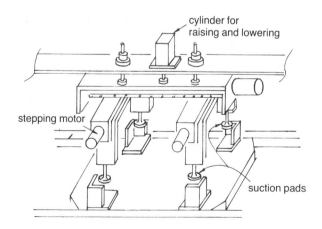

FIGURE 8-8. **Changing Pallet Guides Automatically**

Since workers no longer had to be stationed permanently by the pallet, this change reduced manpower costs by ¥680,000 (about $2810) per month. Other effects included the elimination of unsafe operations and a reduction in the number of defects.

These improvements cost about ¥190,000 (about $785) per month. Thus, SMED has led to net savings of roughly ¥500,000 ($2066) each month.

These improvements, unlike those for press setups, were difficult to break down into discrete elements. The new equipment made it possible for the changeover itself to be made instantly (in approximately ten seconds), but since a whole series of assembly line procedures have to be changed whenever the switch to a new product model is made, the automation of pallet guide changes by itself did not solve the problem of implementing SMED.

The challenge for the future is to broaden the scope of this improvement so as to speed up changes all along the line.

— *(Reported by Iwao Miyazaki, Development and Manufacturing Section)*

Automatic Welding on Washing Machines

A part called a patch plate is automatically welded to the washing machine body during manufacturing (*Figure 8-9*). Patch plates and body sizes differ by washing machine type, and models have proliferated in response to market demand.

Setup changes for automatic welding originally took four hours, during which body placement guides were shifted, photoelectric

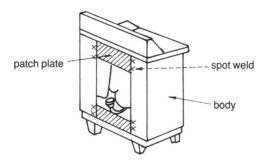

FIGURE 8-9. **Patch Plate on Washing Machine**

tubes for checking materials were repositioned, and clamp strokes were adjusted.

Matsushita Electric has been approaching the problem of speeding up this operation in stages, tackling changes one by one. Some examples from this ongoing process, which began in December 1982, are discussed below.

Body Positioning

Two arms regulate the position of the machine body as a conveyor delivers it to the welding stage. Stroke adjustments are performed because body sizes vary (*Figure 8-10*).

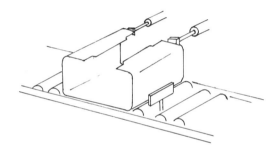

FIGURE 8-10. Positioning Washing Machine Body for Welding

Before improvement, a turning cylinder rod adjusted the stroke (*Figure 8-11*). Positioning occurred while in contact with the product, and minute adjustments (using a monkey wrench) were necessary.

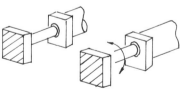

turning cylinder rod adjusts stroke
(positioning by contact with product)
fine adjustments needed (tool: monkey wrench)

FIGURE 8-11. Adjusting Stroke with Turning Cylinder Rod

After improvement, the stroke changed to conform to the dimensions of the machine body (*Figure 8-12*). The measurement of "*a*" varies according to the machine type being positioned for welding. As a result of this improvement, no fine adjustments or tools are necessary.

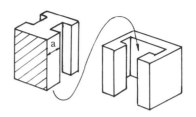

FIGURE 8-12. Improved Welding Position

Repositioning Photoelectric Tubes for Checking Materials

The photoelectric tube that checks for the arrival of washing machine bodies to be welded had to be moved back and forth according to machine body type (*Figure 8-13*). It was secured by two 25-mm nuts.

What in the past had been changed by turning nuts has been improved (*Figure 8-14*) so that the change now takes only one-tenth as long. This slide-on method requires only a hexagonal wrench and an M6 bolt to secure the mount.

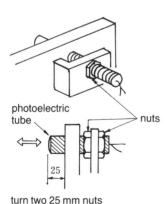

photoelectric tube

nuts

25

turn two 25 mm nuts

FIGURE 8-13. Photoelectric Tube Mounting, Before Improvement

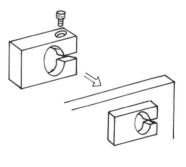

slide-on method, clamped with M6 bolt (tool: hexagonal wrench)

FIGURE 8-14. Slide-On Method for Mounting Photoelectric Tubes

Adjusting Patch Plate Position

After the patch plate is set on the machine body, its position is adjusted as shown in *Figure 8-15*. Since the size of the plate depends on the body type, the contact jigs used in this operation must be changed.

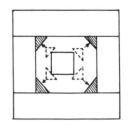

FIGURE 8-15. Position of Patch Plate

In the past, each jig had been secured with two M8 bolts, using a hexagonal wrench. Since there are four positions, this meant handling a total of eight bolts in an operation that took thirty-two minutes (*Figure 8-16*).

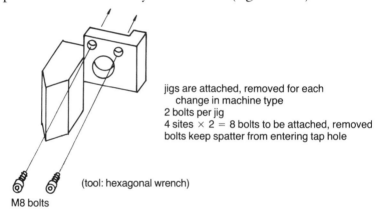

jigs are attached, removed for each change in machine type
2 bolts per jig
4 sites × 2 = 8 bolts to be attached, removed
bolts keep spatter from entering tap hole

(tool: hexagonal wrench)

M8 bolts

FIGURE 8-16. Positioning Patch Plate with Conventional Jigs

The improved method required no tools whatsoever in changing the jigs for different models (*Figure 8-17*). The jig holder is bolted to the main body of the welding machine, and the variable jigs are slid into the holder to perform the change.

Three improvements resulted from these changes:

- Machine body positioning time dropped from twenty-one minutes to ten seconds.

- The time required to reposition the photoelectric tubes was reduced from twenty minutes to two minutes.

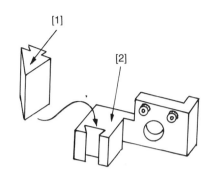

[2] is bolted to the main body of the welding machine and [1] is inserted to perform change (no tools whatsoever needed for change)

FIGURE 8-17. **Improved Jig Mounting for Patch Plate Positioning**

- Patch plate position adjustment time went from thirty-two minutes to one minute.

In the first three months of the program, ten other improvements were made, for a total time reduction of close to four hours (232 minutes). The cost of all these improvements was approximately ¥80,000 ($330).

Although individual changes have been brought down to the single-minute range, the operation as a whole has yet to reach that goal. The strength of the effort is in the persistence of workers involved, however, and the company looks forward to tackling the remaining issues.

—*(Reported by Yoshihiro Masaike, Parts Manufacturing Section)*

Changing Colors for Powder Coating Operations

Home appliances have come out in a wider range of colors in recent years, necessitating frequent color changes in the washing machine painting operation. Setup changes for this high-diversity, low-volume production process involved seven workers and took an hour to complete. Since this arrangement was unresponsive to change, improvements were envisaged that would make it possible to switch to any color quickly. (Until then, the number of colors available had been restricted by machine capacities.)

Originally, the following procedures were involved in color changes (*Figure 8-18*):

- Scrub down booth ceiling and walls.
- Air out booth interior.
- Change heads.
- Change hoses.
- Change duct.
- Make adjustments as necessary.

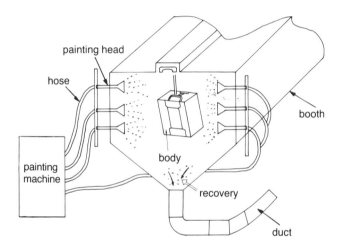

FIGURE 8-18. Painting Setup Prior to Improvement

The improvement program encompassed several significant changes (*Figure 8-19*).

Movable painting machines are now used instead of fixed ones. Each painting machine is used exclusively for a single color and these machines are switched whenever a color change is made.

Painting heads, too, are dedicated to single colors, so that when a color change is made it is sufficient merely to attach hoses to the head corresponding to the desired color.

Heads are made to move both horizontally and vertically, so that paint is concentrated on the washing machine bodies and does not spatter on the walls or ceiling of the booth. This eliminates the need to scrub down and air out the booth interior.

The earlier operation of reclaiming paint from ducts has been

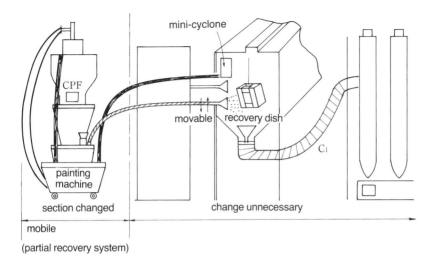

FIGURE 8-19. **Improved Painting Setup**

abolished (and the ducts discarded), and recovery is made from a mini-cyclone. This makes duct changes unnecessary.

These changes had several results:

- Color change time was reduced from sixty minutes and seven workers to ten minutes and two workers.

- Inventories required for color changes were reduced from 300 items to 100.

- Color changes were simplified.

Where it used to take four specialists to handle this operation, any worker can now do the job.
—(Reported by Mitsuo Shoji, Parts Manufacturing Section)

Achieving Instantaneous Press Die Changes

Holes are made in washing machine bodies for mounting towel racks, attaching drain hoses, and mounting hanger hooks (*Figure 8-20*). Both the need for these holes and their locations differ for different models.

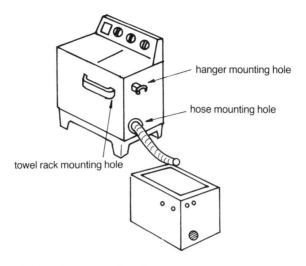

FIGURE 8-20. Placement of Holes in Washing Machine Bodies

Different sections of the assembly line are devoted to different models. A great deal of time was needed to bolt and unbolt punches for different machine types in the course of press operations (*Figure 8-21*). In addition, if one takes into account adjustments needed during die changes, three model changes per day required not only excessive time, but also substantial inventories of half-finished products.

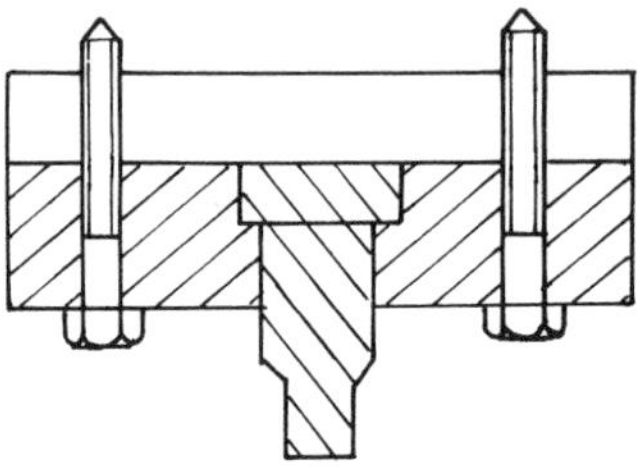

In a program implemented between 1973 and 1975, we worked to solve these immediate problems in a way that would also allow us to deal effectively with the even greater market diversity expected in the future.

FIGURE 8-21. Changing Punches with Bolts

The main improvement was to eliminate the need for bolts in changing punches. Punches are now inserted and removed with the aid of cylinders (*Figure 8-22*). Approximately twenty-five cylinders are inserted in a single die, making five model changes possible. Electric control makes it possible to change these punches almost instantaneously. Thus, different models can be produced one after another

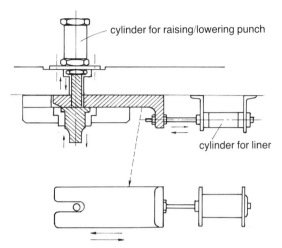

FIGURE 8-22. Changing Punches with Cylinders

by setting the quantities of each model on the electric control panel.

These improvements led to impressive results. Changing one block had previously taken fifteen minutes at each location. Since four blocks were involved in manufacturing bodies for one product, the operation took sixty minutes — seventy including adjustments. This change is now accomplished instantaneously at the flip of a switch.

In addition, with three model changeovers per day, production has doubled and inventories of unfinished products have been greatly reduced.

—*(Reported by Nobuhiro Nishijima, Parts Manufacturing Section)*

Reducing Setup Time for Injection Molding Dies Used for Twin-Tub Washing Machine Plastic Bases

In recent years, the number of washing machine models has increased in accordance with customer preferences and industry diversification. Because operators prefer to avoid taking more time than necessary to perform die changes, the traditional strategy has been to schedule large enough lots to reduce the number of changes needed. With this approach, however, as the number of production models and parts increased, inventories bulged.

Matsushita set to work on SMED when it became obvious even from the standpoint of inventory storage space that this approach could not deal with the problem.

Considering, moreover, that rapid setups had been demanded ever since the injection molding department was inaugurated, we went ahead and laid the groundwork for die size standardization and for the joint use of product extracting machines.

Because the workers were interested in the SMED concept from the start, the road leading to a concrete plan had already been paved. It was felt, furthermore, that since SMED would be run by workers, the most favorable results would be obtained if they were allowed to devise their own techniques for achieving desired goals. The SMED concept, then, was taken up as a theme in quality circle meetings.

The results were demonstrated six months later, when operations that had previously taken seventy minutes were cut to eight minutes and sixteen seconds. This great achievement was the result of the united dedication and enthusiasm of these workers. These results could not have been attained without teamwork, for the workers shared the task equally. They decided on procedures for internal and external setup and eliminated waste from the operation.

Included in the improvement effort were the following items:

Equipment: Mitsubishi Heavy Industries' injection
                      molding machine 850MDW
               Automatic extraction machine
               Automatic product stacking device
               One 20-ton crane
     Dies: Hot runner, 6-12 gates (single
                      and double dies)
  Material: Polypropylene

Results of a Pareto analysis of pre-improvement time required for tooling changes by elemental operation are shown in *Table 8.1*.

With the Pareto analysis as a basis, elemental operations were further subdivided with a view to separating internal and external setup operations, instituting "one-touch" fastening and unfastening, and eliminating adjustments. Some of them are elaborated here.

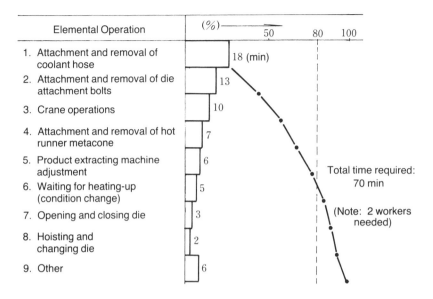

Elemental Operation	(%)	50	80	100

1. Attachment and removal of coolant hose — 18 (min)
2. Attachment and removal of die attachment bolts — 13
3. Crane operations — 10
4. Attachment and removal of hot runner metacone — 7
5. Product extracting machine adjustment — 6
6. Waiting for heating-up (condition change) — 5
7. Opening and closing die — 3
8. Hoisting and changing die — 2
9. Other — 6

Total time required: 70 min

(Note: 2 workers needed)

TABLE 8-1. Pareto Analysis of Pre-improvement Time for Tooling Changes

Simplifying Coolant Hose Connection

More than ten hose connections were previously needed for supplying and draining coolant water. This arrangement was simplified by attaching a coolant water manifold to the die. A total of four connections were provided, with one fixed and one mobile supply and drain connection for each. As a result, connection times were reduced considerably, and both connection errors and water quantity adjustments were eliminated (*Figure 8-23*).

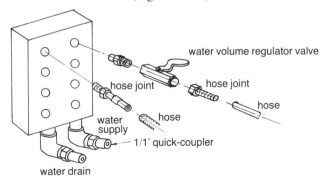

water volume regulator valve

hose joint

hose joint

hose

hose joint

water supply

hose

1/1' quick-coupler

water drain

FIGURE 8-23. Simplified Coolant Hose Connection

Simplifying Die Bolt Attachment and Removal

As mentioned before, die mounting plate sizes and thicknesses had already been standardized. By attaching die locating guides and cradles to fixed plates and attaching cradles to movable plates, we could secure the dies with clamps. It became possible to loosen a secured die merely by turning a clamp bolt one or two turns and then pulling the clamp forward. The clamp itself was kept in a stable position by means of a guide and a spring (*Figure 8-24*).

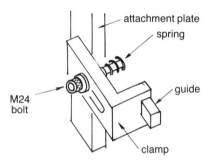

FIGURE 8-24. Simplified Die Bolt Attachment and Removal

Regulating Preparatory Die Temperature and Checking the Electrical System

Hot-runner dies are frequently plagued by heat sensor or heater shutdowns and similar problems. For this reason, Matsushita manufactured a hot-runner preheat regulator that can also check the electrical system.

Reducing Crane Operation Time

Since time is wasted by crane operations when attaching and removing dies, these crane operations were analyzed and wasted movement was eliminated. Operations were simplified, too, by providing traveling and horizontal movement rest position markers with which to line up the crane.

One-Touch Attachment and Removal of Metal Sockets

Screw-type metal sockets for connecting heaters and heat sensors to hot runner dies were replaced with watertight connectors manufactured by the Kontakt Company of West Germany, making one-touch operation possible.

Simplifying Product Extraction Machine Adjustment

The vertical strokes and in-and-out strokes of extraction machines were modified so that the chucks holding the products could be shared by removing or attaching a special block (*Figure 8-25*).

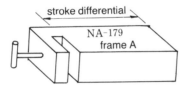

FIGURE 8-25. Simplified Product Extraction Machine Adjustment

Shifting Forming Die Adjustments to External Setup

Two series of limit switches were provided to indicate die open and shut amounts, speeds, and forward and rear movement limits. One series was set to the position of the next die to be attached. When dies were changed, the new switches were exchanged for the old ones by means of a snap switch on the control board.

The results of these various improvements were impressive:

- Tooling change time was reduced from seventy minutes to eight minutes.

- The size of inventory was substantially reduced.

- Lead time was reduced from three days to one day.

- The use of work space became more efficient.

Even better than these results is the fact that the workers no longer dislike die changes.

The issues involved in the field of injection molding processing are too numerous to discuss in detail, but they include shot time reductions (shortening trial cycles, low temperature molding, vacuum molding, increasing materials flow), lowered materials costs, improved yields, electrical power savings, the elimination of finish-machining, die problem prevention, and reduced materials switching times and materials loss.

Every effort has been made to find ways to apply the SMED system to these issues. Although nothing in particular distinguishes this plant from others of the same type, it is certainly true that everyone involved is pushing ahead with undaunted and positive efforts to deal with a broad range of issues. The goal is to have the most technologically advanced resin molding plant in Japan.

—*(Reported by Satoru Michi, Resin Molding Section)*

Changing Yielding Rubber for Automatic Bond Applicator Machines

Yokes of yielding rubber are press-fitted into washing machine drainage tanks and bond is applied automatically to each drainpipe. With the random mixed production of the NA-480 and NA-483L models, various holes are positioned differently, and a tooling change is required each time a different model is encountered. Before improvements were undertaken, tooling setup losses from random production were considerable. Furthermore, performance declined and confusion was created on the line. A scheme for automatic switching had to be devised.

To deal with random production, various methods were considered, including those based on changes by means of selector switches, changes by means of cylinders, and automatic changes by means of model recognition.

Concrete investigation led to the implementation of a system of automatic machine model recognition and, based on this, automatic jig changing routines using cylinders.

Nozzle Movement

Initially, bond was applied automatically to the tank's three drain openings, but the nozzle that was used had to be moved to three positions (*Plate 8-2*).

PLATE 8-2. Nozzle Movement, Before Improvement

The system has been improved by using a chain that is pulled by autotension. The chain moves the cylinder by just the amount required (*Plate 8-3*). The center of the nozzle is moved by the cylinder according to the dimensions shown above the photograph. Model recognition is performed by a hole-detecting photoelectric tube.

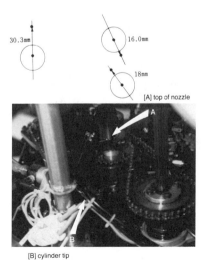

PLATE 8-3. Nozzle Movement, After Improvement

These improvements permit automatic changes and eliminate many of the problems associated with random production.

Guide Pin Movement

Machine model recognition is performed with a photoelectric tube; guide pin holes move by means of a cylinder (*Plates 8-4, 8-5*).

These changes have resulted in savings of ¥ 300,000 ($1240) per month. In addition, safety has improved dramatically due to the elimination of adjustment operations.

—*(Reported by Tadashi Ohiro, Assembly and Manufacturing Section)*

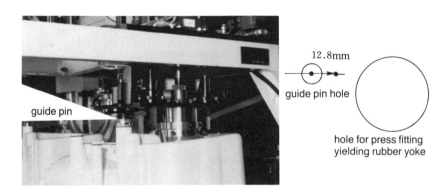

PLATE 8-4. Guide Pin Movement

PLATE 8-5. Guide Pin Movement

9

Setup Improvements Based on the Toyota Production System
Toyoda Gosei Co., Ltd.

THE COMPANY

Since Toyoda Gosei was founded in 1949, we have successfully developed and improved a variety of high polymer products for the automobile industry. We also develop and produce plastic, cork, urethane, and other parts, and have built up an unrivaled market share in many products, including steering wheels, various hoses, and piston caps.

Capital:	¥ 3.3 billion ($13.6 million) (FY 1978; officially listed on the second section of the stock exchange)
Sales:	¥ 106.4 billion ($439.7 million) (FY 1981)
Employees:	4,600
Factories:	8
Product Types:	12,000

Company-Wide Activities Aimed at Lowering Costs

The business environment surrounding the automobile industry showed solid expansion even during the uncertain years of 1977-1978, but from the time of the second oil crisis in 1979, limited customer demand compelled manufacturers to firm up their positions in global small car competition and to switch to a new emphasis on quality. Parts manufacturers, too, were pressed to respond to changing user requirements, to fulfill demands for quality and performance, and to supply items at low prices.

As industry competition grew increasingly heated and global, there was no way to survive except by lowering prices while maintaining or improving quality.

Toyoda Gosei tried to find ways to manufacture products less expensively. In 1976, under the guidance of the Toyota Motor Corporation, we undertook to put into practice the Toyota Production System, whose basic principle is the elimination of inefficiency. Briefly stated, this method lowers prices and raises business efficiency by approaching an ideal situation with these three characteristics:

- Workers, machines, and objects are combined without waste.

- Workers and machines perform only work that increases value added.

- The time it takes to manufacture goods is the total of processing times (i.e., lead times are made as short as possible).

The purpose of these measures, which rest on the twin cornerstones of "Just-In-Time" production and automation with worker involvement, is to manufacture as inexpensively as possible only goods that will sell, and to manufacture them only when they will sell quickly. This method, in other words, lies in the domain of management (*Figure 9-1*).

In October 1978, Taiichi Ohno, the father of the Toyota Production System (and now a consultant), was welcomed as Toyoda Gosei's chairman of the board, and with his direct on-site leadership and the strong support of top company officials, the Toyota Production System was extended — and continues to expand — throughout the company.

Motivation for Tackling SMED

Just-In-Time Production

Just-in-Time (JIT) production, one of the two cornerstones of the Toyota Production System, is an extremely important concept.

When applied to a single industrial process, the JIT concept means making items *when* they are required and in the *quantities* required, all as inexpensively as possible. This is done by minimizing

The objective of the Toyota Production System is to lower costs

Responses to high-diversity, low-volume production

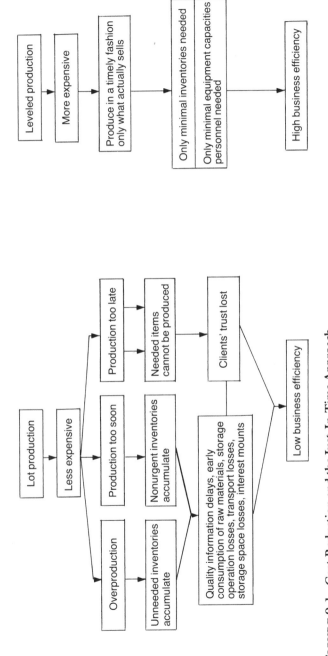

FIGURE 9-1. Cost Reduction and the Just-In-Time Approach

inventory, synchronizing the production processes, and producing in a continuous stream with a minimum of work in process (*Figure 9-2*).

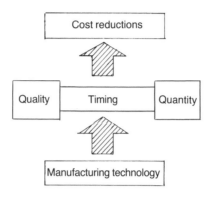

FIGURE 9-2. The Principle of Just-In-Time Production

To deal with high-diversity, low-volume production through the JIT approach, a company must abandon large lots in favor of smaller lots along with level production.

All too often there is a tendency to reduce the number of tooling setups and avoid setup losses by switching to large-lot production. This results in complete confusion as managers try to keep track of inventories and mechanical devices so numerous that one cannot see from one side of the shop to the other. These inventories and devices, in turn, require warehouses.

In principle, however, such a situation is unnecessary as long as a producer has the capacity to manufacture required items in the quantities required whenever an order is received (*Figure 9-3*).

Setup time reductions must be achieved rapidly, for if nothing were done to change the present situation, setup times would lengthen and losses would rise.

Toyoda Gosei's Experience with SMED

The Man-hour Reduction Council inaugurated in 1969 at Toyota Motor Corporation had been urging that tooling setups be

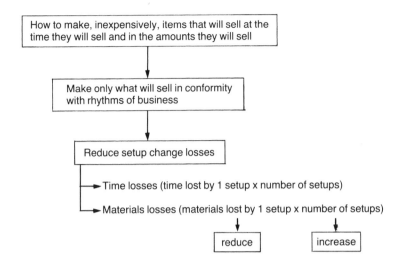

FIGURE 9-3. **Setup Changes and the Just-In-Time Approach**

shortened, but the challenge of SMED was taken up in earnest only in 1972 when, under the leadership of Shigeo Shingo, a setup of less than nine minutes was achieved on a resin injection molding machine.

With the backing of company officials, this improvement led to tremendous progress; a tooling setup that had taken over two hours was reduced to less than ten minutes in 1973 and less than one minute in 1975. SMED succeeded impressively in making it possible to handle a large number and greater diversity of products with existing machinery.

Like priming powder, the effects of this example touched off other improvement activities throughout the company.

On the other hand, means and ends would occasionally be confused. In the midst of daily production activities, it has sometimes been necessary to stop and consider whether the maximum possible savings have actually been realized.

On the basis of these reflections, arrangements have been made in recent years to stimulate the need for setup reductions, and to discover how few mechanical interventions and how little inventory the process involved can tolerate. The goal throughout the company, in other words, has been to develop a robust system of processes responsive to change.

Fundamental Concepts Regarding Tooling Changes

First, it is important to stimulate the need for reducing setup change times. The Toyota Production System makes practical use of *kanban*, indicator cards or signs which, in addition to preventing overproduction and providing information on production and transactions, also act as tools for improvement in systematizing production (*Figure 9-4*). To function this way, the *kanban* must be located so that everyone can see the sequence, amount, and timing of work to be done.

---

1. Ordinary Kanban
   Make in order of kanban only for items sold

2. Signal Kanban
   Make in order that signal kanban come off

Kanban
1 day unit → half day unit → 1 hour unit → 1 sheet unit → 1 piece unit

---

FIGURE 9-4. Examples of Stimulating the Need for Reducing Setup Change Times

As a result, everyone should be able to understand:

- The pace of work (whether fast or slow)

- The order of work in process

- The timing of work in process

- The number of work in process conditions at the outset

- Which operations are standard

- Which operations are nonstandard

The basic approach to reducing setup times includes several key points:

- It is important to have the conviction that drastically shortened tooling setups are possible. Dramatic reductions can be made by starting out with the attitude that a tooling change is merely a matter of removing one die and attaching another. If the setup time can be reduced on one assembly line, then managers and supervisors will gain direct experience of the improvements, making it easier to extend these improvements laterally (to other assembly line operations).

- There are natural stages of setup time reduction, as shown in *Figure 9-5.*

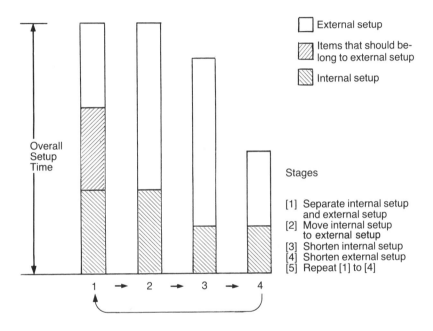

FIGURE 9-5. **Stages of Setup Time Reduction**

- Keeping setup changes away from machine operators merely creates a class of setup experts. Dealing with this issue is one of the principal goals of setup improvements; operators must be involved.

- Centering and locating adjustments should not have to be made. Parts should center on contact and locations should be fixed when parts are pressed together. Adjustments depend on the right "touch" or on luck; differences show up when different people are doing the adjusting. Even the same person may take more or less time to make the same adjustment on different occasions. For all these reasons, adjustments should be eliminated.

- Functional clamps should be used. Screw-type fastenings should be replaced with dovetail grooves, pins, cams, wedges, and the like. Where the use of screws is unavoidable, they should have to be turned no more than once.

- Intermediary jigs should be used. When blades are changed, for example, holders (e.g., intermediary jigs) should be used instead of mounting blades directly onto the head. Dimensions can be set during external setup and holders switched.

- Movements should be linked to one another to facilitate simpler die exchanging procedures (*Figure 9-6*).

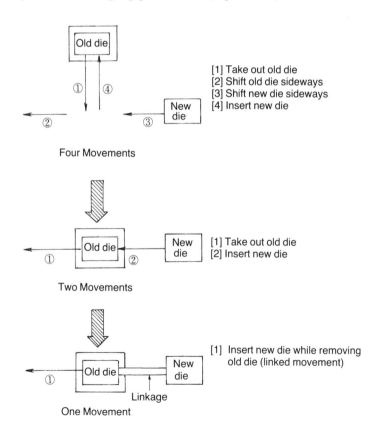

FIGURE 9-6. Simplifying Die Exchange

- Parallel operations should be conducted. Even though the total number of setup man-hours may be unchanged, setup operations are more than halved when two workers instead of one perform the changes where machines are large or processes are long.

- Sequential setup changes should be made when numerous processes are involved (*Table 9-1*).

Example of Change from A to B for Four-Process Product

Processes	No.1	No.2	No.3	No.4
	A	A	A	A
Setup Change No. 1	Setup Change	A	A	A
Setup Change No. 2	B	Setup Change	A	A
Setup Change No. 3	B	B	Setup Change	A
Setup Change No. 4	B	B	B	Setup Change
	B	B	B	B

TABLE 9-1. **Sequence of Setup Changes**

- Setup changes should allow defect-free products to be produced from the very start. It makes no sense to speed up a setup operation without knowing when quality products can be turned out.

- The ideal setup change is no change at all. As long as setup changes are necessary, however, they should be designed to be performed with a "one-touch" motion.

APPLICATIONS OF SMED

Bit Setup in a Process for Machining Fittings

The target process consisted of an automated line in which fittings for rubber hoses are cut from raw castings and pierced in a single flow, from rough machining [Process 1] through threading to inspection [Process 5] (*Figure 9-7*).

Several problems existed in this setup. Processes 1, 2, 4, and 5 each took less than ten seconds, but Process 3, single-purpose drill

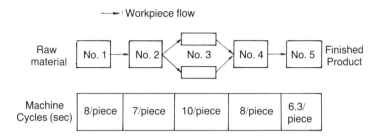

FIGURE 9-7. Process Flow and Machine Cycles

boring (*Figure 9-8*), had a long machine contact time of ten seconds. This was a bottleneck process whose efficiency determined the output of the entire line.

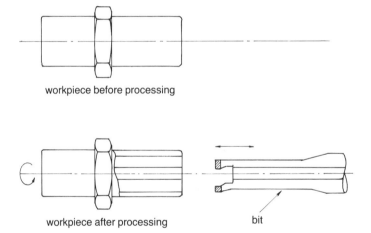

FIGURE 9-8. Bit Position and Workpiece Shapes Before and After Processing

In dealing with this situation, concentration was placed on improving the rate of movement through the process and on producing defect-free items from the very first cycle after a setup change. This latter goal, a basic tenet at Toyoda Gosei, came about because when tools were switched, so-called "trial cutting" would result in the disposal of one out of every six or seven half-finished goods at the setup change stage.

As may be seen from *Table 9-2* and *Figure 9-9*, most of the time was taken up in loosening, tightening, and adjusting screws.

No.	Procedural Steps (in order)	Time Req. (sec)	Observations
1	Loosen 2 A bolts	36	eliminate bolts, use one-touch method
2	Extract tool holder	15	simplify
3	Set new tool holder	15	(same as 2)
4	Tighten 2 A bolts	32	(same as 1)
5	Run machine	20	
6	Remove workpiece, measure	18	to external setup
7	Loosen C	28	
8	Adjust with handle B	32	contact method
9	Tighten C	18	
10	Run machine	20	
11	Remove workpiece, measure	17	to external setup
12	Repeat 5 - 11	665	use intermediary jigs
13	Measure depth with D	24	
14	Run machine	20	
15	Remove workpiece, measure	12	
16	Continuous run	1	
Total: 973 = 16 min. 13 sec.			

TABLE 9-2. Pre-improvement Procedure and Observations

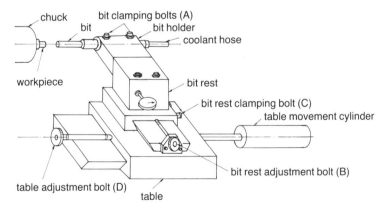

FIGURE 9-9. Sketch of Bit Setting Before Improvement

Thus there were three main issues to be dealt with:

- Eliminating screw fastenings
- Changing bits by mounting them on intermediary jigs and

changing the entire assembly

- Determining whether blade positioning could be moved to external setup

Improvement was achieved (*Figure 9-10, Table 9-3*) principally by using intermediary jigs (*Figure 9-11*) and by making the necessary settings in advance (*Figure 9-12*). After repeated trial and error, it became possible to preset tools as part of external setup.

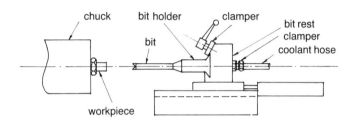

FIGURE 9-10. Bit Setting After Improvement

No.	Procedures	Time(sec) M.O.	Fd.	Manual Operations Automatic (sec)
1*	Detach coolant hose	5		
2	Loosen clamper	4		
3	Extra tool holder	6		
4	Set new tool holder	8		
5	Tighten clamper	5		
6*	Connect coolant hose	5		
7	Start up	1	20	
(8)	Take first workpiece, check dimensions	(20)		MT 20 sec

M.O. = Manual Operations
Fd. = Feeding

total setup time: 34 sec (No.1 - No.7)
No.(8) is external setup
* indicates supplementary step

TABLE 9-3. Bit Setting Procedures After Improvement

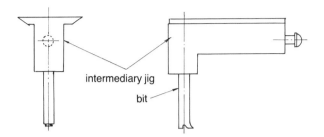

FIGURE 9-11. Bit Set on Intermediary Jig

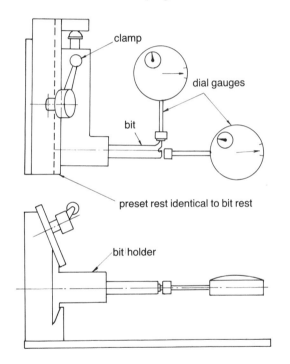

FIGURE 9-12. Bit Presetting Schema

The total cost for implementing this improvement was ¥80,000 ($330) × 21 machines = ¥1,680,000 ($6930) (ten lines). And the results were impressive (*Figures 9-13* and *9-14*): we saved ¥210,000 per month (about $868) on the cost of discarded toolings; two setup engineers were no longer needed; and the rate of movement improved significantly.

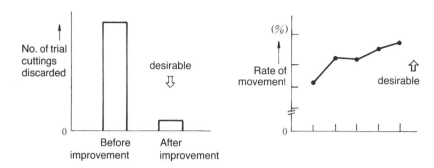

FIGURE 9-13. Ratio of Products Discarded Before and After Improvement

FIGURE 9-14. Changes in Rate of Movement

Die Punch Setup Changes in a Cold-Forging Process

In this process the raw material used in the example above is cold-forged from coil stock. Although all raw parts used to be purchased from the outside, we installed a cold-forging machine in 1982 and began manufacturing parts internally. Starting with only one type of product, we soon found it necessary to shorten setup times because of expanded internal demand for various items and rising volumes. SMED thus came about in accordance with the need — fundamental to the Toyota Production System — to produce the *items* required at the *time* required and in the *quantity* required (*Figure 9-15*).

An American-made cold-forging machine was perfect for producing one item in large quantities, but no consideration had been given to the question of setup changes and, at one hour and forty minutes, individual setups took a long time. Since at this rate either

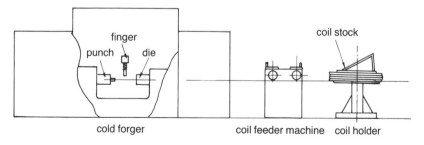

FIGURE 9-15. Outline of Cold-Forging Tooling Porcess

the equipment was not working up to capacity or the company risked moving into large-lot operations, it was necessary to pursue efficient use of the machine along with the aims mentioned above (*Figure 9-16*).

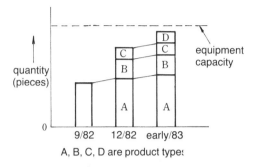

FIGURE 9-16. Changes in Projected Demand

Improvement proceeded in two stages. In the first stage, three major issues relating to operations required by setup changes were identified and dealt with. These were:

1. To consolidate scattered punch and die parts
2. To eliminate die height adjustments
3. To use nut runners for loosening and tightening screws

These changes were made. Parts were consolidated (*Figure 9-17*), the dimensions of other parts were changed to make die height adjustments unnecessary, and tool changes were carried out.

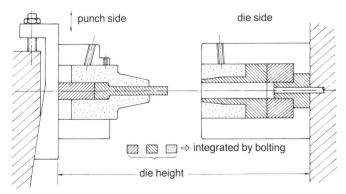

FIGURE 9-17. Cross Sections of Punch, Die

As a result, time was cut from one hour and forty minutes to thirty-one minutes and fifteen seconds (*Figure 9-18*). In addition, process flow, work rate, and safety were improved. The total cost of first-stage improvements was ¥1,200,000 (about $4958).

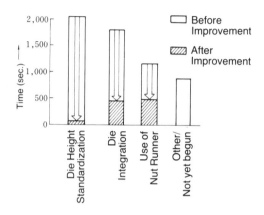

FIGURE 9-18. **First Stage Improvements in Cold-Forging Setup**

For the second stage, the pre-improvement procedures were analyzed (*Table 9-4*) and the following suggested improvements made:

- Bring tools to convenient locations.
- Eliminate the transportation of heavy items (dies, punches.)
- Eliminate adjustments and use one-touch techniques.
- Change part of the procedure.

These suggestions were carried out. The method after improvement is shown in *Figures 9-19, 9-20, 9-21* and *9-22*, and in *Table 9-5*.

The cost to implement second stage improvements was ¥200,000 ($826). As a result of these changes, ¥250,000 ($1033) per month was saved, and fewer mechanical devices were needed (*Figures 9-23, 9-24,* and *9-25*).

In addition to the setup improvements, the two key factors contributing to the success of these activities were the understanding and backing of company officials, and the enthusiasm and persistence of

No.	Procedural Steps (in order)	Time Req'd (secs)	Observations
1	Change lift valve	30	make automatic
2	Loosen lift screw	5	
3	Loosen punch bolts (6)	95	keep tool (nut runner) nearby
4	Loosen die bolts (6)	91	(same as 3)
5	Put punch on bolster	65	eliminate transportation from within machine
6	Put die on bolster	172	(same as 5)
7	Remove die pin	8	
8	Clean punch, die case	15	
9	Take die from cradle	110	(same as 5, 6)
10	Take punch from cradle	85	(same as 5, 6)
11	Tighten punch bolts	60	(same as 3, 4)
12	Tighten die bolts	52	(same as 3, 4)
13	Additional bolt tightening	128	do in steps 11, 12
14	Connect coolant pipe	15	eliminate adjustments
15	Tighten 6 die pressure-fit bolts	37	
16	Change finger blocks, adjust	685	eliminate adjustments, use one-touch method
17	Join dies, adjust	56	combine with punch, die
18	Secure to lift	27	
19	Inch dies together	43	(same as 17)
20	Adjust oil output		(same as 14)
21	Form first product	16	
22	Measure dimensions	85	measure at start, in external setup
	Total: 1915" = 31'55"		

TABLE 9-4. **Pre-improvement Procedure and Observations**

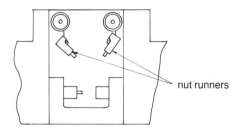

FIGURE 9-19. Nut Runner Schema

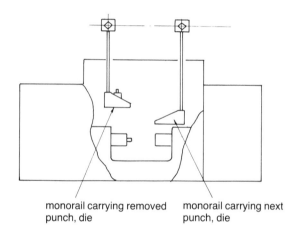

FIGURE 9-20. Die Monorail

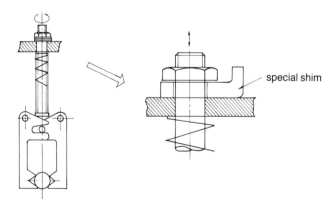

FIGURE 9-21. One-Touch Finger Positioning

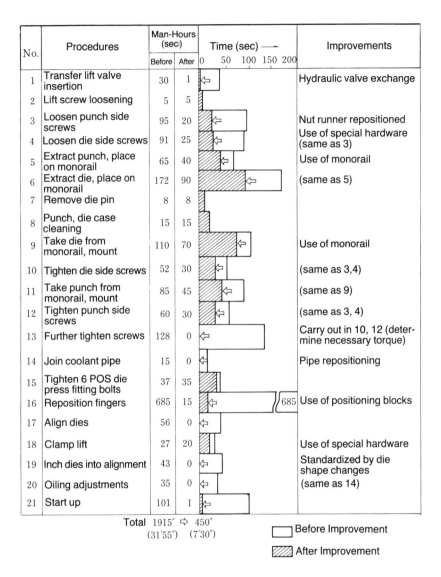

No.	Procedures	Man-Hours (sec)		Time (sec) ⟶	Improvements
		Before	After	0 50 100 150 200	
1	Transfer lift valve insertion	30	1		Hydraulic valve exchange
2	Lift screw loosening	5	5		
3	Loosen punch side screws	95	20		Nut runner repositioned
4	Loosen die side screws	91	25		Use of special hardware (same as 3)
5	Extract punch, place on monorail	65	40		Use of monorail
6	Extract die, place on monorail	172	90		(same as 5)
7	Remove die pin	8	8		
8	Punch, die case cleaning	15	15		
9	Take die from monorail, mount	110	70		Use of monorail
10	Tighten die side screws	52	30		(same as 3,4)
11	Take punch from monorail, mount	85	45		(same as 9)
12	Tighten punch side screws	60	30		(same as 3, 4)
13	Further tighten screws	128	0		Carry out in 10, 12 (determine necessary torque)
14	Join coolant pipe	15	0		Pipe repositioning
15	Tighten 6 POS die press fitting bolts	37	35		
16	Reposition fingers	685	15	685	Use of positioning blocks
17	Align dies	56	0		
18	Clamp lift	27	20		Use of special hardware
19	Inch dies into alignment	43	0		Standardized by die shape changes
20	Oiling adjustments	35	0		(same as 14)
21	Start up	101	1		

Total 1915″ ⇨ 450″
(31′55″) (7′30″)

☐ Before Improvement
▨ After Improvement

TABLE 9-5. Setup Procedure for Cold-Forging Machine After Improvement

the people implementing the changes. Because of the support of these two groups, 95% of the company's goals have been met.
—*(Reported by Noboru Takami, Production Survey Office)*

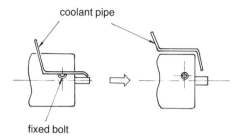

coolant pipe

fixed bolt

FIGURE 9-22. Improved Coolant Pipe Position

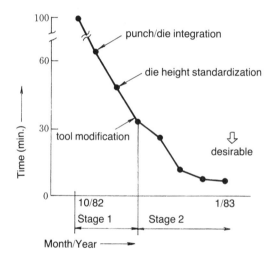

punch/die integration

die height standardization

tool modification

desirable

Time (min.)

10/82
Stage 1   Stage 2

Month/Year ⟶

FIGURE 9-23. Change in Setup Time

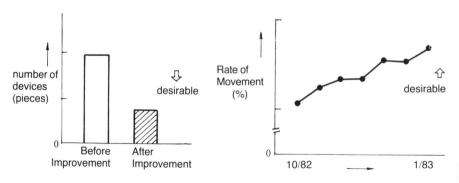

number of
devices
(pieces)

desirable

Before   After
Improvement Improvement

Rate of
Movement
(%)

desirable

10/82 ⟶ 1/83

FIGURE 9-24. Comparison of
Mechanical Intervention Amounts

FIGURE 9-25. Change in
Movement Rate

10

A Quick-Setting
("Q-S") Campaign
Nippon Kogaku K.K. (Oi Plant)

THE COMPANY

From its founding in 1917 to the end of World War II, Nippon Kogaku was Japan's premier producer of military optical products. With the shift to the production of civilian consumer goods after the war, the firm began afresh as an all-around manufacturer of optical devices.

Principal products are Nikon single-lens reflex cameras and compact cameras, all types of lenses, surveying instruments, measurement instruments, microscopes, telescopes, eyeglasses, and semiconductor-related devices. The cameras, lenses, and semiconductor-related devices are manufactured at the firm's main plant in Oi. The company employs about 6,300 people, of whom 2,900 work at the Oi Plant.

Competition in cameras intensified when a worldwide economic slowdown dampened demand, especially for single-lens reflex cameras. For this reason, manufacturers were besieged by demands for broad cost reductions and inventory cuts.

As of March 1983, capital was approximately ¥8.8 billion ($36.3 million). Sales in 1982 were approximately ¥1.135 trillion ($4.68 billion).

Philosophy and Direction

The oil crisis of 1973 brought about broad structural market changes in the optical equipment industry. These rapid and wide-ranging market shifts caused the business financial picture to deteriorate and, in particular, work-in-process (WIP) inventory rose considerably, revealing how ill-equipped previous manufacturing ar-

173

rangements had been for dealing with change. Among various directives from management at that time were the following, addressed to the production division:

- Shorten new-product startup times.

- Reduce production times and WIP inventory.

A number of successful policies were devised with respect to the first of these points. A discussion of issues bearing on the second follows.

The final assembly operation in processing and assembly industries like Nippon Kogaku consists in principle of a flow of individual items. In the past, however, from the raw material stage through various kinds of processing up to final assembly, parts used in parts assembly and overall assembly were processed in comparatively large lots. The distinction between the allowances needed for production arrangements and for product quantities, moreover, was not entirely clear, obscuring the extent of needed work in process. Thus, four issues were given serious consideration:

- Processing had been carried out with comparatively large lots.

- Some parts involved unnecessarily overlapping processes.

- The required degree of work in process was unclear.

- No one had sought to discover why waiting for work in process was necessary.

We began concrete activities after reinterpreting the directives from management as follows: *Construct a production system that can respond without wastefulness to market changes and that, moreover, by its very nature reduces costs.*

Motivation for and Steps Involved in Tackling SMED

To "respond without wastefulness to market changes," the first requirement was to cut processing times to the minimum by using small lots, ultimately lots of one.

Many large and small problems needed to be solved to lower costs as time went on. Among these, setup changes — which had always been taken as givens and which had consequently been ignored — constituted one of the most troublesome bottlenecks in the whole process. Because of this, an average 20% reduction in setup times was included among the manufacturing section's annual objectives. The situation did not progress satisfactorily, however, whether in response to having talked about the concept of "average" improvement, or because the problem was approached with thinking extrapolated from that of the past.

At this point, a different method of persuasion was tried. Rather than cutting setup times for a hundred machines by an average of 10%, employees were told, it would be more valuable to cut the setup time for one machine by 99%. In addition to stressing the need for a complete change of conceptual approach, management presented case studies from other companies and, as much as possible, arranged for supervisors to visit other firms.

Along with the direct guidance of Mr. Shingo, repeated visits to M Heavy Industries's S Plant, which had already achieved several successes with SMED, spurred on improvement efforts.

What was gained from Mr. Shingo's guidance and from various plant visits can be summarized as follows: *The biggest obstacle is deciding that SMED will not work. SMED will be achieved more than 50% of the time if everyone is determined, no matter what, to bring it about.*

By following this advice, we have steadily continued to increase the number of setup times brought into the single-minute range (*Figure 10-1*).

Mr. Shingo teaches that adjustments should be eliminated in favor of settings. Perhaps because this advice sank in, SMED came to be referred to on the shop floor as "quick setting," or "Q-S," and this has become the company's official term for it.

APPLICATIONS OF SMED

Improving Collet Changes on a Semiautomatic Lathe

When collets are changed during setup on a semiautomatic lathe, numerous trips have to be made between the front and back of the machine to remove and attach the collet and adjust the amount it is opened and closed. In addition, when a collet is secured by being

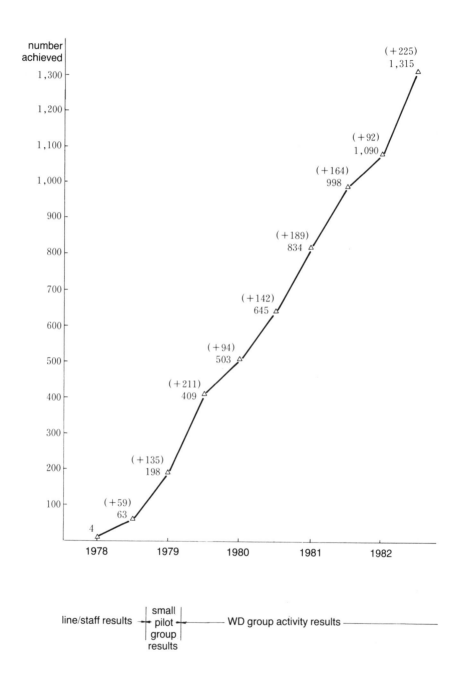

FIGURE 10-1. **Number of Q-S Operations Achieved**

driven onto the main spindle with a No. 4 Morse taper, longitudinal reproducibility deteriorates to approximately 0.05–0.10 mm (*Figure 10-2*).

To solve these problems, the main body of the collet was divided into two sections, the Morse taper section and the head; only the (threaded) head and core were then changed during setup (*Figure 10-3*). After improvement, it became possible to change heads and

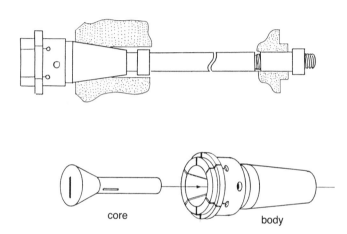

FIGURE 10-2. Collet Adjustment Before Improvement

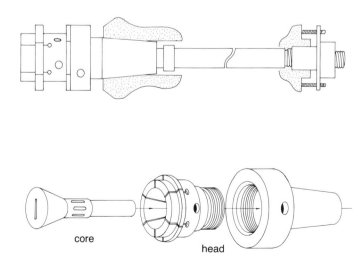

FIGURE 10-3. Collet Adjustment After Improvement

cores working only from the front of the machine, which reduced collet-changing time from ten minutes to two. Also, because of the poor longitudinal reproducibility in pre-improvement collets, approximately five minutes had been needed to correct tool position. Reproducibility became 0.01 mm following improvement, however, making dimension adjustments unnecessary.

Q-S on a Multipurpose Turret Lathe

Three kinds of improvement for this operation were planned:

1. Standardize turret head reference planes.
2. Set vertical position more quickly.
3. Eliminate adjustments in setting horizontal position.

As shown in *Figure 10-4*, the turret head's horizontal and vertical position reference surfaces were corrected and ground. A jig was installed that ran right up against the tool holder. By this means, the position of the tool holder could be regulated by matching the holder to a model of the workpiece to be processed, and quick-set attachment by the contact method became possible.

Next, as shown in *Figure 10-5*, a vertical positioning jig was secured, and by changing standard stoppers and special (fine adjustment) screws for each workpiece, it was possible to quick-set vertical position dimensions.

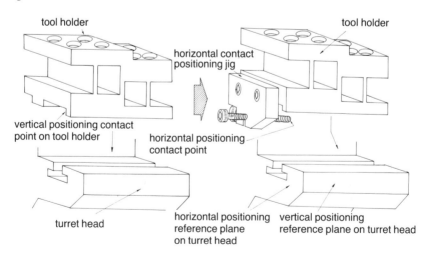

FIGURE 10-4. Standardizing Turret Head Reference Planes on Multipurpose Lathe

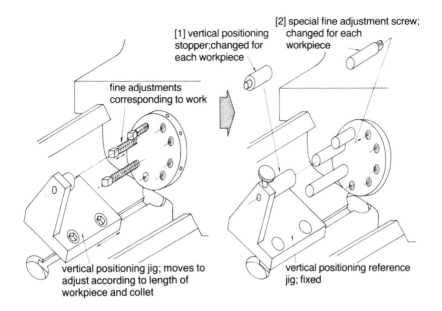

FIGURE 10-5. Setting Vertical Position on Multipurpose Lathe

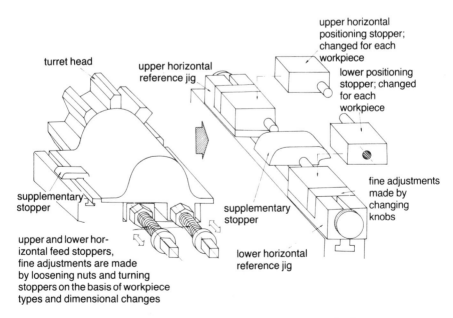

FIGURE 10-6. Setting Horizontal Position on Multipurpose Lathe

Finally, as shown in *Figure 10-6*, horizontal positioning reference jigs were selected and affixed, and the turret head was positioned by exchanging upper and lower stoppers for each workpiece. Fine adjustment knobs were then used to make allowances for slight dimension changes caused by thermal deformation, etc.

Together, these improvements shortened the setup time from four hours and eight minutes to nineteen minutes (*Figure 10-7*).

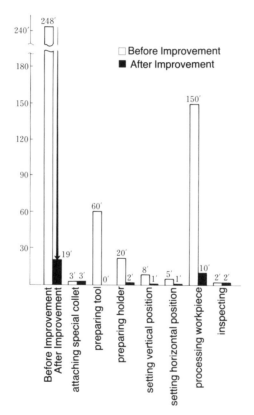

FIGURE 10-7. **Q-S Results**

Mounting Replacement Gears

The machine in this example threads lens fittings. A gear-changing setup is required, depending on the leads and thread lengths for individual fittings.

Although this change of gears is but one operation within the setup, it had been an obstacle to the achievement of a quick-setup change. The change had previously taken from ten to twenty minutes, depending on the operator's experience and level of skill.

Figure 10-8 shows the attached state. The previous method of replacement, shown in *Figure 10-9*, used a paddle that was secured while adjusting backlash.

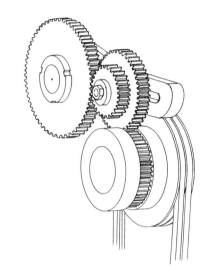

FIGURE 10-8. Replacement Gears Before Improvement

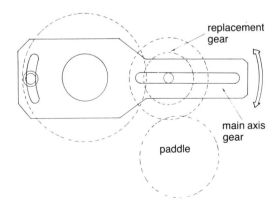

FIGURE 10-9. Paddle Before Improvement

To improve this operation, a paddle was devised with sites for the attachment of two replacement gears, so that the operation could be accomplished merely by changing gear engagement (*Figure 10-10*). This method is extremely effective for machines that process only two kinds of parts, but it cannot deal with three kinds or more.

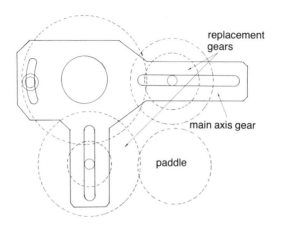

FIGURE 10-10. Paddle After Improvement

In addition, cassette-type paddles were devised (*Figure 10-11*). Replacement gears are attached to the cassette plate, which is sandwiched into the cassette-type paddle and secured by using an air

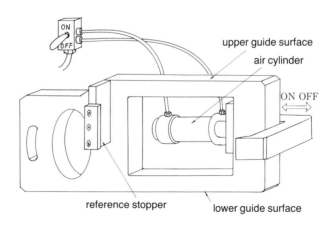

FIGURE 10-11. Cassette-Type Paddle

cylinder (*Figure 10-12*). The completed setting is shown in *Figure 10-13*.

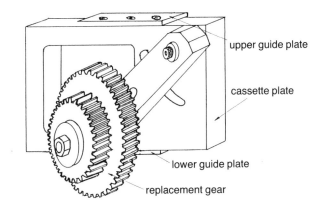

FIGURE 10-12. Cassette Replacement Gear

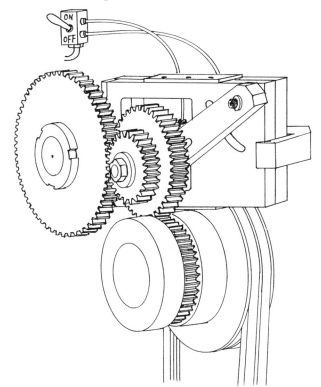

FIGURE 10-13. Completed Setting

By using the cassette method, it has been possible to cut replacement gear changing time to thirty seconds. In addition, variations in backlash settings caused by differences in operator skill have been eliminated, making fixed gear attachment possible.

Indexing with an All-Purpose Engraving Machine

In this operation, an index mark is engraved on a camera lens fitting. The setup consists of the following steps, with the positioning operation of the second step accounting for approximately 70% of the setup time:

- A special collet for each workpiece is attached to a dividing head with a three-way clamping chuck.

- The spindle and direction of rotation are positioned.

- The depth of the blade cut into the item to be processed is set.

If the second operation could be eliminated, ten minutes could be cut from the setup time. It was therefore decided to investigate the possibility of improving the collet (*Figure 10-14*), as described below.

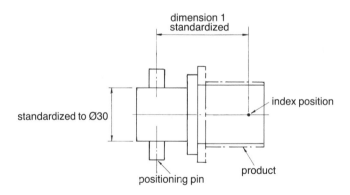

FIGURE 10-14. **Collet Improvement**

1. First, the previous collet was machined to standardize its attachment diameter at Ø30 mm (*Figure 10-15*).
2. Next, locating pins were mounted on the attachment diameter section to eliminate the operation of positioning in the

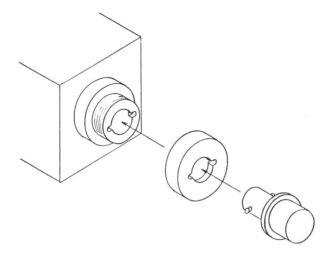

FIGURE 10-15. Base Collet Improvement

    direction of collet rotation.

3. Third, dimension 1, from the rotation-wise positioning pin to the index position, was standardized to eliminate the operation of positioning along the spindle.

4. Simultaneously with the above three improvements, the dividing head with the three-way clamping chuck was abandoned and an index collet for milling was appropriated as a base collet. (In a later improvement, attachment and positioning of the collet were made a one-touch operation.)

As a result of these changes, setup time dropped from twenty-four minutes to five (*Figure 10-16*).

The one remaining aim is to improve cutting depth settings and proceed with reducing times until the setup is instantaneous.

A Process Computer Lathe

This is a hydraulically driven process computer cycle lathe engaged principally in turning the exteriors of camera lens fittings. The problem was examined on the basis of results, such as those in *Figure 10-17*, yielded by an analysis of current setup operations.

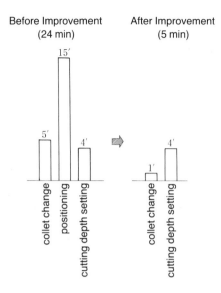

FIGURE 10-16. Setup Improvement Results

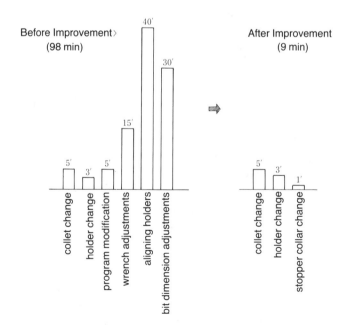

FIGURE 10-17. Setup Elements and Results of Improvement

To reduce various adjustments taking up about 85% of the setup, workpieces were to be grouped together.

- *Workpiece shapes:* bring close to tool positions
- *Elements of processing:* standardize tool shapes
- *Order of processing:* standardize program

The number of workpieces was restricted in accordance with these three principles and, taking machine capacity into consideration, eight workpieces were dealt with as follows:

1. By means of grouping, the order of processing was standardized to outer diameter finishing, end surface finishing, and beveling. Program changes became unnecessary.
2. The number of adjustments declined for all stoppers. After further investigation, all stopper adjustments were eliminated by using stopper collars (*Figure 10-18*).

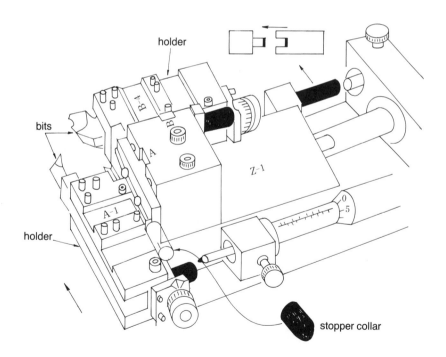

FIGURE 10-18. Hood Setup Scheme

3. Setups were conducted using various combinations of tools classified according to the eight workpiece shapes. Also, tool changes were handled by exchanging holders, with the base holder secured at the side of the machine. Adjustments were eliminated, moreover, by using stopper collars for contact method positioning (*Figures 10-18, 10-19*).

4. A dock for switching from rapid traverse to tool feeding was positioned by the contact method (*Figure 10-20*).

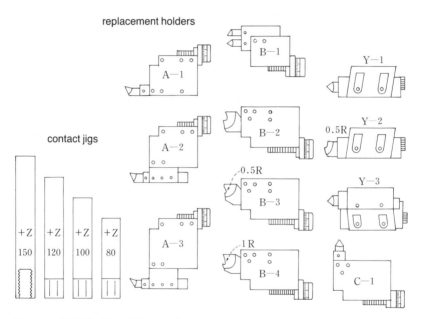

FIGURE 10-19. Visual Control

Accumulated improvements made it possible to cut setup time considerably, from ninety-eight minutes to nine, with three setup operations carried out per day.

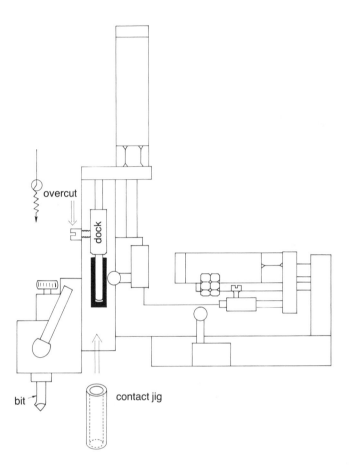

FIGURE 10-20. Positioning for ALK Overcut Quick-Feeding

Benchless Processing of Nylon

Ten types of fittings used for camera zoom lenses are processed, for a total of 8,000 items per month. Roughly twenty setup changes are carried out each month. Each consists of several steps:

- Attaching a shearing tool
- Centering

- Determining overall length
- Determining drill depth

Observing that the material being cut was nylon, the group investigated ways to improve shearing blades. They also looked for ways to eliminate manual determination of length, which required a special stopper for each workpiece.

First, they carried out a function analysis of processing elements to see whether processing time itself could be cut along with setup time.

Centering adjustments were eliminated by exchanging safety razors for the blades on the previous tools. In addition, two processes were conducted simultaneously with two razor blades combined, and holders were constructed to incorporate overall length stoppers. As a result, processing time was reduced to one-fourth of what it had been, and setup time was cut in half. Product quality improved as well, since processing using razors almost never produced returns.

Spacers for determining overall length had to be changed for each order. To make this operation easier, attachment holes were lengthened so that bolts did not have to be removed (*Figure 10-21*).

What had been a twenty-minute setup was cut to three minutes, and processing time was reduced from sixty seconds to fifteen.

— *(Reported by Tsuneo Morishima, First Machine Section, and Jiro Igarashi, Second Machine Section)*

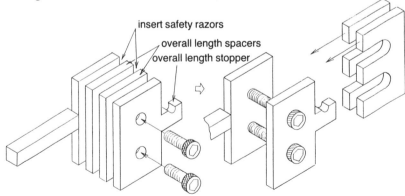

insert safety razors
overall length spacers
overall length stopper

FIGURE 10-21. **Improved Holder**

11

Using SMED on a Farm Machinery Processing Line
Kubota, Ltd. (Sakai Plant)

THE COMPANY

The Sakai plant is Kubota, Ltd.'s principal facility for the manufacture of farm machinery, one of the mainstays of the company. The plant produces a wide variety of equipment, including small and large tractors, tillers, large combines, and large and small diesel and air-cooled engines. These products are sold both domestically and abroad.

The plant lot size is 200,000 square meters, the total building area 130,000 square meters, and the total number of employees about 2000.

The Problem

With limited growth potential and intensifying competition in the domestic market, the firm has been strengthening its expanded export orientation. To compete overseas, low production costs and a broad product line are needed. In addition, domestic demand is shifting from an emphasis on machinery for rice cultivation toward non-rice agricultural machinery, spurring the current move to low-volume production of a variety of machine types.

As a result of both slower market growth and changes made over many years in the Sakai plant, factory production lines had become scattered, forming isolated pockets that had given rise to inefficiencies in transportation, in mechanical intervention, and in management. Production efficiency had dropped, and the situation had gotten to the point where drastic changes were needed.

The U.S. Production System

For these reasons, an interim plan for strengthening the production system was developed and inaugurated in 1976. The nucleus of this plan is something we call the "U.S. Production System." Based on the concepts of production leveling and synchronization, the system aims at building an efficient process founded on the elimination of waste and on low-volume production of a variety of products. Methods used by the system are shown in *Table 11-1*.

The two following points are crucial to putting the U.S. Production System into practice:

- *Implementation of a multiprocess layout:* The production line should be redesigned to create a multiprocess system that eliminates waste in materials flow and in management.

- *Implementation of level assembly production:* While "mixed assembly" makes it possible to synchronize production with demand to a significant degree, progress should be made toward eliminating all overproduction by leveling assembly and anterior processes.

These two critical features of the U.S. Production System depend on sharp cuts in setup times. First, by reorganizing multiprocess lines and creating a flow of production processes, we were able to work toward a reduction in man-hours. With setups as they had been conducted in the past, however, the flow of processes was impeded and it was necessary to intervene in the middle of processes.

The Move to SMED

It was in response to this problem that the need for setup time reductions arose. At the same time that assembly leveling was proceeding, a major problem was created by a prerequisite condition — that of changing the line over to small-lot production. This provided the impetus for tackling SMED.

Apart from this, another motivation for attempting SMED was that shortened setup times were necessary to complete the urgent task of building a flexible production facility. The U.S. Production System, moreover, considers as waste anything that does not pro-

Needs	Basic Approach to Production	Fundamental Strategy	Expanded Strategy 1	Expanded Strategy 2	Expanded Strategy 3
producing what the customer demands (responding with diverse machines, linked manufacture and sales)	lead time reduction	leveled production	leveling	production planning methods / leveling methods / setup change reductions	
		improved ordering, production and inventory system			
		later processes take over			
producing at minimum cost (cost reduction)	the elimination of waste due to: • overproduction • delays • transport waste • processing errors and defects • operations which do not add value	Just-In-Time production (synchronization)	small-lot transport	organize, improve types of packing / delivery lot improvement shipment methods / establish locations	
			"super-market"	multiple process layout / cycle time operations / single item flows / operations improvement	
			multiple process production		
		personnel reduction	"human automation"	"full-work, no-work"	
			standard operations	manuals for: • defining standard operations • combining standard operations • directing standard operations	
			difficulties		
satisfying demands for quality (quality assurance)	build quality into processes (leave later processes to customer)	making the workplace understandable	shutdown principles	establish line indicator boards / rules for dealing with shutdowns / shutdown devices at fixed places	implementation handbook
			the 4 S's (an orderly workplace)	"foolproof" methods / comprehensive checks	

TABLE 11-1. The So-called "U.S. Production System"

duce added value, and on that basis, SMED was needed to eradicate a huge area of inefficiency.

There was an even more critical issue: thorough implementation of SMED was the key to securing the same kind of productivity improvements that the Toyota Production System had already brought to automobile and farm machinery plants in Japan.

It took much painful effort to find ways to move everyone away from a long-ingrained large-lot orientation and from the notion that setup operations are intrinsically time-consuming. We had to instill in our people the desire to take up the challenge of dramatically shortening setup times and to discover how to begin working toward SMED.

As mentioned above, we sensed a strong and urgent need to give precedence to building a multiprocess layout and to implementing level assembly production. As the inaugural act of our SMED campaign, we welcomed Mr. Shingo who, in the midst of a busy schedule, gave a talk and made an initial on-site advisory visit. This visit had the salutary effect of raising our spirits as we faced the challenge of SMED.

We proceeded to build SMED model machines that showed what certain measures would enable us to do. We chose as our models either the machines on each line or in each shop whose setup took the most time, or those that underwent the greatest number of setup changes. We then carried out successive demonstration setups, each with the goal of cutting setup time either by 90% or to less than thirty minutes. These demonstration setups became part of our regular program. They were very effective in fostering improvements and mutual edification among the shops, and helped to raise consciousness in the plant as a whole.

The achievement of our goals on the models encouraged the idea that anything can be accomplished by trying, and this attitude quickly spread throughout the firm. A new atmosphere developed and a new way of thinking was encouraged. A setup newsletter was published, case studies were compiled, and workers began hanging emblems on their machines to boast of setup achievements.

The principal authors of practical improvements in the plant were the key people who worked full-time to promote the U.S. Production System, the quality control circles of the manufacturing sections, and the improvement teams. In particular, the precision machining of parts and the rebuilding of large equipment proceeded with the support of the Production Technology Division.

As we moved toward single-minute setups, one technique that left a particularly vivid impression concerned screw fastenings. With screws, it is really the last thread that does the tightening and the first thread that does the loosening. A careful look shows that machines and jigs are full of screws, and that screws are used to fasten virtually everything. Most of these items cannot be unfastened without removing screws.

With this in mind, we mounted a drive to pursue the problem of screw fastenings. We focused in on screws and made improvements so that either no screw would be turned more than once, or one-touch methods of securing would be used. In one shop, screws that had to be turned more than once during setup operations were painted red while efforts were made to reduce their number or eliminate them entirely. In another shop, knock pins were driven into bolts to prevent nuts from being loosened by any more than one turn.

These screw improvements were carried out by various schemes in different shops and achieved considerable success. In spite of this, however, we were keenly aware of not having pursued the matter to the limit by eliminating screws altogether.

From this experience we learned once again how important it is to delve into the phenomena around us from the point of view of functions and effects. This, indeed, is why the SMED system has been called "a way of thinking."

APPLICATIONS OF SMED

Below, we present three cases drawn from our numerous applications of SMED: that of the screw improvements mentioned above, the application of the concept to line processes as a whole, and the case of a multiple-axis drill press.

Screw Improvement

Examples of concrete improvement are shown in *Figure 11-1*. It is important to rethink fastening methods from scratch, taking into account the magnitudes and directions of the forces acting on screws.

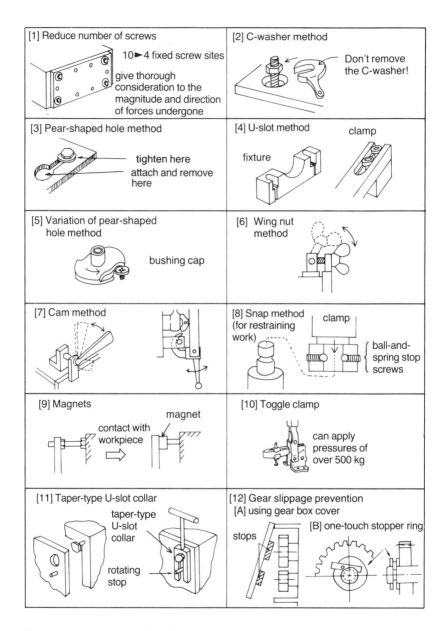

FIGURE 11-1. Examples of Screw Improvement

In the matter of screws, it is extremely important also to devise solutions for the tools used in setup operations:

- Reduce the variety of tools, make screws uniform, and standardize tools even if screws are of different sizes.

- If there is no obstacle to the operation, secure wrenches or handles to screws to eliminate having to pick up and put down tools.

- Keep tools nearby and arranged neatly. Label tool hooks or keep tools together on boards.

These measures will contribute greatly to time reductions. They are actively incorporated, too, in the following examples.

SMED Applied to an Air-Cooled Engine Connecting Rod Processing Line

On a line for processing the connecting rods that lie at the heart of air-cooled engines, aluminum die-cast raw material was finished by moving through the following processes:

1. Reference hole processing
2. Bolt hole processing
3. Tap oil hole processing
4. Large end cutting
5. Cap attachment process (clamping)
6. Boring
7. Washing

Equipment on the line was arranged in a U-configuration and the single-item-flow multiprocess operation was carried out by three female part-time workers and one male worker.

Figure 11-2 shows pre-improvement setup times by process. The operation took a total of five hours and forty-two minutes. During setups, a male worker with previous experience on this line came from another production line to help the three women and one man who handled the line during normal production. He and the other male worker performed the setup operation together. While this was going on, the female workers waited, passing the time by cleaning up around the machines.

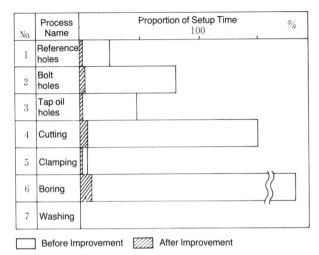

No.	Process Name	Proportion of Setup Time	%
1	Reference holes		
2	Bolt holes		
3	Tap oil holes		
4	Cutting		
5	Clamping		
6	Boring		
7	Washing		

☐ Before Improvement   ▨ After Improvement

FIGURE 11-2. Setup Times by Process

Considerable resources were wasted because of the unconscious assumption that changing setups was man's work and by other problems referred to below. We tried to improve the operation in two ways: achieving setups in less than ten minutes, and having the setup changes performed by women. As a result of surveys and analyses, specialized jigs were adopted for nearly every operation and these jigs were exchanged, but several problems arose:

1. Some of the jigs and parts to be changed were too heavy for women to handle easily.

2. Whenever jigs or parts were exchanged, chips had to be removed and cutting oil wiped off with petroleum jelly before the next jig was put into place. This took a tremendous amount of time in the second and fourth processes, which involved index-type machines. In the third process, too, there was a problem in that if an oil hole drill (which normally should not have to be taken off during setup changes) were not taken off, it would get in the way and the jig could not be removed.

3. Centering adjustments were required when a jig, cleaned off with petroleum jelly, was lifted onto the table. These would have been unnecessary if the jig were already correctly centered on contact, but since this was not done, adjustments had to be made every time a setup change took place. This

was a major cause of long setup times. Furthermore, this adjustment problem was a barrier to the performance of setup changes by female part-timers.

An important element of the SMED improvements on this line was the *subplate method*, i.e., the adoption of intermediary jigs. By exchanging only subplates and leaving the jigs themselves as they were, changing parts in setup operations became easier. In addition, this eliminated cleaning operations and superfluous fastening and unfastening of drills accompanying jig changes, and did away with the need for jig centering adjustments — the most time-consuming operation of all. With a single stroke, this intermediatry jig method solved all of the problems mentioned above.

Another cleverly conceived and very effective improvement was the combined use of workpiece guides in a boring process. In the past, guide bars had been straight. When the diameters of holes at the large end changed, special guides were put in, and time was needed to remove several auxiliary parts. If these guide bars were tapered, however, a spring at the back would push the guide into any size hole, so that the amount by which a guide bar entered a hole depended on the size of the hole. Since these guide bars also guided the workpiece into position, combined use was possible and the changing operation was eliminated.

A concrete description of improvements for each process is shown in *Figure 11-3*.

Setup times for each process after improvement are shown in *Figure 11-2*. Overall, time was reduced dramatically, to 4% of the previous time; where the total of pre-improvement setup times for all processes had been five hours and forty-two minutes, the total after improvements was thirteen minutes and fifty-two seconds. Each individual process, moreover, was successfully brought down to the single-minute range. In addition, it became possible for women to perform setups without outside help.

Improvements were achieved, too, in quality and safety, as adjustments were eliminated from all processes and setup changes no longer involved heavy jigs.

These improvements were achieved at a materials cost of approximately ¥220,000 ($909).

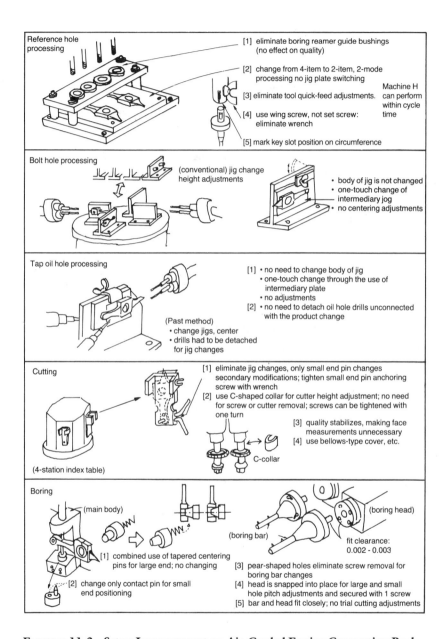

Reference hole processing

[1] eliminate boring reamer guide bushings (no effect on quality)

[2] change from 4-item to 2-item, 2-mode processing no jig plate switching

[3] eliminate tool quick-feed adjustments.

[4] use wing screw, not set screw: eliminate wrench

[5] mark key slot position on circumference

Machine H can perform within cycle time

Bolt hole processing

(conventional) jig change height adjustments

• body of jig is not changed
• one-touch change of intermediary jog
• no centering adjustments

Tap oil hole processing

[1] • no need to change body of jig
• one-touch change through the use of intermediary plate
• no adjustments

[2] • no need to detach oil hole drills unconnected with the product change

(Past method)
• change jigs, center
• drills had to be detached for jig changes

Cutting

[1] eliminate jig changes, only small end pin changes secondary modifications; tighten small end pin anchoring screw with wrench

[2] use C-shaped collar for cutter height adjustment; no need for screw or cutter removal; screws can be tightened with one turn

[3] quality stabilizes, making face measurements unnecessary

[4] use bellows-type cover, etc.

C-collar

(4-station index table)

Boring

(main body)

(boring head)

(boring bar)

fit clearance: 0.002 - 0.003

[1] combined use of tapered centering pins for large end; no changing

[2] change only contact pin for small end positioning

[3] pear-shaped holes eliminate screw removal for boring bar changes

[4] head is snapped into place for large and small hole pitch adjustments and secured with 1 screw

[5] bar and head fit closely; no trial cutting adjustments

FIGURE 11-3. Setup Improvement on Air-Cooled Engine Connecting Rod Processing Line

The Small Tractor Case Processing Line — Using SMED on Multiple-Axis Drill Presses

On a line for processing cases for small tractors, aluminum die-cast raw material was finished by milling, boring, piercing, tapping, and washing. Commercial multiple-axis drill presses and tapping machines were used for the piercing and tapping processes, and although various off-line machines were used as well, long setups were a common problem. On the drill presses that required the most time, setup changes took from two to four hours. The times required for elemental setup operations before improvement are shown in *Figure 11-4*. Special jigs were used for various workpiece shapes, and these jigs were changed during setup operations.

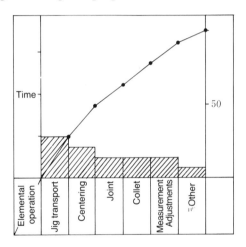

FIGURE 11-4. Pre-improvement Times for Elemental Operations in Multiple-Axis Drill Press Setup Changes

The first problem involved jig removal and transportation. After the jig and machine table were cleaned and tubing was removed from the jig, there was a time-consuming and unsafe operation in which a crane moved the jig to an off-line storage area over the tops of other machines and delivered the next jig in the same fashion.

To make matters worse, there was only one crane. An extraordinary amount of time was taken up in waiting for the crane and by the poor organization of tools and of the jig storage area. Moreover, since jigs and cluster plates were changed separately, similar operations were needed for the cluster plates.

The second problem was that, since jigs and clusters were mounted separately, they had to be aligned with each other, and these adjustments took still more time. After alignment was carried out, the next problem was that of joining cluster shafts and machine-driven shafts. With two or three shafts things were bad enough, but once there were ten or more, inserting one's hands in narrow joint windows and making connections in the proper order was extremely difficult. Even more time was wasted, moreover, by the fact that the joints had developed flaws through the years and connections would stick and be difficult to make.

The following measures were crucial in improving the multiple-axis drill presses (*Figure 11-5*):

Consolidating jigs and cluster plates. By means of two or three posts, jigs and clusters were combined so that they could be mounted, removed, and stored together. This eliminated the need to make centering adjustments between the two, and cut in half the number of transport operations to and from the machine. It also made possible the next measure.

Eliminating crane operations. A roller conveyor was installed between machines so that insertion and removal could be carried out by pushing or pulling techniques. In addition, storage was provided for the jig combinations. We struggled with the problem of how to move what by consolidation had become 300- to 400-kilogram jigs on the machine tables. After various investigations and improvements, we adopted an air mat system. We were able to reduce times and make setup operations easy even when a jig was secured to the table as is.

Improving joints. We simplified connections by repairing the nicked sections of the shafts, etc., so that parts would slip together smoothly. In another measure effective in cutting times, we color-coded corresponding joints and indicated key groove positions on sleeve exteriors.

While setup changes before improvement had taken three hours and thirty minutes, we were able, after improvement, to complete them in five minutes and thirty-eight seconds — less than 3% of the

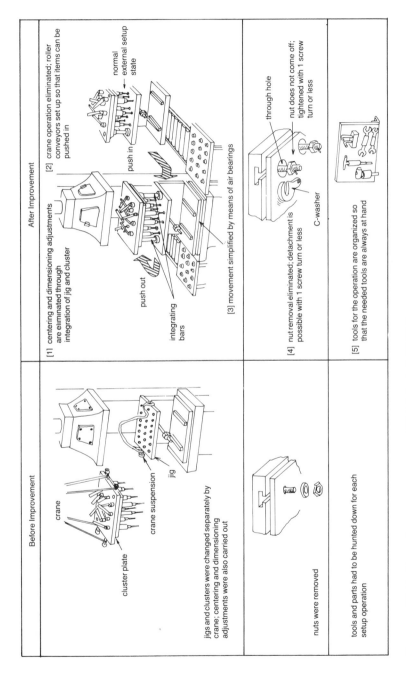

Before Improvement	After Improvement
crane cluster plate crane suspension jig jigs and clusters were changed separately by crane; centering and dimensioning adjustments were also carried out	[1] centering and dimensioning adjustments are eliminated through integration of jig and cluster push out integrating bars [2] crane operation eliminated; roller conveyors set up so that items can be pushed in normal external setup state push in [3] movement simplified by means of air bearings
nuts were removed	[4] nut removal eliminated; detachment is possible with 1 screw turn or less through hole nut does not come off; tightened with 1 screw turn or less C-washer
tools and parts had to be hunted down for each setup operation	[5] tools for the operation are organized so that the needed tools are always at hand

FIGURE 11-5. Setup Improvements on a Multiple-Axis Drill Press

former time. Costs were approximately ¥100,000 ($413) for materials. The elimination of crane operations and centering adjustments was linked to quality stabilization and significantly improved safety.

These improvements, of course, allowed immediate lateral movement to other machines on the line. They also had a tremendous effect in allowing movement to similar machines throughout the plant.

In the three examples presented above, significant advances were occasioned by improvements linked to setup man-hour reductions and that consequently brought to light problems of equipment failure and defective materials as well as hidden inefficiencies.

The manufacturing plant was the focal point of the above improvements. A proliferation of such ingenious improvements has contributed greatly to revitalizing the workplace and improving its structure.

— *(Reported by Kanenori Nakamura, Technology Development Section)*

12

Setup Improvements Based on Shop Circle Activities
Toyota Auto Body Co., Ltd.

THE COMPANY

Toyota Auto Body Co., Ltd. is located in the city of Kariya in Aichi Prefecture, where its specialized plant produces bodies for passenger cars, trucks, and commercial vehicles by means of pressing, plate-work, painting, and assembly processes.

Numerous body types are produced — four passenger car types, five truck body types, and three commercial vehicle body types — and each production line is a mixed, multi-body line. In numbers of auto bodies, the firm is responsible for over 10% of total Toyota production.

APPLICATIONS OF SMED

Simplifying Materials Setting Changes

As shown in *Figure 12-1 (left)*, although the press line was a single line from machines 1–6, intermediate processes fed into the line according to the shapes of the parts involved. When this happened, a materials rack was placed between machines 1 and 2 to feed into the main line. Each time this took place, considerable setup time was required to set up the materials rack with a crane and to put the material in place.

To improve this process, rather than use a crane with a high operating load, we arranged to move the operation to external setup (*Figure 12-1, right*). We made the materials racks so they could slide up and down and, with a conveyor running underneath a materials rack between machines 1–6, materials could be delivered by sliding up the rack.

205

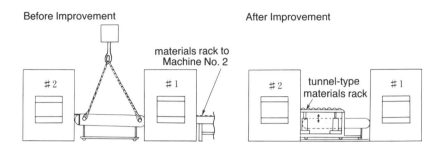

FIGURE 12-1. Simplification of Materials Setting Changes

Improved Setup for Accessory Transfer Die Equipment

Because the number of transfer-die processes varied, setups for installing a conveyor to remove and then move products took considerable time, as shown in *Figure 12-2 (left)*.

To improve this setup, a stage was attached to the transfer die (*Figure 12-2, right*). Products could then be moved by mechanical fingers, thereby eliminating conveyor equipment.

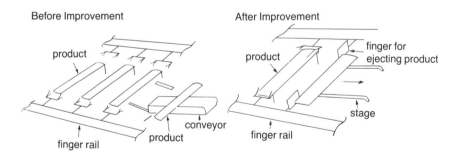

FIGURE 12-2. Improved Setup for Accessory Transfer Die Equipment

Improved Setting of Dies on a Fixed Bolster

Previously, a hoist crane had been used to transport dies for insertion into and removal from a small press (*Figure 12-3, left*).

To simplify the die placement, we set a roller conveyor into the bolster so that dies could be inserted and removed without using machines (*Figure 12-3, right*).

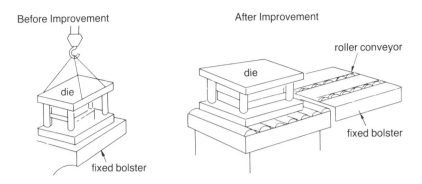

FIGURE 12-3. Improved Setting of Dies on a Fixed Bolster

Improvement in the Attachment and Removal of Air Hoses for Automation

Air hoses had been used for automation, but setups took time because hoses were manually attached to and removed from dies in the course of internal setup (*Figure 12-4, left*).

The improvement was to attach and remove air hoses during external setup. A packing-type quick joint was mounted on the bolster, so that air would be automatically fed in or cut off as the press moved up and down (*Figure 12-4, right*).

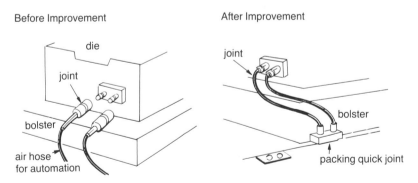

FIGURE 12-4. Improvement in the Attachment and Removal of Air Hoses for Automation

Die Positioning

Dies were set in place by fitting die-locating jigs into slots on the bolster and on the bottom of the die (*Figure 12-5, left*). The fine adjustments involved, however, took a great deal of time.

To improve the positioning of dies, locating stoppers were mounted on a moving bolster and corresponding sections cut out of the lower press die (*Figure 12-5, right*). When these came into contact as the crane was lowered, the die was set in place without fine adjustments.

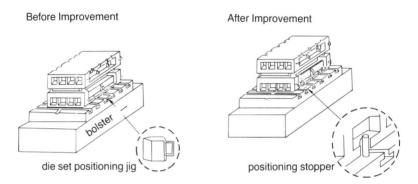

FIGURE 12-5. Die Positioning

Setting Coil Sheet Feed Volume

Coil sheet feed adjustments needed for particular types of products used to be made by combining four cylindrical spacers and using adjustment screws (*Figure 12-6, left*). These feed volume adjustments, however, took a long time.

For each product type, a special arch-shaped stroke gauge was made so that one-touch adjustment settings became possible (*Figure 12-6, right*).

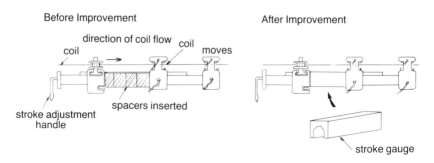

FIGURE 12-6. Setting Coil Sheet Feed Volume

Simplified Die Positioning

Center keys, located at the front and back and left and right, made positioning difficult and time-consuming when attaching or removing a die on a bolster, since it had to take place at four locations simultaneously (*Figure 12-7, left*).

To simplify this procedure, the left-to-right position on the bolster is determined first. Setup time is reduced by providing a spring-action bobbing center key, since centering can be divided between the two surfaces (*Figure 12-7, right*).

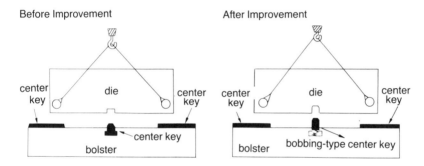

FIGURE 12-7. Simplified Die Positioning

Microshear Piling Setup Improvement

Pilings made of material cut to planks on a microshear were secured by fitting the piling stopper to the cut dimension of the raw material (*Figure 12-8, left*).

Now, by linking the microshear adjustment stopper and the piling stopper, piling stopper adjustments have been eliminated and setup time reduced (*Figure 12-8, right*).

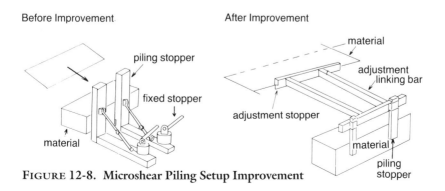

FIGURE 12-8. Microshear Piling Setup Improvement

Improving Setup by Means of a Feed Line Blanking Die Strike Die

For a spring stock blanking die with few processing strokes, a surface plate was used, and setup took a long time because bolts were used for attachment (*Figure 12-9, left*).

After improvement, a gap is preserved between the upper and lower dies with urethane stock so that the die can be struck directly (*Figure 12-9, right*). The surface plate is abandoned and bolts are eliminated from both the upper and lower dies.

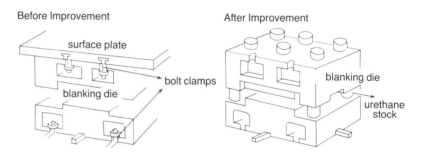

FIGURE 12-9. Improved Setup by Means of a Feed Line Blank Die Strike Die

Automating Deck Front Guard Frame Spot-Welding

Decks (the loading areas on trucks) are put together on two lines, and to spot-weld front guard frames on each of them, workers would choose either RX-34, C-157 or C-030 spot-welding guns and then do the welding (*Figure 12-10, left*). With the integration of

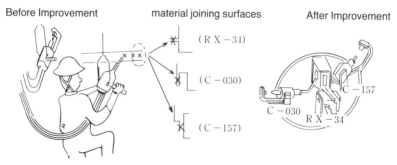

FIGURE 12-10. Elimination of Gun Selection Time Through the Automation of Deck Front Guard Frame Spot-Welding

decks, selection changes become more frequent, requiring more time and increasing worker fatigue.

To eliminate the increased time and fatigue that result from these gun selection changes, the three types of spot-welding gun are now set on a round plate (*Figure 12-10, right*). Rotating the plate automates the gun selection process.

Eliminating Setup Operations for Urethane Bumper Loading Pallets

When a loading pallet for urethane bumper products was full, a preparatory operation was needed in which that pallet was shunted aside and the next loading pallet was moved into loading position. Positioning pallets required repeated adjustments and production had to wait until all the preparations were completed (*Figure 12-11, left*).

A positioning guide to control the pallet was then installed and a feed mechanism and loading pallet were linked and automated. By this means, pallet-moving preparations were reduced by half and positioning adjustment operations and waiting were eliminated (*Figure 12-11, right*).

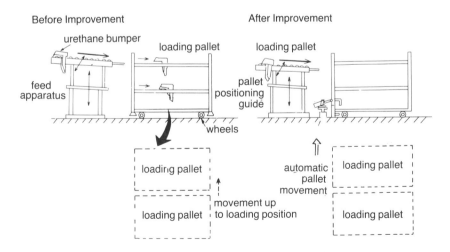

FIGURE 12-11. **Elimination of Setup Operations for Urethane Bumper Loading Pallets**

Improved Separation of a Hat-Shaped Cutting Die

Formerly, two types of die were used for hat-shaped cutting, making it necessary to set the dies in place for each separation (*Figure 12-12, left*).

Now, two types of hat shapes are incorporated in a single die, which can be separated by changing the length of the strike block (*Figure 12-12, right*).

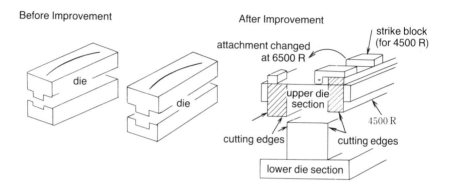

Before Improvement

After Improvement

FIGURE 12-12. Improved Separation of a Hat-Shaped Cutting Die

Reducing Setup Times for Changing Automatic Patch Machine Attachments

On automatic patch machines for a deck sheet metal shearcross process, two types of gusset shearcross are spot-welded with an automatic machine. Since gusset shearcross dimensions vary, there was a special attachment for each. According to the order of assembly, they were changed by loosening two bolts per side with a wrench (*Figure 12-13, left*).

After improvement, it was possible to change attachments by a one-touch plug-in method (*Figure 12-13, right*).

Reducing Loading Process Setup Times by Using a Tunnel Conveyor

Before improvement, the press line consisted of a single line from machines 1–6 (*Figure 12-14, upper*), but depending on fluctua-

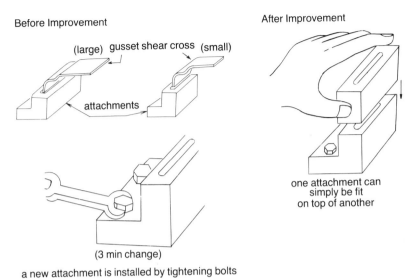

FIGURE 12-13. **A Deck Sheet Metal Shearcross Process**

tions in the number of processes for the parts involved, the loading position would shift either to behind machine 5 or to behind machine 6. Each change took considerable time.

After improvement, goods were loaded at a fixed location (*Figure 12-14, lower*). A turntable was attached to the conveyor, which could then be rotated for loading and unloading, and storage facilities could be set up at the next location after the halted process.

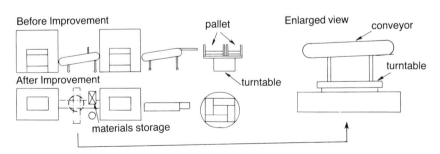

FIGURE 12-14. **Reductions in Loading Process Setup Times Through the Use of a Tunnel Conveyor**

13

Comprehensive Development of the SMED Concept to Include Affiliated Plants
Arakawa Auto Body Industries K.K.

THE COMPANY

In the thirty-five years since its founding in 1947, Arakawa Auto Body, a member of the Toyota group, has continued to develop along with the automobile industry and is currently one of the foremost makers of automobile bodies in Japan.

The firm is expanding in two directions, producing land cruisers and Coaster, High Ace, and Commuter microbuses on the one hand, and all types of interior accessories for passenger cars on the other.

After the company's founding in Nagoya, we began operations at our current main plant in Toyoda City in 1962 and have since expanded at a rapid rate.

Arakawa Auto Body's plants are specialized by product. The main plant produces auto bodies, the Kotobuki and Toyohashi plants specialize in interior accessories for passenger cars, and the Sarunage plant specializes in interior metal fittings, such as seat frames and seat tracks, and in specially equipped vehicles.

The diversification of demand in the auto industry has required manufacturers to avoid large-lot production in favor of level production of various product quantities and types. Setup changes, of course, have proliferated as a result, creating an urgent need to shorten setup times. To raise operating rates, improvements to reduce setup times have been implemented, with simultaneous investments in suitable equipment and preventive maintenance (PM) strategies for press dies, machines, and the like.

These measures, however, have never gone beyond the superficial question of raising operating rates. This is because, rather than shortening setup times themselves, solutions have tended to lower the number of setups. In other words, by enlarging lot sizes, they merely gave the appearance of cutting setup times. This was actually

215

counterproductive, because it led to inventory accumulation and consequent losses.

It was in 1977 that the company chose to develop the Toyota Production System as a means of streamlining operations. We put into place an efficient system of producing "required items when they are required and in the quantities required." SMED was implemented as part of this strategy, as the decision was made to build a workplace that was both strong and resilient in the face of change.

Improvement has required a number of stages:

1. Development of a new consciousness within the plant.
2. Clarification of the distinction between internal setup and external setup. This includes shifting the preparation of materials, tools, and die transportation machinery to external setup.
3. A shift from internal to external setup. Setup must be complete before machine operation, and standardization of tool shapes is necessary.
4. A reduction in internal setup time. In this stage, methods must be designed for attachment and removal of parts, wasted movement eliminated, parallel operations adopted, and one-touch techniques implemented by standardizing die tools.
5. Reduction in external setup time. This is done by improving the removal and storage of die materials and by improving transportation operations.
6. Creation of written procedures and operations training to guide standard operations and implement demonstration setup changes.

APPLICATIONS OF SMED

Improved Setup on a Cutting Press for Vinyl Interior Coverings (Kotobuki Plant)

Reducing Setup Times for a 150-Ton Hydraulic Press

At the Kotobuki plant, production of door trim for passenger cars incorporates the following steps (*Figure 13-1*):

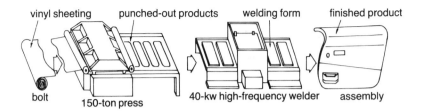

FIGURE 13-1. Door Trim Process

- A raw bolt of polyvinyl sheeting is punched out with a 150-ton hydraulic press.

- The piece punched from the polyvinyl sheet is welded to a board and pad with a 40-kw high-frequency welder.

- The trim is assembled.

Small quantities of a wide variety of door trim are produced according to design differences in shape, color, type of material, etc. It was thought quite reasonable, before improvements were carried out on the 150-ton hydraulic presses and the 40-kw high-frequency welders, that inventories would accumulate because of large-lot production. To reduce such inventories, setup times were shortened and the number of setups increased proportionately, so that work in process involved small lots. This is reasonable, but there was no progress in the reduction of setup times.

So that the need for shortened setup changes would become apparent through the job itself, we shifted, step by step, to small-lot production and began implementing multiple setup changes without waiting for setup time reductions.

As a result, to the extent that setup times remained as long as they had been previously, shortages of goods and the like began to appear, and it was then that the need for SMED was recognized throughout the plant.

Reducing Setup Times

In this example, the following operations are performed on the 150-ton hydraulic press (*Figure 13-2*):

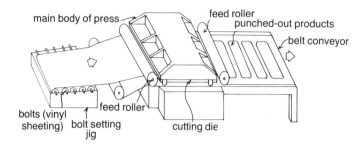

FIGURE 13-2. 150-Ton Hydraulic Press

- Five raw bolts of polyvinyl sheeting are mounted on a raw bolt setting jig.

- Raw bolt feed rollers feed sheeting into the press.

- Blades mounted on the press stamp out the sheeting.

- The stamped-out items are sent from the press by means of a belt conveyor.

As shown in *Figure 13-3*, setup before improvement took twelve minutes and thirty seconds; after improvement, setup time had been successfully lowered to one minute and thirty seconds.

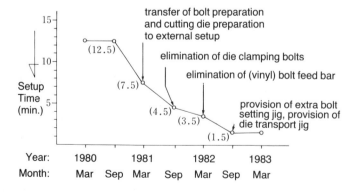

FIGURE 13-3. Setup Times on a 150-Ton Hydraulic Press

Shifting Bolt Preparation to External Setup

Before improvement, bolt preparation had been performed during internal setup. This was changed so that the next bolts are prepared while the machine is running (*Figure 13-4* and *Plate 13-1*). By

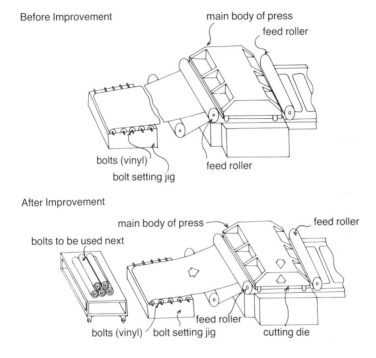

FIGURE 13-4. Shifting Bolt Preparation to External Setup

Before Improvement   **After Improvement**

PLATE 13-1. Bolt Preparation

shifting bolt preparation from internal to external setup in this manner, it became possible to do away entirely with this particular setup operation, which had previously required three minutes and thirty seconds.

Shifting Blade Preparation to External Setup

Blade preparation had been an internal setup operation before improvement, but in the new configuration, blades can be prepared on a blade preparation bench while the press is running (*Figure 13-5* and *Plate 13-2*).

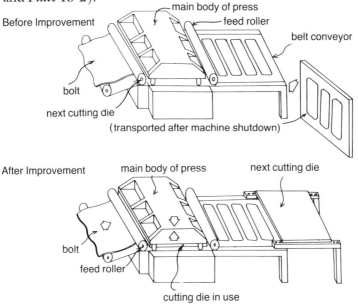

FIGURE 13-5. Shifting Blade Preparation to External Setup

Before Improvement   After Improvement

PLATE 13-2. Blade Preparation

Eliminating Adjustment Operations by Doing Away with Cutting Die Clamping Bolts

Before improvement, the procedure for removing and attaching cutting dies was as follows:

1. Loosen four bolts and remove punch die cradle.
2. Pull cutting die out of press.
3. Insert next cutting die into press.
4. Mount cutting die on cutting die cradle, tighten four bolts.

This setup procedure took three minutes and thirty seconds (*Figure 13-6, top*).

Precision was not required in this operation, since the die was attached with bolts only to keep it from falling. Improvement, then, proceeded from the observation that bolts would be unnecessary as long as a jig were attached to prevent the die from falling. Thus, the die had merely to be placed on the two L-shaped jigs mounted for this purpose (*Figure 13-6, bottom* and *Plate 13-3*).

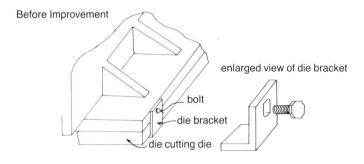

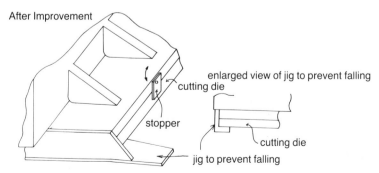

FIGURE 13-6. **Elimination of Cutting Die Attachment Bolts**

PLATE 13-3. Cutting Die Attachment After Improvement

After improvement, the order of operations was as follows:

1. Raise stopper.
2. Pull cutting die from press.
3. Place next cutting die on jig to prevent falling and insert in press.
4. Lower stopper.

Setup time was successfully cut by three minutes, to thirty seconds.

Reducing Setup Time by Eliminating Bolt Feed Rods

Before improvement, five bolt ends were pulled into the press by means of a feed rod (*Plate 13-4, left*). The procedure was as follows:

1. Cut off the bolt in use.
2. Catch onto the end of the new bolt with the feed rod and pull it into press.
3. Change the feed length on the 150-ton hydraulic press.

This setup operation took two minutes.

Despite the fact that the bolt in use was being fed automatically into the press, the new bolt had to be pulled into the press by means of a feed rod because the bolt in use and the new bolt were not attached to one another. If the end of the bolt in use were joined to the leading edge of the new bolt, the feed rod could be eliminated. On

| Before Improvement | After Improvement |

PLATE 13-4. Feeding New Bolts

the basis of this observation, the operation was improved by stapling together the two bolt edges (*Plate 13-4, right*).

The operation after improvement proceeded as follows:

1. Cut the bolt in use with scissors.
2. Staple the leading edge of the new bolt to the edge of the bolt in use.
3. Change feed length on the 150-ton hydraulic press.

This made it possible to cut setup time to one minute.

Shifting Operations to External Setup by Using an Extra Jig for Holding Bolts

Before improvement there was only one jig to hold bolts, so after the bolts in use were gone, new bolts had to be set on this jig.

The order of operations was as follows:

1. Remove locating stoppers on holding jig.
2. Pull steel rods out of used bolts.
3. Place current bolts onto cart.
4. Set steel rods in new bolts.
5. Mount new bolts on holding jig.
6. Attach locating stoppers to holding jig.

This setup operation took two minutes (*Figure 13-7, top*).

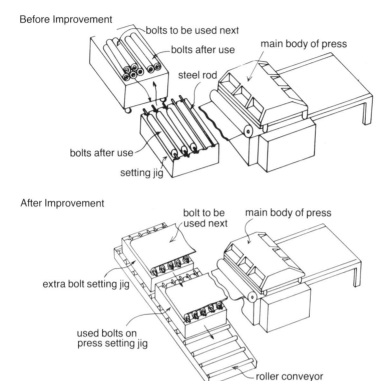

FIGURE 13-7. **Shifting Operations to External Setup by Means of an Extra Jig for Holding Bolts**

The situation was improved by installing an extra bolt-holding jig onto which new bolts could be mounted while the press was running (*Figure 13-7, bottom,* and *Plate 13-5*).

Before Improvement   **After Improvement**

PLATE 13-5. **Mounting New Bolts**

With the new order of operations it has become possible to exchange holding jigs while the press is in operation, reducing setup time to zero.

Shortening Setup Time for Cutting Die Preparation

Although cutting dies were originally prepared in an internal setup operation, this operation was shifted to external setup with the use of a blade preparation bench. While dies were being prepared, however, they were transported by two people; the operation still took one minute and thirty seconds. To reduce external setup time, the die storage rack was moved next to the press and a cart was provided so that dies could be transported by a single worker (*Plate 13-6*). As a result, a one-minute reduction in external setup time was possible.

PLATE 13-6. Transporting Cutting Dies

Shortening Setup Time for a 40-kw High-Frequency Welder

The 40-kw high-frequency welder is a machine for welding three parts: boards, pads, and pieces cut from bolt material (*Figure 13-8* and *Plate 13-7*).

With the experience we gained in making setup improvements in the previous processes involving the 150-ton hydraulic press, we were able to cut welder setup time from ten minutes and thirty seconds to ten seconds by shifting internal to external setup and by improving internal setup operations (*Figure 13-9*).

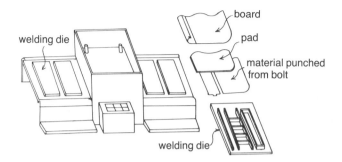

FIGURE 13-8. 40-kw High-Frequency Welder

PLATE 13-7. 40-kw High-Frequency Welder

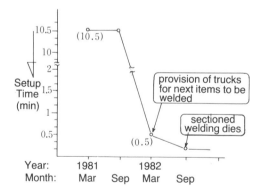

FIGURE 13-9. Setup Times for 40-kw High-Frequency Welder

Shifting Welding Die Preparation to External Setup by Providing a Setup Bench

Before improvement, welding die preparation had been part of internal setup and had involved the use of a hoist (*Plate 13-8, left*). The operation was moved from internal to external setup by using a setup bench for the preparation of welding dies (*Plate 13-8, right*). This shift from internal to external setup cut setup time from ten minutes and thirty seconds to thirty seconds.

Before Improvement   After Improvement

PLATE 13-8. Welding Die Preparation

Eliminating Hoist Delays by Using Sectional Welding Dies

Although we managed to move welding die preparation to external setup, the external setup operation still made use of a hoist.

Hoist delays during the external setup of welding dies occurred because the hoist was used by other machines also. To shorten internal setup time even further by abandoning the use of the hoist, we set about making the welding dies lighter. As shown in *Plate 13-8, left*, welding dies before improvement were of the single-body type and built to the appropriate specifications.

After improvement, parts of different specifications were made into welding sections, so that it was possible to change only those parts (*Plate 13-9*). The weight of a welding die section after improvement was 8 kg, as contrasted with the 30 kg of a single-body type die before improvement. Die size was reduced as well, to one-fourth of what it had been previously.

This change eliminated the need for a hoist and cut setup time from thirty seconds to ten seconds.

— *(Reported by Hiromitsu Fujieda, Technical Staff)*

PLATE 13-9. Sectional Welding Die

Using SMED on a 500-Ton Press (Sarunage Plant)

A 500-ton crank press using sixty-two dies had been processing approximately 70,000 interior fittings per month. In the same period, from eight to one hundred die changes would take place, with each change taking from twenty-five to thirty minutes. This situation led inevitably to large-lot production and so engendered inventory losses.

With our full energies, we tackled the problem of eliminating this sort of overproduction. On the basis of a detailed breakdown of setup operations on the 500-ton press line, shown in *Figure 13-10*, we devised and put into operation the rigorous plan for improvement shown in *Table 13-1*. (Please refer also to *Figures 13-11, 13-12, 13-13* and *Plates 13-10, 13-11, 13-12*).

Reducing Internal Setup Times

Improved die positioning method. Accurately lining up the center of the material supplied and the center of the die was the most time-consuming element of die attachment operations. Before improvement, as shown in *Figure 13-14 (left)*, alignment was a taxing operation involving the use of positioning blocks, scales, etc. After improvement, die-locating guides were sunk into the top of a bolster and positioning plates were installed on twenty-three of the dies used, so that one-touch positioning could be completed by fitting a die onto the bolster. This made possible both the elimination of adjustments and significant reductions in setup times (*Figure 13-14, right*).

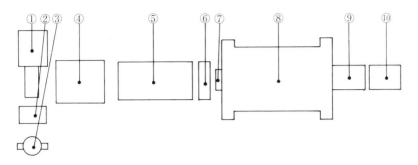

No.	Name of Machine	Setup Operation
1	uncoiler	coil change
2	coil lift car	transport operation (between [1] and [3])
3	coil changer	new coil preparation and old coil storage
4	leveler	operation to regulate plate thickness
5	looper table	operation to raise and lower table
6	coil centering apparatus	coil centering adjustments
7	coil feed regulator	coil feed regulation
8	500 ton press	die attachment and removal
9	product ejection conveyor	set conveyor position
10	polyethylene box changer	positioning and storage

FIGURE 13-10. Setup Procedures on 500-Ton Press Line

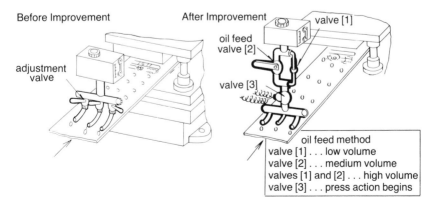

FIGURE 13-11. Oil Feed Valve

Operation \ Item	Details of Improvement	Result
Internal Setup		
1. upper and lower die clamping bolt removal	assign bolts exclusively to this operation and modify storage methods	reduced adjustment time for bolt attachment and removal
2. die removal transport	explained in improvement example [3]	transport to die storage area is moved to external setup
3. bolster, ram cleaning		
4. die transport	improved retrieval of dies from storage (numerical, color coding) As in item 2, transport to press in external setup	delivery to press is moved to external setup
5. die positioning	explained in improvement example [1]	positioning with a scale; gauge adjustment operations are eliminated
6. attachment of upper and lower die sections	provide attachment U-grooves in dies; do away with blocks	
7. stroke adjustments	standardize die heights	elimination of stroke adjustment operations
8. material feed pitch adjustments	as in improvement example [2]	elimination of trial runs on the basis of feed pitch scale measurements and adjustment operations
9. align material feed centers	install cassette width gauges by raw material type	elimination of material feed center alignment operations
10. oil feed adjustments for press coils	improved method uses 3-step (high, middle and low) oil feed cocks, thus making fine adjustments easier	reduction in oil feed adjustment time
11. chute setting	sectional dies make this a one-touch operation	attachment time reduction
12. air hose attachment	group air hoses	attachment time reduction
13. trial run, inspection		
External Setup		
1. coil transport	improved methods of retrieving dies from storage (numerical, color codes)	reduced time for selecting coils put aside for storage
2. coil disposal	use a speed vise for final disposal of coils after use	reduction in coil disposal time
3. uncoiler	install a rotating coil holding rack near uncoiler and eliminate coil changing and transport operations	elimination of internal setup transport from coil storage area to uncoiler
4. settings on coiler leveler	bring down to the single minute range by linking the two leveler plate thickness adjustment handles together with a chain	reduction of leveler plate thickness adjustment time
5. scrap disposal	attach light for summoning lift	does away with waiting for transport device

Table 13-1.   Outline of Improvements

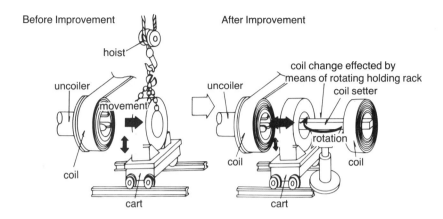

FIGURE 13-12. Coiling Mechanism

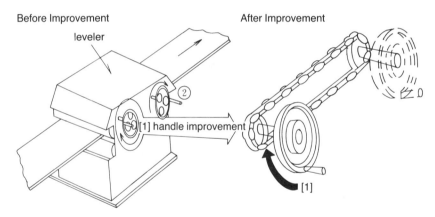

FIGURE 13-13. Handle Improvement

PLATE 13-10. Improvements on 500-Ton Press—I

PLATE 13-11. Improvements on 500-Ton Press—II

PLATE 13-12. Improvements on 500-Ton Press—III

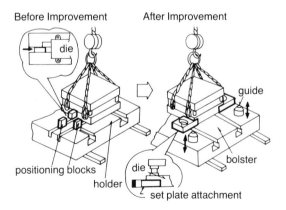

FIGURE 13-14. Improved Die Positioning Method

Improved method for setting material feed pitch. This operation required a considerable amount of time because of various adjustments involved. As shown in *Figure 13-15 (left)*, trial strikes were made with each die matched to a graduated scale already set on the machine, and pitch was set by means of fine height adjustments made while this was going on.

Fine adjustments and errors arising from misread graduations were eliminated by setting a pitch gauge, which had been preset for the feed pitch of each die, into the moving part of the machine that determined feed volume (*Figure 13-15, right*, and *Plate 13-13*).

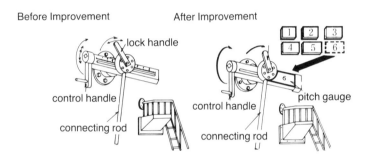

FIGURE 13-15. Setting Material Feed Pitch

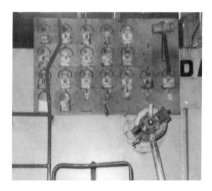

PLATE 13-13. Setting Material Feed Pitch

From Internal to External Setup: Improving Die Changing Method

During die changes in the past, the old and new dies were trans-ported to and from a storage area by crane in an internal setup oper-ation. To cut the time required, two special die-changing carts of the type shown in *Figure 13-16* were provided. The old die was loaded on one, while the new die was prepared on the other in an external setup operation.

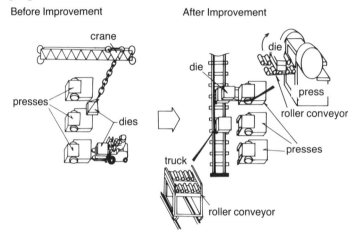

FIGURE 13-16. **Improved Die Changing Method**

Such activities aimed at SMED improvements began early in 1977. Where at first the average setup change had taken twenty-seven minutes, by the end of 1982 it was possible to reduce this aver-age to four minutes and thirty seconds, a considerably greater reduc-tion than originally planned (*Figure 13-17*).

The first stage of improvement was to improve die attachment speed by standardizing press dies and mounting press die positioning hardware. Shortly thereafter, a number of other changes were insti-tuted:

- Installation of cassette-type gauge for work feed pitch (elimi-nation of adjustments)

- Installation of cassette-type gauge for coil centering (elimina-tion of adjustments)

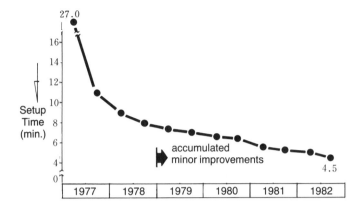

FIGURE 13-17. Successive Setup Improvements on 500-Ton Press

- Provision of special die transport truck (moving internal to external setup; elimination of crane delays)

- Standardization of clamps and tools (simplified attachment and removal)

- Operations training (elimination of losses and errors in procedures and movement)

With a third cluster of improvements early in 1978, setup time was brought down into the single-minute range:

- Installation of rotating coil holding rack (elimination of crane delays)

- Creation of a setup standards manual (support improvement)

- Establishment of fixed storage addresses for materials and dies (speedy retrieval, elimination of choice)

Thereafter, refinements and minor improvements further reduced setup by about half.

We are in the process of implementing SMED on other assembly lines. One example is shown in *Figure 13-18* and in *Plate 13-14*.

No	Observations	Before Improvement	After Improvement
1	Spot-welding jig integration Subsequent processes were often delayed because jigs had to be changed among three types of products to be spot-welded.	5 min changes made among 3 jigs tightened with wrench	3 sec jig rotated locked with pins triple rotary jig
2	Eliminating mounting bolts for spot-welding jigs The attachment and removal of bolts when mounting spot-welding jigs took a great deal of time.	5 min R jig L jig tightened with wrench	3 sec R jig R and L jigs changed by means of half-revolutions L jig
3	Spot-welder coordination 20-25 wasted trips between Machine A and Machine B were made every day because of small-lot, leveled production.	Machine A Machine B 20-25 trips per day made between the machines 	1 spot-welder, A and B switched B jig A jig handle locks jig A jig

Observations

One-touch changes were devised for jig sections and workpiece positioning blocks.

Subsequent operations are frequently delayed due to the use of mistaken combinations of jig sections (A) and blocks when these parts are changed by fastening and loosening bolts.

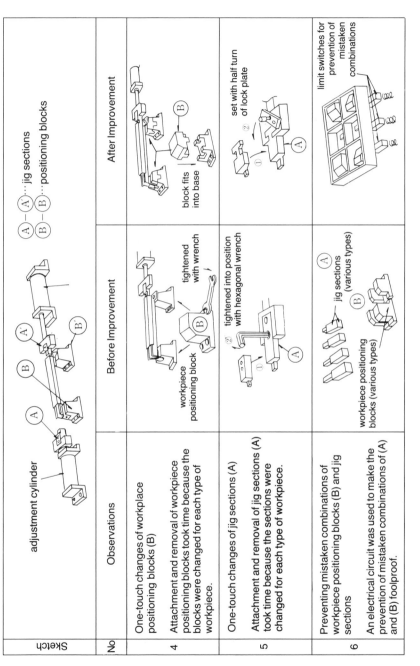

Sketch		adjustment cylinder (A) (B) (A) (B')	(A)—(A)···jig sections (B)—(B)···positioning blocks
No	Observations	Before Improvement	After Improvement
4	One-touch changes of workplace positioning blocks (B) Attachment and removal of workpiece positioning blocks took time because the blocks were changed for each type of workpiece.	workpiece positioning block (B) tightened with wrench	block fits into base (B)
5	One-touch changes of jig sections (A) Attachment and removal of jig sections (A) took time because the sections were changed for each type of workpiece.	① ② tightened into position with hexagonal wrench (A)	① ② set with half turn of lock plate (A)
6	Preventing mistaken combinations of workpiece positioning blocks (B) and jig sections An electrical circuit was used to make the prevention of mistaken combinations of (A) and (B) foolproof.	workpiece positioning blocks (various types) jig sections (various types) (A) (B)	limit switches for prevention of mistaken combinations

FIGURE 13-18. Other Setup Improvements at Sarunage Plant

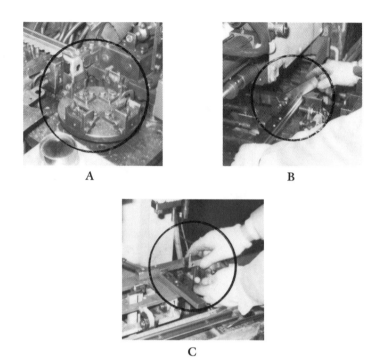

PLATE 13-14. Other Setup Improvements at Sarunage Plant

IMPROVEMENTS AT AFFILIATED PLANTS

The principle behind streamlining operations in affiliated plants is exactly the same as in our company: what in the Toyota Production System is referred to as JIT production. This means producing, in a timely fashion, "the required items when they are required and in the amounts required." The key to attaining this objective lies in building a production system that can respond promptly to change. To promote the realization of this sort of system in practice, we have established a system of guidance for affiliated plants on the basis of the issues presented below.

First, within our purchasing department there is a purchasing management office that offers technical guidance on production and everyday management to affiliated plants.

In addition, based on the needs of affiliated plants, guidance in the effort to raise productivity takes two forms — the "soft" advice offered by the purchasing management office, and the "hard," practical leadership of the productivity improvement office.

Moreover, a press subgroup (twenty firms) and interior trim subgroup (ten firms) have formed within the Mutual Benefit Association of the affiliated plants. Each subgroup is divided into groups of five or six companies. Each company, in turn, strives to raise its level of technology by carrying out monthly activities aimed·at higher productivity (e.g., reducing work in process, improving operations, promoting the 5 S's,* cutting setup times). Members of our purchasing management and productivity improvement offices participate in these meetings and give active guidance on practical improvements.

In the plants of one of our affiliates, the SMED concept was successfully applied to small press processes involving dies on 40- to 50-ton presses.

Setup procedures on a certain press took forty-four minutes and six seconds from the time the press was stopped until it was restarted. This was improved along SMED lines and, as a result of repeated on-the-job worker training, it was possible to realize a substantial reduction in setup time, to four minutes and forty-two seconds. The principal improvements are presented below, and summarized in *Table 13-2*.

Providing Special Die Carts

At the end of a processing run, the die used was extracted from the press by lift, transported to a designated area and kept there. A similar operation took place in moving from the first process to the next. Because of this, waiting for lift transportation at later processes turned out to be a considerable impediment.

Then rollers were installed at the rear of the press bolster, allowing dies to be pushed in and out and stored temporarily. For transportation, a special cart was stationed at the rear of the press area and used for external setup. This method made it possible to reduce die removal time to less than one-tenth of what it had been. In addition, free bearings were mounted in the bolster to speed up the insertion of dies (*Plate 13-15*).

---

* EDITOR'S NOTE: The so-called 5 S's are key words that all begin with an "S" in Japanese. They are: *seiri* (pigeonholing), *seiton* (orderliness), *seiso* (the act of cleaning), *seiketsu* (the state of cleanliness), and *shitsuke* (the practice of discipline).

Before Improvement

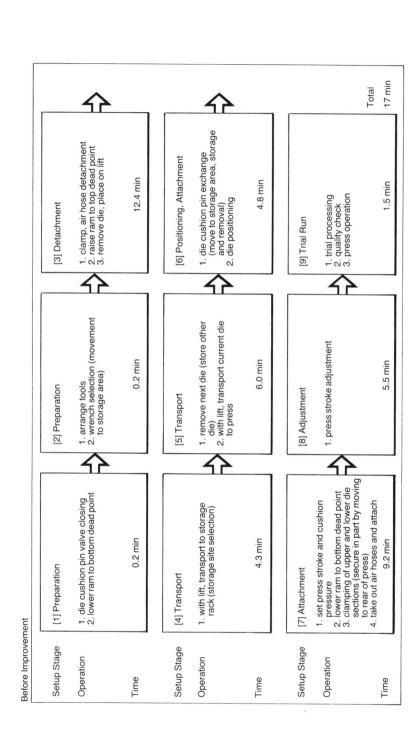

Setup Stage	[1] Preparation	[2] Preparation	[3] Detachment
Operation	1. die cushion pin valve closing 2. lower ram to bottom dead point	1. arrange tools 2. wrench selection (movement to storage area)	1. clamp, air hose detachment 2. raise ram to top dead point 3. remove die, place on lift
Time	0.2 min	0.2 min	12.4 min

Setup Stage	[4] Transport	[5] Transport	[6] Positioning, Attachment
Operation	1. with lift, transport to storage rack (storage site selection)	1. remove next die (store other die) 2. with lift, transport current die to press	1. die cushion pin exchange (move to storage area, storage and removal) 2. die positioning
Time	4.3 min	6.0 min	4.8 min

Setup Stage	[7] Attachment	[8] Adjustment	[9] Trial Run
Operation	1. set press stroke and cushion pressure 2. lower ram to bottom dead point 3. clamping of upper and lower die sections (secure in part by moving to rear of press) 4. take out air hoses and attach	1. press stroke adjustment	1. trial processing 2. quality check 3. press operation
Time	9.2 min	5.5 min	1.5 min

Total
17 min

After Improvement

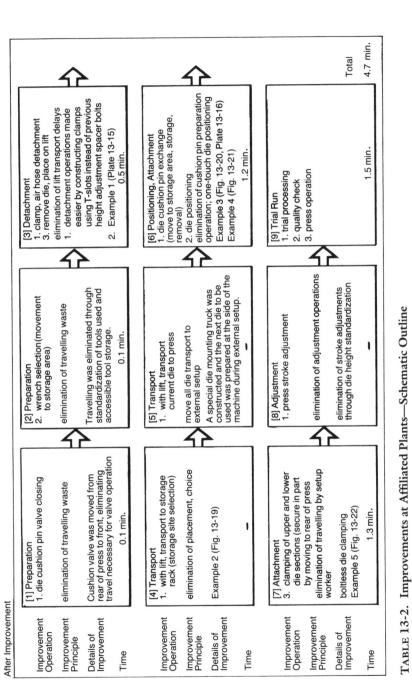

Improvement Operation	**[1] Preparation** 1. die cushion pin valve closing	**[2] Preparation** 2. wrench selection (movement to storage area)	**[3] Detachment** 1. clamp, air hose detachment 3. remove die, place on lift
Improvement Principle	elimination of travelling waste	elimination of travelling waste	elimination of lift transport delays 1. detachment operations made easier by constructing clamps using T-slots instead of previous height adjustment spacer bolts
Details of Improvement	Cushion valve was moved from rear of press to front, eliminating travel necessary for valve operation	Travelling was eliminated through standardization of tools used and accessible tool storage.	2. Example 1 (Plate 13-15)
Time	0.1 min.	0.1 min.	0.5 min.

Improvement Operation	**[4] Transport** 1. with lift, transport to storage rack (storage site selection)	**[5] Transport** 1. with lift, transport current die to press	**[6] Positioning, Attachment** 1. die cushion pin exchange (move to storage area, storage, removal)
Improvement Principle	elimination of placement, choice	move all die transport to external setup	2. die positioning elimination of cushion pin preparation operation; one-touch die positioning
Details of Improvement	Example 2 (Fig. 13-19)	A special die mounting truck was constructed and the next die to be used was prepared at the side of the machine during external setup.	Example 3 (Fig. 13-20, Plate 13-16) Example 4 (Fig. 13-21)
Time	–		1.2 min.

Improvement Operation	**[7] Attachment** 3. clamping of upper and lower die sections (secure in part by moving to rear of press	**[8] Adjustment** 1. press stroke adjustment	**[9] Trial Run** 1. trial processing 2. quality check 3. press operation
Improvement Principle	elimination of travelling by setup worker	elimination of adjustment operations	
Details of Improvement	boltless die clamping Example 5 (Fig. 13-22)	elimination of stroke adjustments through die height standardization	
Time	1.3 min.	–	1.5 min.

Total 4.7 min.

TABLE 13-2. Improvements at Affiliated Plants—Schematic Outline

PLATE 13-15. Special Die Carts

Controlling Dies

The indiscriminate storage of dies arising from increases in the number of dies kept on hand meant that a great deal of time was needed for die storage, temporary storage during removal operations, and die selection.

Die removal was facilitated by marking dies with color codes and location numbers before storing them. In addition, the orientation of dies during use was taken into account in storing them, so that a lift operator could attach lift hooks to the die without getting off of the lift (*Figure 13-19*).

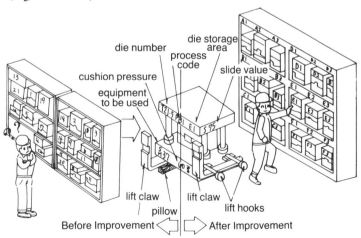

FIGURE 13-19. Die Control

Eliminating Selection in Cushion Pin Setup Changes

Since, depending on the part to be processed, cushion pins varied in length, number to be used, and place of attachment, the selection, removal, and disposition of the pins during each setup took more time than did other operations (*Figure 13-20, left*).

In one improvement, interfering parts of die cushions and unneeded pins were eliminated, making it possible to handle a number of processing parts without changing cushion pins. By committing pins of the correct di-

PLATE 13-16. Cushion Pin Setup

mensions, number, and location, we were able to eliminate pin changes. For specially designated dies that could not be handled in this manner, moreover, travelling choice was reduced to zero to allow cushion pins to be stored (*Figure 13-20, right,* and *Plate 13-16*).

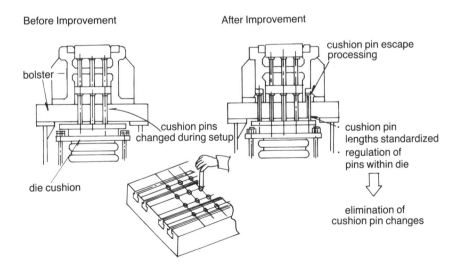

FIGURE 13-20. Elimination of Cushion Pin Changes

Positioning One-Touch Dies

The method shown in *Figure 13-21 (left)* was used to position dies, but since the identification of patch plates A and B took place at the back of the die, several adjustments were needed for final positioning.

The various adjustments were eliminated and one-touch positioning made possible by the following (*Figure 13-21, right*):

- Attachment of die positioning guides in the center of the bolster.

- Attachment of front and back stoppers at the rear of the guides.

- Installation of guide engagement slots in the center of the die bed.

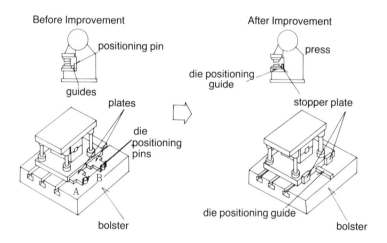

FIGURE 13-21. Die Positioning

Shortening Die-Clamping Times

To eliminate die-bolting operations, a one-touch method was devised by securing the die bed with lever-applied hand clamps that made use of bolster slots (*Figure 13-22*). Clamping had previously been done by rotating the upper die toward the back of the machine, but this wasted movement was eliminated by installing a horizontally slotted ram face and attaching the die on the ram side.

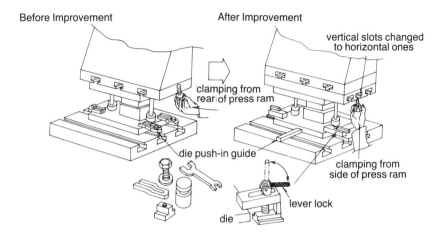

FIGURE 13-22. Shortened Die-Clamping Times

In sum, implementing the SMED system in our firm and in affiliated plants has brought remarkable results. It goes without saying that the extension of this approach to our production facilities as a whole is indispensable. Smoother production and minimized lead times are two primary benefits of the Toyota Production System, but the process has also fostered solidarity among our factories and affiliated plants. We intend to pursue SMED to the limit as we take up the challenge of efficient production.

— *(Reported by Akira Maruyama, Production Technology Office)*

14

SMED Developments in Producing Slide Bearings

T. H. Kogyo K.K.

THE COMPANY

T.H. Kogyo is a world-class manufacturer of sliding bearings, including engine bearings, bushings, and thrust washers for automobiles. Founded with capital of ¥ 180,000 ($744) in 1939 in the city of Nishio, Aiichi Prefecture, the company began machining all automobile bushings for Toyota Motor Corporation's cars in 1947. In 1958 it inaugurated a new aluminum die-casting plant, and in 1969 built a factory that specializes in processing half-bearings. The company employs roughly 1,000 workers and managers.

APPLICATIONS OF SMED

Concrete SMED Developments

Skillful use of the SMED system can produce striking results, but it is important to quantify plant needs, goals, and objectives at the start. Only then should managers try to select techniques best suited to the achievement of those goals, to implement them, and to verify the results.

At T.H. Kogyo we wanted, first of all, to make actual running time — that is, the time spent actually producing goods — as long as possible. We decided to put our efforts into improvements aimed at reducing setup times, since these occupied a substantial portion of machine shutdown time (*Figure 14-1*).

As we proceeded, we noted the extreme importance of three basic improvements:

- Shortening die exchange operations in each setup

247

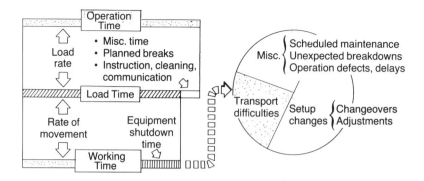

FIGURE 14-1. Production Time and Machine Shutdown Time

- Shortening or shifting to external setup the adjustment operations incidental to die exchange operations

- Eliminating or drastically condensing fine adjustment operations that arise as part of internal setup after normal operation (continuous running) has begun

These improvements increase productive capacity by reducing equipment shutdown time and stretching actual running time. If the time required for individual setups is shortened sufficiently, impressive results can be achieved even if the number of setups is increased.

(Production capacity of run per line 10, example of 3 specialized lines: no setups, stock adjustment type)

Line	Part	No/Run	Run 1	Run 2	Run 3	Run 4	Run 5	Run 6	
1	A	10							a b c d
2	B	6							a b c d
3	C	4							a b c d
Load Ratio			100%	67%	67%	67%	33%	100%	e
Stock Ratio			33%	33%	33%	33%	0 %	33%	f

FIGURE 14-2. Conventional Production Scheme

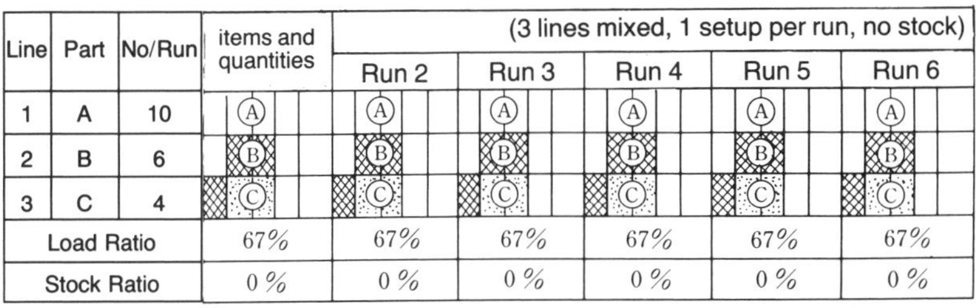

Line	Part	No/Run	items and quantities	(3 lines mixed, 1 setup per run, no stock)				
				Run 2	Run 3	Run 4	Run 5	Run 6
1	A	10	Ⓐ	Ⓐ	Ⓐ	Ⓐ	Ⓐ	Ⓐ
2	B	6	Ⓑ	Ⓑ	Ⓑ	Ⓑ	Ⓑ	Ⓑ
3	C	4	Ⓒ	Ⓒ	Ⓒ	Ⓒ	Ⓒ	Ⓒ
Load Ratio			67%	67%	67%	67%	67%	67%
Stock Ratio			0 %	0 %	0 %	0 %	0 %	0 %

FIGURE 14-3. **Balanced Production Scheme**

Leveling Numbers of Mechanical Interventions

For instance, one example for leveling the number of mechanical interventions is illustrated in *Figure 14-2* and *Figure 14-3*. Although the total loads for the three lines shown in the two figures are substantially the same, the setup changes shown in Figure 14-3 make it possible to cut inventories drastically and perform stable operations repeatedly. It is important to cut setup times, diminish lot sizes, and even loads simultaneously; no more than partial success can be expected with shortened setup times alone.

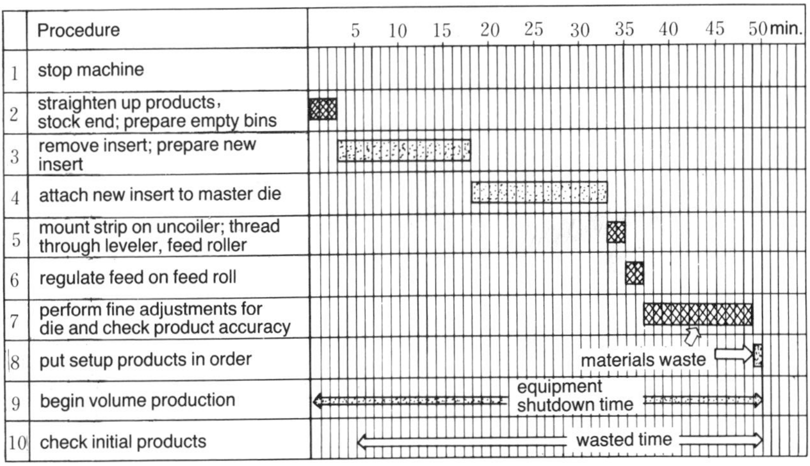

	Procedure	5 10 15 20 25 30 35 40 45 50 min.
1	stop machine	
2	straighten up products, stock end; prepare empty bins	
3	remove insert; prepare new insert	
4	attach new insert to master die	
5	mount strip on uncoiler; thread through leveler, feed roller	
6	regulate feed on feed roll	
7	perform fine adjustments for die and check product accuracy	
8	put setup products in order	materials waste
9	begin volume production	equipment shutdown time
10	check initial products	wasted time

FIGURE 14-4. **Press Operation Setup Before Improvement**

Concrete Ideas for Cutting Setup Times (I)

The procedures and times involved in a press setup operation before improvement are shown in *Figure 14-4*. In addition to the time wasted by lengthy mechanical operations, materials were wasted because dimensioning adjustments during setup resulted in the production of defective goods.

This example illustrates what we can call the "hard" and "soft" aspects of SMED. Hard aspects are those physical changes to equipment and tools that reduce setup times. Soft aspects are any changes in procedures that increase productivity and reduce waste by, for example, saving materials or reducing worker fatigue. While the hard aspects are central, the soft elements should never be ignored.

Figure 14-5 shows that the time-consuming operations have been eliminated and machine shutdown time has been reduced by 90%. These results are brought together in *Table 14-1*.

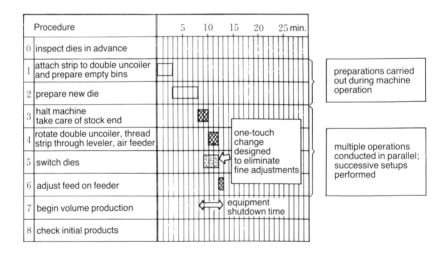

FIGURE 14-5. **Press Operation Setup After Improvement**

Item	Corresponding Procedure Nos.		SMED Category		Effect	
	Fig. 14-4	Fig. 14-5	Soft	Hard	Time Reduction	Finding
1 Change in procedures	2, 5	1,2	*		5 2	
2 Switch to parallel operations and consecutive setups		3, 4 5, 6	*		8 5	
3 External setup	3,4			*		○
4 One-touch change		4,5,6		*	32 4	○
5 Elimination of fine adjustments	7			*	12 0	○

TABLE 14-1. SMED Improvements—I

SMED Software Improvement

Concrete Ideas for Cutting Setup Times (II)

Let us next consider the case of successive setup changes. In a series of processes such as those shown in *Figure 14-6*, a total of forty-

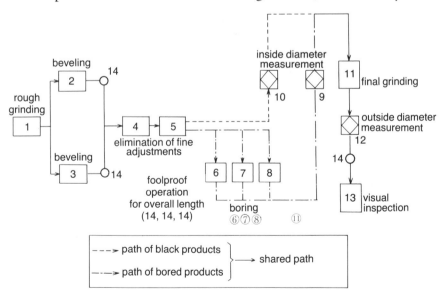

FIGURE 14-6. Outline of Processes for Machine Processing Operations

eight minutes or more is needed when setups for the various process-es follow one after another. If, however, four workers (A, B, C, and D) proceed with setup changes in a designated order, as shown in *Figure 14-7*, the changes can be completed in twenty minutes. This improvement shows that without spending any money it is actually possible to cut the time required for a sequence of steps by as much as 58%.

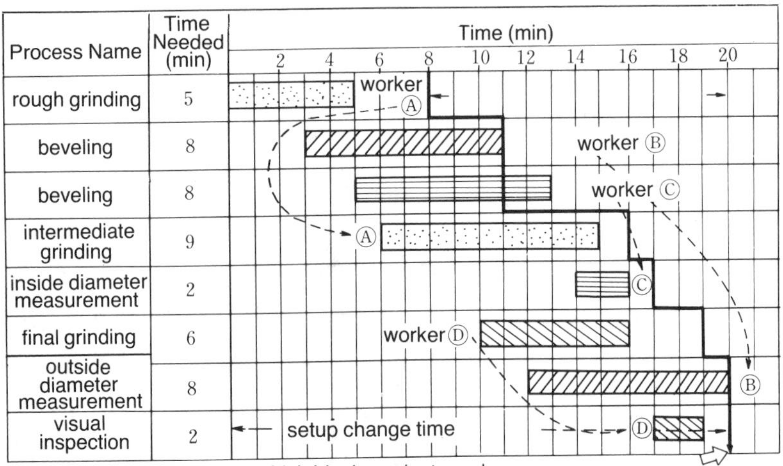

Process Name	Time Needed (min)	Time (min)
rough grinding	5	worker Ⓐ
beveling	8	worker Ⓑ
beveling	8	worker Ⓒ
intermediate grinding	9	Ⓐ
inside diameter measurement	2	Ⓒ
final grinding	6	worker Ⓓ
outside diameter measurement	8	Ⓑ
visual inspection	2	setup change time Ⓓ

Note: This is a mixed line in which black products and bored products are alternated, and boring machine (6, 7, 8) setups are completed while black products are being processed.

product flow

FIGURE 14-7. Sequence of Setup Change Combinations for Black

The Leader's Role

The role of top managers is crucial to SMED software improve-ments. *Table 14-2* shows concrete examples of tasks leaders, mana-gers, and supervisors perform and how they go about dividing setup time and post-setup quality assurances into stages.

The Flow of Setup Change Operations

To shorten setup times, it is important to begin by treating ex-ternal setup as a whole. Distinguishing between external setup (which begins with advance preparation) and internal setup (which

A. Advance Preparation Steps

(1) Separate external setup and internal setup.

(2) Determine the order of internal setup operations, including both successive and parallel operations, for tools and equipment required for internal and external setups, the standard number of devices on hand, the workers needed for external setup, external setup maintenance criteria and internal setup inspection criteria.

(3) Following internal setup procedures, direct and train workers needed for internal setup and give them skill in setup change operations.

B. Preparation Steps Immediately Preceding Operation

(1) Confirm *kanban* for next device; have dies, jigs, blades, tools, materials and standard on-hand devices, etc. transported to specified locations.

(2) Verify transported items and perform checks in accordance with internal setup inspection criteria.

C. Internal Setup Operation Implementation Steps

(1) Gather internal setup operation personnel and, where necessary, give instructions relating to important points involved in the operation.

(2) Confirm whether or not operation is running smoothly and give instructions or guidance where necessary.

(3) Begin to lead off raw materials and standard on-hand devices from the process for which internal setup has been completed; conduct product quality checks.

(4) Confirm completion of internal setup operation for entire process; have dies, jigs, blades, tools, materials and standard on-hand devices, etc. used up until now moved to specified locations; have workers attend to operation.

D. Items to Note

(1) Setup workers are normally made up of a "setup man" and a line operator, but suitable preparatory training for a leader or other setup man or line operator designated as a relief worker must not be neglected.

(2) It is critical for the leader himself to be more skilled in the setup change operation than any of the workers involved.

TABLE 14-2. The Role of the Leader

begins with last-minute preparation), *Figure 14-8* shows product flow and *kanban* information, signaled in advance by setup *kanban*, recording this information by means of the *kanban* signals and flows of physical objects (dies, tools, raw materials) around a central processing line.

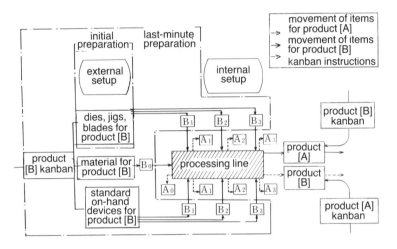

FIGURE 14-8. **Product Flow and Kanban Information**

SMED Hardware Improvement

Although software improvements eliminate waste, inconsistencies, and irregularities in operations, these improvements are just the first step in achieving the benefits of SMED. Hardware improvements are also necessary. Specific hardware improvements might include:

- Standardizing die height and positioning values

- Making it possible to clamp or release items by means of a single turn

- Eliminating the clamping of upper dies by adopting floating dies

- Using pear-shaped holes so that bolts are loosened — but not detached — by a single turn
- Shifting tool alignment to external setup
- Applying the cassette concept to die-casting dies

Speedy Die Exchanges

In the past, since press die heights were irregular, shut height used to be adjusted as part of internal setup (*Figure 14-9*). By making all die heights uniform, it was possible to eliminate shut height adjustments. Similarly, dies needed to be positioned during internal setup, because they were not all the same size. Standardizing sizes and attaching positioning plates to the bolster made it possible to eliminate this operation.

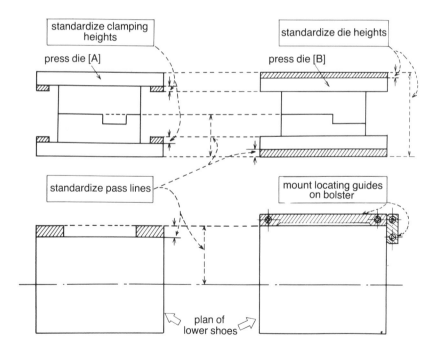

FIGURE 14-9. Press Die

Figure 14-10 shows an improved clamping device. Once die heights and sizes were uniform, attachment bolts of fixed dimensions could be used, making it possible to integrate bolts, clamps, and blocks. This device was further improved by inserting a spring so that the washer would not fall off.

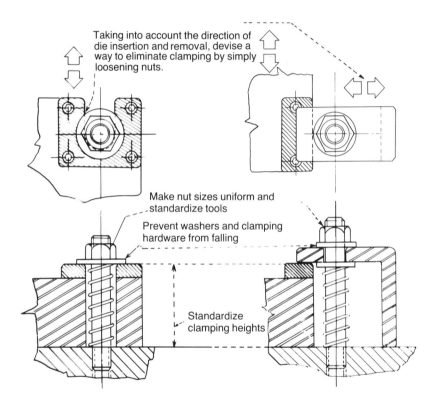

FIGURE 14-10. **Clamping Device**

Speedy Die and Jig Changes

Before improvement, the lower and upper dies had each been secured with four bolts. The upper die was pushed upward and springs inserted so that the press die would rise naturally, thus eliminating the need to clamp the upper die by creating a floating die (*Figure 14-11*). In addition, we devised a way to diminish the shock of the press by inserting a cushion in the upper die.

Clamping of the upper die section is eliminated and
only the lower die is secured to the bolster (floating die)

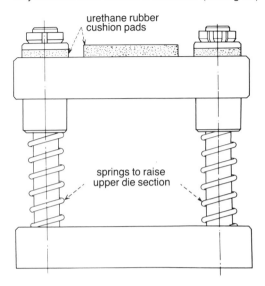

FIGURE 14-11. Floating Die

Because the original holes were round, two bolts had to be
turned a number of times and then taken off when a jig was removed.
These holes were modified to a pear shape, so that one turn of the
bolts was sufficient to clamp or release the die, and bolt removal was
unnecessary (*Figure 14-12*).

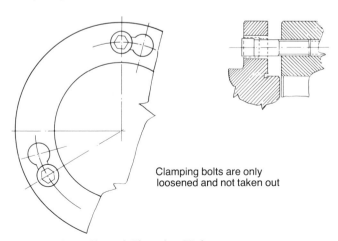

Clamping bolts are only
loosened and not taken out

FIGURE 14-12. Pear-Shaped Clamping Holes

The Elimination of Fine Adjustments

Two tools are used to machine the end of a bearing. Centering these tools used to take some forty minutes of internal setup time. To improve this procedure, we made two intermediary jigs that could be attached alternately when centering was done in advance, as part of external setup. With this method, the internal setup operation could be completed in one minute and forty-five seconds (*Figure 14-13*).

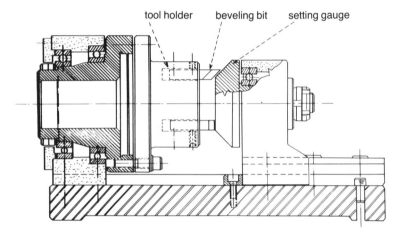

FIGURE 14-13. **Centering Tools in External Setup**

Moving from SMED to OTED

After SMED improvements are completed, the next challenge is OTED (One-Touch Exchange of Die), that is, making setup changes in less than a minute. The fundamental SMED concepts are, of course, applicable here, but it is necessary to give special consideration to the following:

- Elimination of adjustments
- Freedom from screw fastenings
- Moving toward strength and precision
- Precise and close fits
- The functional burdens of dies vis-à-vis machines

- The separation of die material and die function
- Insertion methods
- The Least Common Multiple (LCM) method

Some examples are presented here.

Elimination of Fine Adjustment Screws within a Machine

Guides were originally lined up with the aid of bolts. Adjustments were eliminated by doing away with adjustment bolts, constructing spacers, and adopting a system of switching spacers. Moreover, the use of spacers rather than bolts meant that there were no longer any screws to be tightened or loosened, and with no screws or bolts to be turned, wrenches and screwdrivers were no longer needed (*Figure 14-14*).

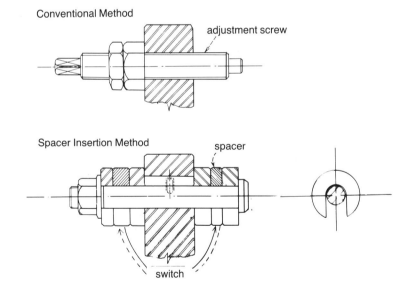

FIGURE 14-14. **Elimination of Fine Adjustment Screws within a Machine**

Other Examples

Figures 14-15, 14-16 and *14-17* describe some other ways the SMED system has been used at T.H. Kogyo.

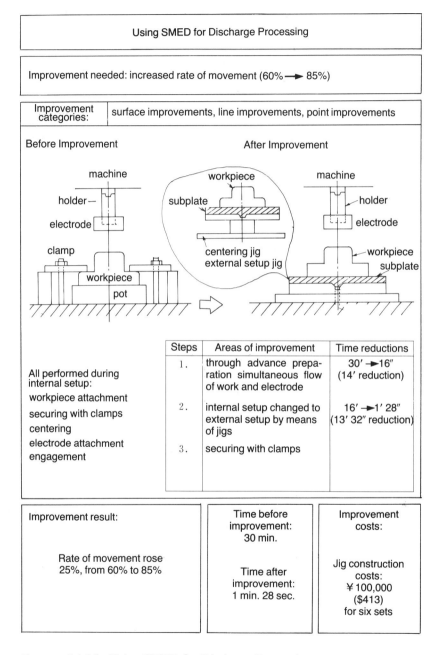

Using SMED for Discharge Processing

Improvement needed: increased rate of movement (60% → 85%)

Improvement categories:	surface improvements, line improvements, point improvements

Before Improvement

After Improvement

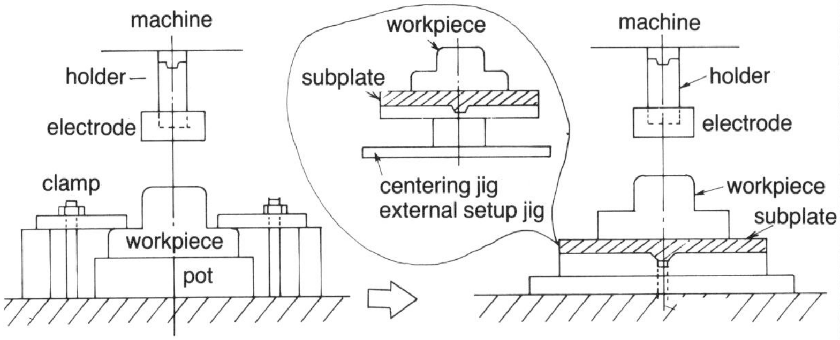

All performed during internal setup:
workpiece attachment
securing with clamps
centering
electrode attachment
engagement

Steps	Areas of improvement	Time reductions
1.	through advance preparation simultaneous flow of work and electrode	30′ → 16″ (14′ reduction)
2.	internal setup changed to external setup by means of jigs	16′ → 1′ 28″ (13′ 32″ reduction)
3.	securing with clamps	

Improvement result:	Time before improvement:	Improvement costs:
Rate of movement rose 25%, from 60% to 85%	30 min. Time after improvement: 1 min. 28 sec.	Jig construction costs: ¥100,000 ($413) for six sets

FIGURE 14-15. Using SMED for Discharge Processing

Using SMED for a 70-Ton Press Molding Process

Improvement needed: inventory reduction
50% reduction of overtime (70 hr/month → 35 hr/month)

Before Improvement

(1) the whole operation was conducted as internal setup
(2) the operator handled the procedure alone
(3) shut height adjustments were needed because die heights were not uniform

(1) die height preparation performed as external setup
(2) die heights standardized

(1) guides installed to position die when set into press

(1) parallel operations instituted
(2) chute securing bolts eliminated (one-touch operation made possible through the use of magnets)

Step 3
(1) parallel operations instituted
(2) chute securing bolts eliminated (one-touch operation made possible through the use of magnets)

Step 1

(1)

(2)

standardization of heights

Step 2

guide   guide
guide   guide

in   die

Step 3 (2)

magnet

Step 3
(1) Procedure Chart

	Procedure (worker A)		Procedure (worker B)
1	withdraw air with air feeder	1	align levelers
2	move chute	2	align air feeder guides
3	loosen die bolts	3	attach BLK
4	remove die	4	change gauges
5	change fingers	5	align sight guides
6	insert die	6	set foolproof length device
7	tighten die bolts	7	check initial products
8	attach chute	8	

Improvement Results

●—● setup changes
○—○ overtime

H   min   Step 1
70 16
60 14   Step 2
50 12
40 10
30   8
20   6   Step 3
10   4
     2

Over-
time   1978 1979 1980 1981 1982

Time before improvement:
15 min.

⇩

Time after improvement:
3 min.

Improvement costs:

¥ 20,000
($83)

FIGURE 14-16. Using SMED for a 70-Ton Press Molding Process

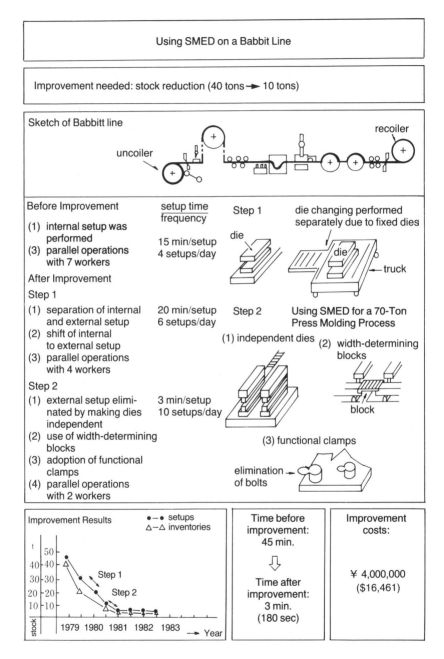

Using SMED on a Babbit Line

Improvement needed: stock reduction (40 tons → 10 tons)

Sketch of Babbitt line

recoiler

uncoiler

| Before Improvement | setup time / frequency | Step 1 | die changing performed separately due to fixed dies |

Before Improvement

(1) internal setup was performed — 15 min/setup
(3) parallel operations with 7 workers — 4 setups/day

After Improvement

Step 1

(1) separation of internal and external setup — 20 min/setup
(2) shift of internal to external setup — 6 setups/day
(3) parallel operations with 4 workers

Step 2

(1) external setup eliminated by making dies independent — 3 min/setup
(2) use of width-determining blocks — 10 setups/day
(3) adoption of functional clamps
(4) parallel operations with 2 workers

Step 1   die changing performed separately due to fixed dies
die   die   truck

Step 2   Using SMED for a 70-Ton Press Molding Process

(1) independent dies   (2) width-determining blocks

block

(3) functional clamps

elimination of bolts

Improvement Results   •—• setups   △—△ inventories

1979 1980 1981 1982 1983 → Year

Step 1   Step 2

Time before improvement: 45 min.

⇩

Time after improvement: 3 min. (180 sec)

Improvement costs:

¥ 4,000,000 ($16,461)

FIGURE 14-17. Using SMED on a Babbitt Line

15

Examples and Effects
of the SMED System
Glory Industries K.K.

THE COMPANY

During its early years, Glory Industries, which began operations in March 1918, processed industrial machinery and ship engine parts, etc., under contract with other firms. After 1950, taking advantage of the development of coin-counting machines for the Mint Bureau, the company devoted its energies to developing its own line of manufactured products. Today it is expanding into new products, and produces coin-counting machines, automatic coin-wrapping machines, coin sorters, bill-counting machines, change machines, vending machines, coin lockers, energy-saving automatic bank tellers, and the like. Production therefore tends to be of the high-diversity, low-volume type.

Before improvement, the company's production methods took the form of lot processing, which could easily handle high-diversity, low-volume production in both parts processing and assembly. The resulting long production times and numerous intermediate interventions made the process inefficient, and because diversity could be accommodated, the number of products tended to proliferate. As pressures intensified for faster product delivery, the firm began to consider how its operations could be improved.

In the parts processing department, in particular, unnecessary interventions and lot inspections were common, due to a layout based on machine type and inefficiencies in the transportation of equipment and materials. Furthermore, transportation routes were not fixed, and production could be managed only by an experienced coordinator.

To make improvements, it was first necessary to train and motivate personnel. Accordingly, we began by trying to spread industrial engineering (IE) concepts: company managers participated in Shigeo Shingo's IE course at the Institute of Management Improvement, and we also had Mr. Shingo visit the firm regularly. Along with receiving his diagnoses and advice, we held in-house IE training sessions for shop leaders.

At present, improvements are being promoted in the form of independent activities within each shop, with shop leaders playing a central role.

The layout of the parts processing department was changed so that machines were arranged according to the order of processes and transportion, and inspection and waiting times were shortened. This resulted in a single-item-flow production system and in small-lot, divided production; the concomitant frequency of setup changes meant that setup time reduction became indispensable for increasing productivity. Improvements began with the introduction of QDC dies at the company's sheet metal plant and with jig positioning and workpiece clamping systems at the machine plant. Conveyor lines were introduced for transportation within the plants.

Below, we consider several cases of improvements aimed at shortening setup times.

APPLICATIONS OF SMED

Improvements on a Multipurpose Press

For simple items produced in very small lots, processing was carried out with multipurpose dies on a 25-ton press.

Because there were approximately thirty hole diameters involved, centering and slide adjustments were performed when dies were exchanged. To position the product, the product was scribed, punches were aligned, and contact standards were adjusted. Adjustment sites were therefore numerous and each setup change took thirty-five minutes.

As a result of our improvements, the die set is now always secured to the 25-ton press. By changing the kinds of punches and boss-securing bosses according to hole diameters, punches and bosses for holes of all diameters can be attached at a single touch (*Figure 15-1*). The product is now positioned with a gauge, and parts used

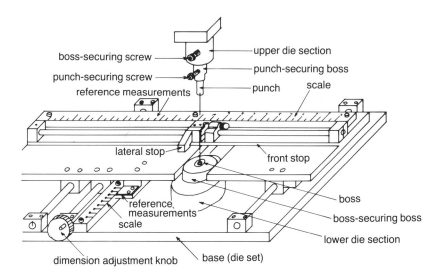

FIGURE 15-1. Improvements on a 25-Ton Multipurpose Press

infrequently can be adjusted by using a reference scale. By this means, setup time was cut to five minutes.

Improvement for a Multipurpose V-Bending Die

As with the multipurpose press above, in this example no special V-bending dies were manufactured, and a 25-ton press was used. Because dies had to be changed according to plate thickness, however, thirty minutes were needed for die preparation, exchange, and the alignment and measuring of the product.

In the improved operation, dies for securing upper and lower dies are permanently attached to the 25-ton press and made so that, by mere insertion, V-die punches in the upper die and V-groove dies in the lower die can be changed in accordance with plate thickness (*Figure 15-2*). Bending-angle adjustments are eliminated by standardizing the die heights and punches with respect to plate thickness. Bending measurements can set contact standards by means of a gauge, and adjustments can be made using a reference scale for parts used infrequently. These improvements lowered setup time to four minutes.

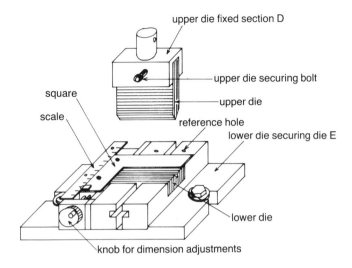

FIGURE 15-2. Improvement for a Multipurpose V-Bending Die

Improved Tip Changing on a Spot Welder

The tip of a spot welder is selected and changed according to the thickness of the plate to be welded, the material involved, its shape, etc. To dissipate heat generated during welding, copper tubing circulates coolant through the tip. This means that coolant hoses must be changed at the same time tips are changed (*Figure 15-3*).

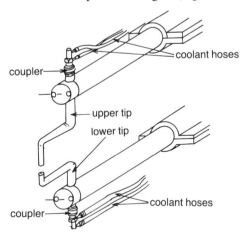

FIGURE 15-3. Spot Welder Tips

Before improvement this operation took thirteen minutes, since it involved a threaded connection and pipe seal was wrapped around the threads before a new tip was screwed on (*Figure 15-4, left*).

In the improved process the connection is made with an air hose high coupler. Since this coupler can prevent coolant leakage, it is now possible to carry out the setup change in three minutes (*Figure 15-4, right*).

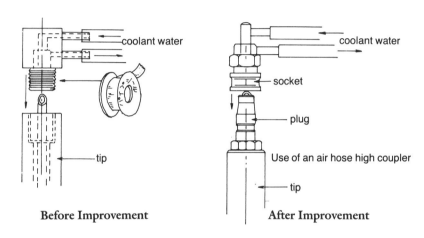

FIGURE 15-4. **Tip Changing on Spot Welder**

Improved Caulking Table Mounting Hardware

Previously, on a rotating friction mechanism-type caulking machine, the caulking table and mounting hardware fit into a socket. A wedge was needed to remove them. Since several sizes of caulking table were used, an operation to center the table with the punch was carried out after the table was attached to the mounting hardware. Setup changes took five minutes (*Figure 15-5*).

One-touch mounting and removal were made possible by integrating the caulking table onto a straight shaft and using a milling chuck on the mounting section (*Figure 15-6*). Adding pilot holes to the mounting section eliminated the operation in which the table was centered with the punch. These improvements have made it possible to complete the setup in thirty seconds.

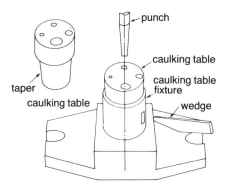

FIGURE 15-5. Caulking Machine Setup Before Improvement

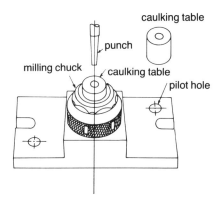

FIGURE 15-6. Improved Caulking Machine Setup

Clamp Improvement

Originally, bolts and clamps had to be removed when circumferential cutting was done on an end mill because they would get in the way (*Figure 15-7*). This procedure took one minute.

Now, end mill circumferential cutting can be done immediately, since an improved clamp can be turned and pushed down simply by loosening a nut by one-half revolution (*Figure 15-8*). This has reduced the time required to twelve seconds.

— *(Reported by Ichiryo Ozaki, Production Technology Section)*

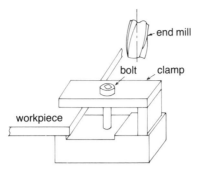

FIGURE 15-7. Clamp Removal from End Mill

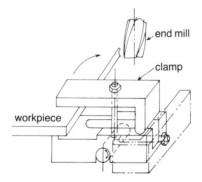

FIGURE 15-8. Improved Clamp Removal from End Mill

16

Achievement of SMED Through Company-Wide Activities
Kyoei Kogyo K.K.

THE COMPANY

Kyoei Kogyo produces supplies for offices, homes, and factories in its plants in Hiratsuka and Kyoto. The company, with headquarters in Tokyo, was founded in 1948 with capital of ¥440 million (about $1.8 million). It employs approximately 500 workers.

Each year, approximately 300,000 filing cabinets are made in Kyoei Kogyo's plants, accounting for a market share of roughly 70%. More than the large number of units we produce, the high degree of customer confidence in our products makes us proud. Each of our employees shares the technical capacity to send highly dependable products to the companies we serve.

Ever since the company's founding, we have devoted unceasing efforts to improving our equipment and to increasing our technical mastery in order to provide goods worthy of the firm's reputation for reliability. By continuing to strive for company-wide standardization and quality control, we earned MITI's Ministerial Prize, the highest honor a manufacturer can receive.

Achievements like this surely derive from the energy we have poured into equipment improvements and technical education; our motto is "high quality, high efficiency, and low cost." Recently, however, customer needs have diversified and we have entered an age in which we can no longer be satisfied merely with standardization.

Orders for diverse goods have increased, as have demands for custom-made items that cannot be handled as continuous orders. In addition, shipments must often go out within one to three days of receiving an order. It has become necessary to devise ways to plunge swiftly into production without diluting the quality of our goods.

271

At this juncture, we adopted the SMED concept and, benefiting from Mr. Shingo's guidance, we have followed this approach for the past several years. Not knowing where to start at first, we implemented changes as instructed by Mr. Shingo. We also have adhered to his strong advice that we try things out. "If you can't figure out how to do something," he said, "talk it over with your machines." In addition, making use of IE and other techniques, groups from each shop have actively put forward proposals for improvement and tested them (*Figure 16-1*).

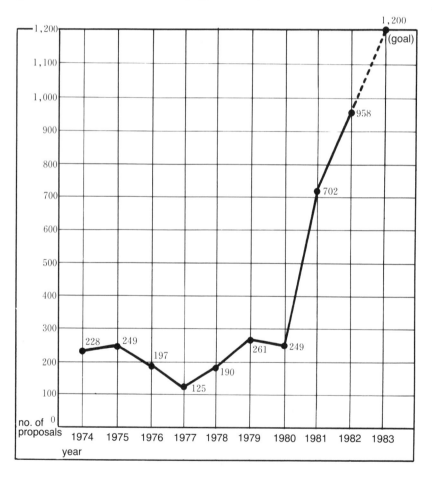

FIGURE 16-1. Total Annual Numbers of Proposals

We asked Mr. Shingo to visit the firm every two months, and during those two months we came up with as many issues as possible and tried to put into practice our own ideas for dealing with them. At his next visit, we reported to Mr. Shingo on this process and on our results, received his advice and criticism, and concentrated on making sure that his guidance was reflected in the next issues we took up.

Group proposals have now increased, and there has been a rapid rise, too, in the annual number of proposals made — roughly a fourfold increase since this method was inaugurated. With our objectives clearly before us, we hope to continue with even greater efforts in the future.

Below, we present several examples of improvements for press dies and setup methods.

APPLICATIONS OF SMED

Improvement in Strike-Adjusting Type Cutting and Piercing Dies

Before improvement (*Figure 16-2*), the process had several characteristics. First, when the workpiece dimension Y was standard, only two quick processes were needed to complete processing; but when dimension Y varied, the punch on X had to be detached, and processing encompassed four operations. Second, since die heights were irregular, heights had to be matched and adjustments carried out for each operation. Third, a skilled worker was needed to set up the punch on X.

This process was changed in three significant ways (*Figure 16-3*). First, dies on the left and right were made independent, so that even if dimension Y varies, left-to-right adjustments can be made on a slide rail [5]. Positioning is determined with a knock pin [9], and the die is bolted down. Bolts are designed to carry out their functions with one turn or less. Second, because die heights are standardized to the press being used, no height adjustments are needed. Third, since strike-type dies are involved, there is no attachment operation whatsoever for the upper die, and the lower die need be only lightly attached.

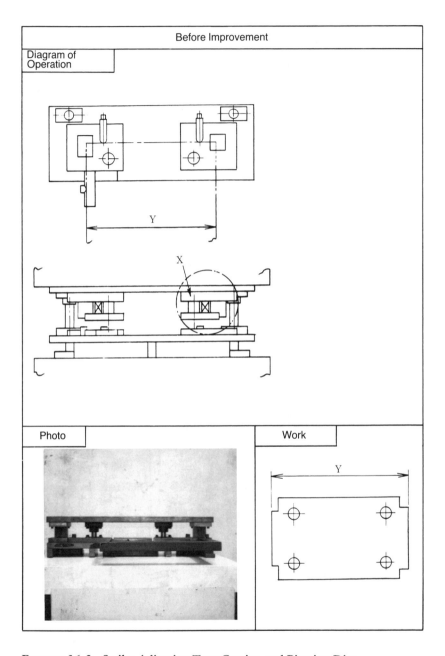

FIGURE 16-2. Strike-Adjusting Type Cutting and Piercing Dies
Before Improvement

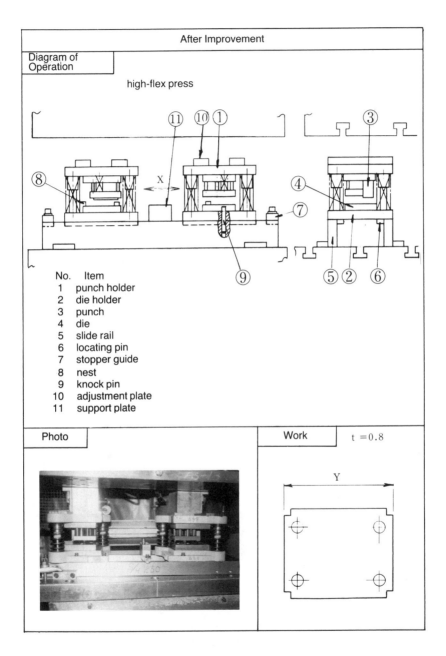

After Improvement

Diagram of Operation

high-flex press

No.	Item
1	punch holder
2	die holder
3	punch
4	die
5	slide rail
6	locating pin
7	stopper guide
8	nest
9	knock pin
10	adjustment plate
11	support plate

Photo

Work   t = 0.8

FIGURE 16-3. Strike-Adjusting Type Cutting and Piercing Dies After Improvement

The effects of this change were pronounced:

- *Setup time reduction.* Before improvement the setup had taken one worker fifteen minutes. After improvement it took one worker one and a half minutes. With ten setups a day, about thirty-nine hours were saved each month.

- *Improved safety.* Since adjustments can be made with few openings where the workpiece enters, strike dies are safe.

- *Ease of operation.* Setup and processing operations became easy even for unskilled workers.

These changes were effected at a cost of approximately ¥100,000 ($413) for one die; the usable parts of existing dies were also utilized.

Improvement of Two-Story Strike-Type Bending Dies

The arrangement before improvement is shown in *Figure 16-4*. Processes were divided into *A* and *B*, and either two presses were used or two types of die were lined up on one press. When the two processes were carried out on the same press, time was required for die shut height adjustments. Since the press brake was a long machine, additional delays were occasioned by left-to-right height determinations when lining up the two dies. In addition, technical skill was required to achieve precise bending angles and flat surfaces.

Figure 16-5 shows the improvements made. Processes *A* and *B* have now been broken down vertically into a two-step process, with *A* on the first story and *B* on the second story. Both upper and lower stories have been made into strike-type dies. The upper die attachment process has been eliminated; it is sufficient to tighten the lower die lightly. Process *A* involves a flat surface and since it would be unstable merely to press down with [3] in process *B*, die adjustment blocks [7] are used to create stability.

As a result of these changes, the following effects were observed:

- *Setup time reduction.* Before improvement, each setup had taken one worker thirty minutes. After improvement, it took one worker three minutes which, with four setups a day, meant about forty hours saved each month.

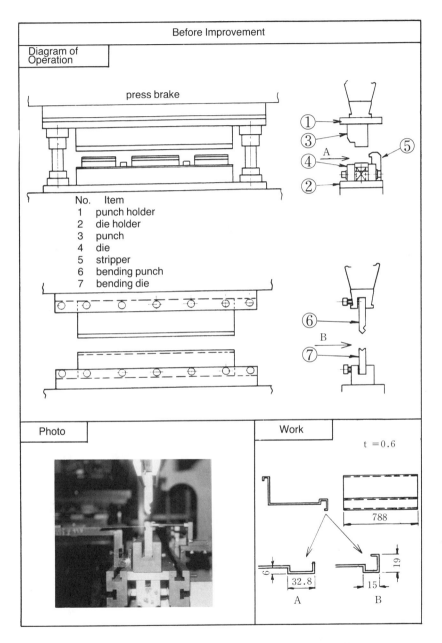

FIGURE 16-4. Two-Story Strike-Type Bending Dies Before Improvement

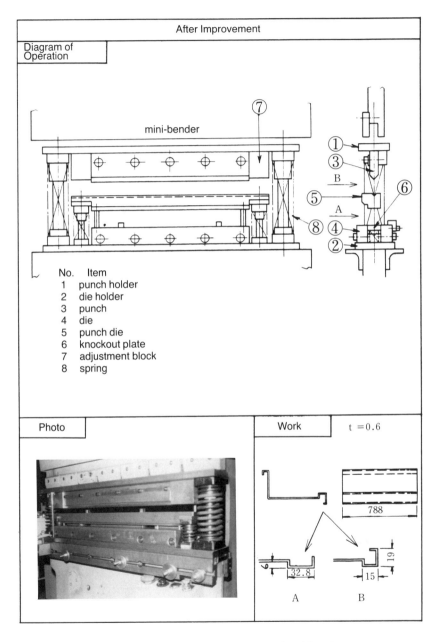

FIGURE 16-5. Two-Story Strike-Type Bending Dies After Improvement

- *Improved safety*. Strike dies are safe because they can be adjusted with few openings for the workpiece to enter.

- *Improved operations*. The worker no longer needs to move sideways, so fatigue diminishes and operating rates rise.

- *Ease of operation*. Setup and processing operations have become easy even for unskilled workers.

This was done at an estimated cost of approximately ¥500,000 ($2066) for one die.

Improved Setup Methods for a Long Bending Die

Before improvement, as shown in *Figure 16-6*, a bending die two or three meters long was taken by two workers from a specific die rack far away, transported to the appropriate press, and mounted. Upper and lower dies were transported separately. On occasion, dies were in danger of being dropped because of crossed signals between the two workers, and some injuries occurred. Setups were also troublesome and lacking in safety because the upper dies were stored upside down and had to be righted after they had been delivered to the press.

To improve the setup, a movable die storage truck was built immediately adjoining the press so that dies no longer had to be brought from remote storage (*Figure 16-7*). Upper and lower dies are set into position on this truck, and items liable to fall are attached with auxiliary fixtures. When a setup is carried out, the truck is moved so as to align the die and press center. Because rollers are provided underneath, the die moves easily when pushed sideways. Attachment sites on the dies have been modified to permit alignment of dies and press holders.

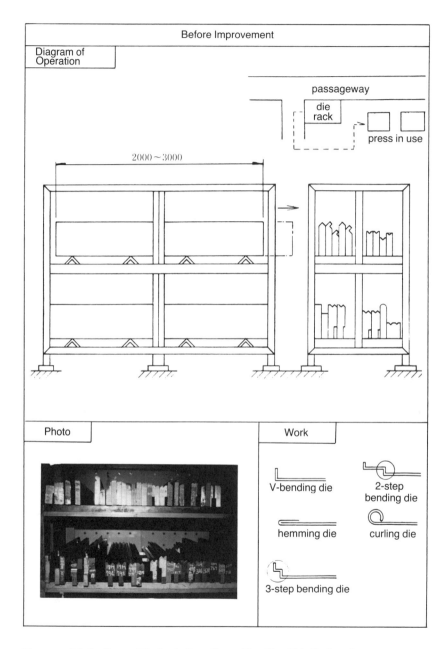

FIGURE 16-6. Setup Methods for a Long Bending Die Before Improvement

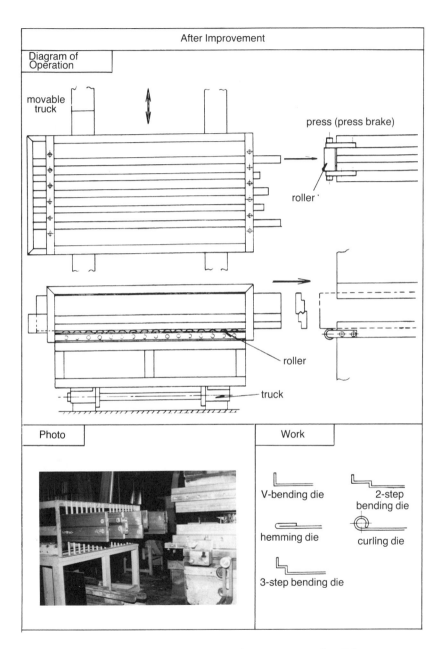

FIGURE 16-7. Improved Setup Methods for a Long Bending Die

Among other effects of this improvement are the following:

- *Setup time reduction.* Before improvement each setup took two workers ten minutes to perform. After improvement, it took one worker two and one half minutes which, with eight setups a day, meant about fifty-one hours saved each month.

- *Improved safety.* Eliminating die transportation and the positioning of upper and lower dies eliminated the danger of dies falling and hands getting caught.

- *Easier setups*

This was done at an estimated cost of ¥100,000 ($413), which covered the purchase of materials; workers did nearly all the required construction.

Improved Transfer Die Setup Operations

As shown in *Figure 16-8*, before improvement, the setup operations for transfer dies required tightening two of the four bolts in the upper and lower dies, a task that involved groping into the frame from the back of the press. Because die heights were not fixed, slide adjustments were made for each changeover. Die positioning involved centering with the shank and measuring by forward and backward rotation. Dies were slid off a forklift to be mounted on the press.

Figure 16-9 shows the changes that were introduced. First, the number of die-clamping bolts has been reduced to two each for upper and lower dies so that clamping can be done from the front of the press. In addition, special clamps are used that take die heights and spaces into consideration. Next, all die heights have been made uniform, eliminating slide adjustments. Positioning blocks are attached to the sides of the die and press, so that one-touch setting occurs when a die is pushed back. Finally, the die to be exchanged is placed on rollers in front of the press and free bearings are attached to the bolster so that the die can be moved manually by light pushes.

Among the effects of these changes:

- *Setup time reduction.* Before improvement, each setup had taken two workers four hours to perform. After improvement, it took three workers ten minutes which, with seven setups per month, meant a savings of approximately fifty-two and a half hours.

- *Material savings.* Pool production fell to one-third of the previous level and the number of pallets used for storage dropped from sixty boxes to twenty. The remainder were used in other ways.

- *Ease and cleanliness of operation.* The operation became easier because groping inside the press frame was eliminated. In addition, workers' uniforms stayed cleaner.

All of this was done at an estimated cost of ¥450,000 ($1860) for ten dies and five presses.

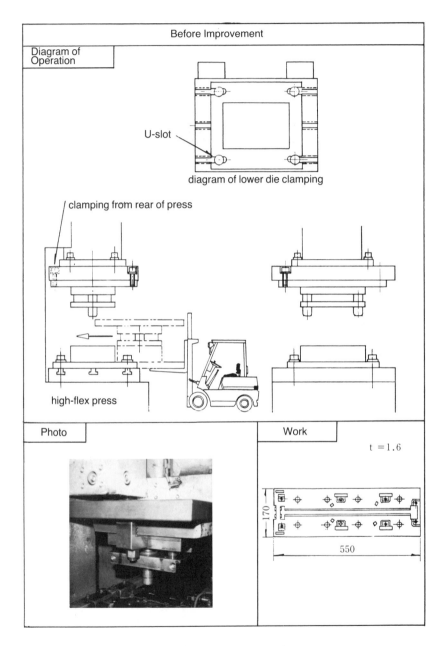

FIGURE 16-8. Transfer Die Setup Operations Before Improvement

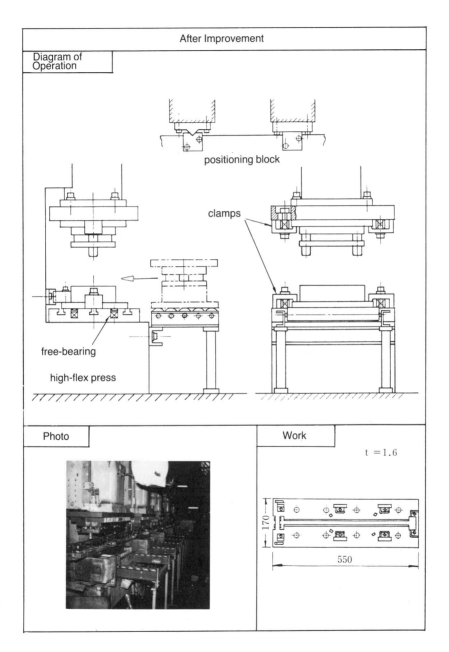

FIGURE 16-9. Improved Transfer Die Setup Operations

17

SMED in Tire
Manufacturing Processes
Bridgestone Tire Co., Ltd.

THE COMPANY

Bridgestone Tire, Ltd. was founded in 1931 in the city of Kurume, in Fukuoka prefecture. It was the first tire maker in Japan funded with domestic capital, and its basic philosophy was to produce tires domestically in Japan, using indigenous technology. In addition to serving the needs of domestic users by selling low-priced, quality goods, the company wanted to try to cover the costs of rubber imports by exporting manufactured goods.

After overcoming numerous difficulties and achieving the goal of domestic production, the firm has promoted bold, positive methods of management, and in 1981 ranked at the top of the domestic rubber industry and fifth in the world.

In addition to tires and tubes, Bridgestone produces in its twelve domestic and five overseas plants belts, hoses, fenders, and other items for industrial use; it also makes golf balls and miscellaneous other goods. Headquartered in Tokyo, the company in 1982 had sales of ¥490 billion (over $2 billion) and employed 17,400 workers. In June of that year, it was capitalized at ¥26.83 billion (close to $111 million).

APPLICATIONS OF SMED

Improving Drum Width Changes for Tire Molding

This is an operation in which tires are made by assembling prefabricated sections.

In tire molding operations, it is necessary to mold a number of tire sizes on a single molding machine. Jigs, as well as drums, are

287

switched according to tire size. To cut the switching time, entire drums used to be changed after being prepared in external setup.

With the increasing trend toward high-diversity, low-volume production, the number of drums proliferated. Not only did these require considerable investment, but there was no space around the molding machines. Thus, it became necessary to reduce the length of time required for setup operations by some other means.

Figure 17-1 shows the operation before improvement, and *Figure 17-2* the operation after improvement. Studies of the type and magnitude of forces acting on the drums revealed that springs and bands could provide sufficient clamping force. As a result, it was possible to eliminate clamping and loosening operations for forty-eight bolts, thus shortening setup time considerably.

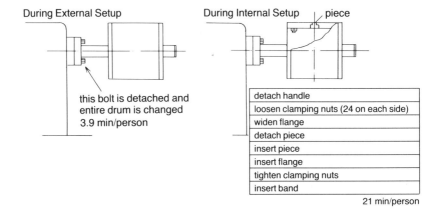

FIGURE 17-1. **Drum Width Changes for Tire Molding During Internal and External Setup**

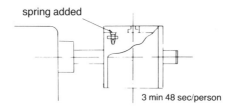

FIGURE 17-2. **Improved Drum Width Changes for Tire Molding**

PCI Change Improvement

This process prevents thermal contraction and improves the performance of vulcanized tires. PCI rims must be changed according to tire size, but because this was done behind the vulcanizing machine, the operation was hampered by space restrictions. Moreover, the weight of the rims made the changeover difficult.

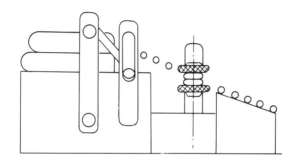

detach bolt and change integrated ring

insert knob (a)	insert knob (b)
set shoe	set shoe
detach bolt	detach bolt
detach bottom ring	detach bottom ring
reverse	prepare ring
detach bolt	detach bolt
detach top ring	detach top ring

60 min/2 people, 4 sets

FIGURE 17-3. PCI Change Before Improvement

Before improvement, this was a two-man operation (*Figure 17-3*). To make the job easier and less time-consuming, several improvements were made (*Figure 17-4*):

- Rims were divided into two sections and only the necessary sections were switched (no bolting or unbolting).
- Scaffolding was installed.
- A storage area was provided for spare drums.
- Operating procedures were changed.

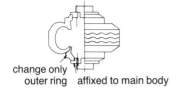

change only outer ring affixed to main body

detach bottom ring (a)	detach bottom ring (b)
set bottom ring	set bottom ring
detach top ring	detach top ring
set top ring	set top ring
reversal operation	ring preparation
set bottom ring	

2 min 48 sec/2 people, 4 sets

FIGURE 17-4. PCI Change After Improvement

As a result of these improvements:

- Changeover time was reduced from sixty minutes for two workers to two minutes and forty-eight seconds for two workers preparing two sets.

- Rim weights were reduced by one half.

- Safety and organization were improved by the installation of scaffolding and a storage area.

The cost of making these improvements was ¥55,000 ($227) per set for rims and attachments, and ¥10,000 ($41) per machine for scaffolding and storage areas.

Reduced Times for Changing Rubber Extrusion Mouthpieces

This is a process in which rubber sheets produced by a kneading process to become tire surfaces are shaped by an extruding machine.

Specific shapes were extruded with a holder bearing a mouthpiece. They were then attached to the front of the extruding machine. Lengthy mouthpiece changeovers not only lowered the operating rate of the machine, but also adversely affected weight and product quality. As a result, adjustment operations proliferated and chaos resulted.

The operation before improvement is shown in *Figure 17-5*, and the operation after improvement in *Figure 17-6*. Two main changes were made:

- Identical holder spares were constructed, so that the next mouthpiece could be prepared in external setup.

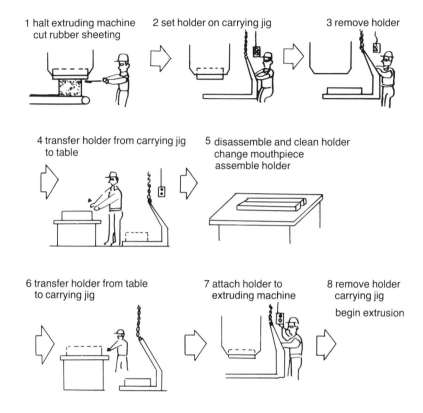

FIGURE 17-5. **Changing Rubber Extrusion Mouthpieces**

- A holder switching jig was made, which not only exchanged holders, but made it possible to perform holder disassembly, mouthpiece exchange, and holder assembly.

As a result of these changes:

- Changing time was reduced by three-fourths, from two minutes to half a minute, making small-lot extrusion possible.

- Quality during changeovers stabilized at an early stage when adjustments were eliminated.

- It became possible to make the switch by push-button control.

- Holders no longer had to be moved for disassembly.

All of this was done at a cost of ¥480,000 ($1983) per machine.

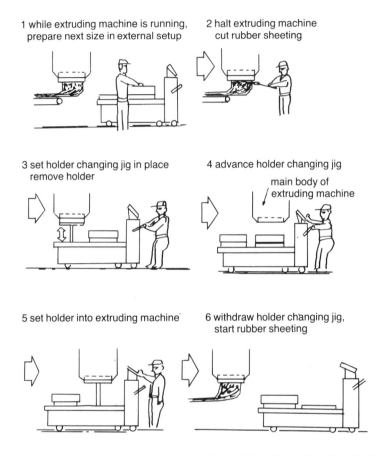

FIGURE 17-6. Reduced Times for Changing Rubber Extrusion Mouthpieces

One-Touch Rubber Extrusion and Indicator Line Setting

This is a process in which rubber sheets produced by a kneading process to become tire surfaces are given specific shapes and marked with indicator lines.

To facilitate product classification, from one to five sizes of indicator lines were made in five colors on rubber given a specific shape on an extruding machine. Setting and adjusting these marks took a great deal of time (*Figure 17-7*).

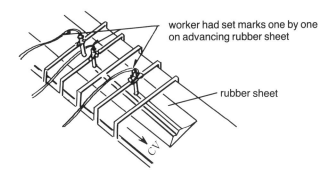

FIGURE 17-7. Rubber Extrusion and Indicator Line Setting

Figure 17-8 shows what we did to improve this procedure. Since the position at which indicator lines were set was determined from the center, we constructed an indicator line setting device. Preparation during external setup became possible, and the device could be automatically dropped and set when the leading edge was detected.

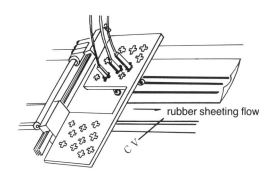

FIGURE 17-8. One-Touch Rubber Extrusion and Indicator Line Setting

Before improvement, twelve to thirteen meters of the sheet had been used by the time the operation was running satisfactorily. After improvement, less than one meter was needed.

Moreover, by shifting the marking to external setup and automating the setting of the indicator line, it became possible to reduce the chaos involved in switching tire sizes.

These improvements were done at a cost of ¥ 300,000 ($1240).

Improved Switching of Bead Molding Formers

This is a process in which rubber is coated onto bead wires and a predetermined number are wound together.

Winding formers must be changed according to tire size. Since this takes time with heavy formers, a way was sought to lighten the work and simultaneously reduce the time it took (*Figure 17-9*).

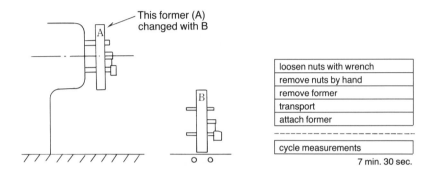

FIGURE 17-9. Switching Bead Molding Formers Before Improvement

After improvement, the operation consisted of the following:

• A four-point truck for attaching, removing, and storing formers was constructed (*Figure 17-10*).

• The first former was loaded onto the truck's holding dish and the next former was set by rotating the dish 90° (*Figures 17-10, 17-11*).

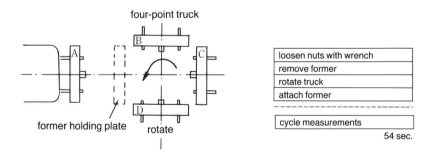

FIGURE 17-10. Four-Point Truck for Switching Bead Molding Formers

Former Truck Movement

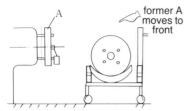

reduction in time for mounting
and removal of formers

FIGURE 17-11. Use of Four-Point Truck for Switching Bead Molding Formers

FIGURE 17-12. Former Clamping Holes

- Attachment and removal were simplified by making former clamping holes pear-shaped (*Figure 17-12*).

The results of improvement were pronounced. Because formers no longer had to be lifted, the work was lighter. Furthermore, with a reduction in the number of operating steps and simplification of individual steps, changeover time was reduced from seven and a half minutes to fifty-four seconds.

The improvement was accomplished at a cost of ¥50,000 ($206) for the four-point truck.

Improvement of Operations for Setting Rubber Sheets on Cords

This is a process in which rubber sheets are joined to rubberized cords at specific gauge, width, and setting positions.

Fairly long changeover times were needed because the setting positions for the sheets had to be changed in response to cord sizes. This required precise positioning adjustments. Before improvement, a rule was used to measure the distance from the center to the cutter, and clamping was done with screws (*Figure 17-13*).

After improvement, as shown in *Figure 17-14*, operations were moved to external setup by means of a position-setting spacer, and locating pins for setting the spacer were attached at the center of the shaft and on cutters.

As a result of this improvement, the need for fine adjustments was eliminated. Furthermore, with a time reduction from the previous one minute and twelve seconds to twelve seconds, near one-

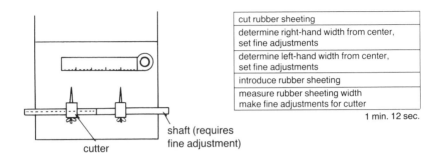

cut rubber sheeting	
determine right-hand width from center, set fine adjustments	
determine left-hand width from center, set fine adjustments	
introduce rubber sheeting	
measure rubber sheeting width make fine adjustments for cutter	

1 min. 12 sec.

FIGURE 17-13. Setting Rubber Sheets on Cords

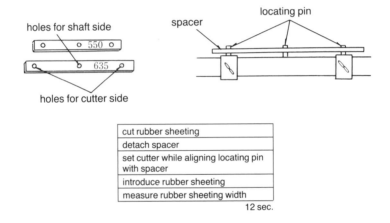

cut rubber sheeting
detach spacer
set cutter while aligning locating pin with spacer
introduce rubber sheeting
measure rubber sheeting width

12 sec.

FIGURE 17-14. Improved Operation for Setting Rubber Sheets on Cords

touch changeovers became possible. In addition, product quality stabilized.

The improvement was accomplished at a cost of ¥ 20,000 ($83) for spacers (for materials only; construction was done in-house). The locating pins were made in-house; no special costs were incurred.

THE INTRODUCTION OF A SYSTEM
OF DEMONSTRATION SETUPS

In 1977, concurrently with activities to improve production efficiency, our adoption of the SMED system yielded substantial results. In the past two or three years, however, results have not materialized in proportion to our efforts. For this reason, we have decided to approach SMED by introducing a system of demonstration setups and training activities.

Plant managers, section chiefs, department heads, and related personnel observe actual setup operations in the shop, look for problem areas, exchange opinions, and work toward solutions. Public notice of demonstration setups is given at the work site, and a record of accomplishments for all setup operations is posted.

Education and training are carried out to foster the capacity to recognize problems and to solve them, and we have made a game of setup improvements and instituted a system of cooperation among all employees.

The results of these setup improvement efforts are shown in *Figure 17-15*.

— *(Reported by Masashi Komata)*

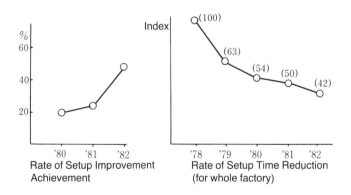

FIGURE 17-15. Results of Setup Improvements

18
Using SMED for Aluminum Die-Casting Dies
Tsuta Machine and Metals Co., Ltd.

THE COMPANY

Founded in 1922, Tsuta Machine has gone through a number of transformations and currently produces aluminum alloy die castings. Monthly production averages 300 tons. Various kinds of machine processing, precision machine parts construction, and machine design are carried out at our machine division. For aluminum die castings, in particular, we perform integrated production, from die design to product machining. Tsuta Machine has both headquarters and plant in Himeji City. The company employs 230 workers.

IMPLEMENTING SMED

Although we had heard there were plants in which die-casting die changes were being performed within five to ten minutes, we could not imagine how. We had assumed it was probably a matter of casting machines with low relative die closing capacities, and so doubted Mr. Shingo's claim at a lecture he gave for us that eight to fifteen minutes was sufficient for switching dies on machines of 800 or more tons.

In addition, we learned from Mr. Shingo that there were procedures for introducing SMED into a plant, and for the first time we heard the terms "internal setup" (IED) and "external setup" (OED).

Half a year later, we were surprised when we actually saw a 70-ton crank press die-changing operation for which Mr. Shingo was providing guidance. We were determined to tackle die changes for die-casting machines, and resolved to reduce our setup time to nine

299

minutes or less. On reflection, we realized that the difference between die changes on a press and on a (side-opening) die-casting machine was merely a matter of whether the dies were attached vertically or horizontally.

Our guiding thought was that separating IED and OED, assigning IED(internal setup) operations as much as possible to OED(external setup), and eliminating die height adjustments on the press would mean the elimination of tie bar nuts. With this knowledge we soon grew confident that the difference involved was simply one of attachment orientation. Having actually observed SMED on a press, we became eager to achieve the same results.

First, we divided the operations into internal and external setup, by asking ourselves whether any operations could be performed without stopping the machine and transferring to external setup all those we were able to identify. We also thoroughly improved internal setup operations (*Table 18-1*).

An overview of the improvements shows:

- Elimination of extrusion rod links (screw connections abandoned in favor of a system of engagement)

- Elimination of individual coolant hose connections (coolant lines grouped by attaching a manifold)

- Elimination of preheating in internal setup (moved to external setup)

- Elimination of die-closing adjustments (die thicknesses standardized for each machine)

- Reduction of the number of die clamps (from sixteen to eight) by attaching a die cradle; four clamps were set on the fixed section and four on the movable section

To accomplish this, first we divided quantity casting dies at the die-casting plant into three categories:

A. Two-part dies (fixed die and mobile die only)
B. Four-part dies with horizontal cylinders (with right and left movable cores; removed as one piece)
C. Four-part dies with vertical cylinders (with right and left movable cores; removed as two pieces)

	Category	Description of Improvement (Implementation)	Method
IED 1	close coolant cock and all hydraulic valves	turn off coolant water cocks before last shot; do not shut hydraulic valves	
4	detach coolant hoses	concentrate coolant lines	use manifold and couplers
5	remove knockout joint clamping nuts	eliminate by means of stripper plate spring and extrusion rod	
6	loosen tie bar	not needed when die thicknesses are standardized	
7	remove clamps on movable die	improve clamps; standardize bolt diameters	use ratchet wrench
8	raise die with hoist	set at specific location in external setup	
9	remove knockout joint	(same as 5)	
10	remove clamps on fixed die	(same as 7)	
11	with hoist, remove die from machine	time reduced by joint use of horizontal die insertion rack and hoist	
12	with hoist, insert die in machine	(same as 11)	
13	align sleeves (use jig)	time reduced through die standardization and positioning	use positioning stoppers and cradles
14	attach fixed jig clamps	(same as 7)	
15	attach knockout joint	(same as 5)	
16	tighten knockout joint, attach nuts	(same as 5)	
17	attach movable die clamps	(same as 7)	
18	attach coolant hoses	(same as 4)	
19	adjust die closing force	(same as 6)	
21	preheat, set operating conditions	advance preheating in external setup	
OED 2	prepare next die		
3	put tools in order		
20	prepare pallet for castings		

TABLE 18-1. Overview of Improvements

We then devised different methods of combining these dies for attachment (*Figure 18-1*):

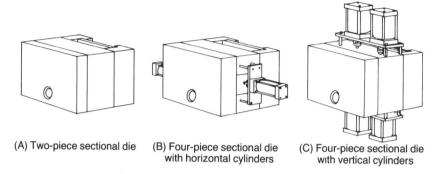

(A) Two-piece sectional die   (B) Four-piece sectional die   (C) Four-piece sectional die
                    with horizontal cylinders   with vertical cylinders

FIGURE 18-1. Methods for Combining Dies

A-A, A-B, A-C
B-A, B-B, B-C
C-A, C-B, C-C

To move the dies, we decided to use hoists and roller conveyors in combination. This made it possible to reduce the changeover time from two hours to twenty minutes; but we still had not reached the single-minute level.

At this point we took up the next improvement. By simplifying centering for the connection of sleeves and die sleeves and by providing die cradles, we came closer to breaking the ten-minute mark, bringing the time down to eleven minutes. Using Mr. Shingo's book *Fundamental Approaches to Plant Improvement*,* we next set about studying procedures introducing SMED. We first selected two machines of 250-ton die-closing capacity and decided to use two-part dies of type A.

To train for single-minute die changes, we used either Saturdays or Sundays, when the production line was shut down. We also practiced internal setups three times to increase our skill. There was some uncertainty at first, but looking at our procedures chart as we

---

* EDITOR'S NOTE: This book is not available in English translation.

conducted parallel operations, we verified each movement at the signal of a whistle and checked for safety as we proceeded.

Although it was only a dry run, the first time we aimed for a SMED change in this way, we easily finished in less than ten minutes. As we became more accustomed to the operation, we were able to complete two dry runs in five minutes without any trouble.

The machine operators, who had previously thought it reasonable for a die change to take two hours, were convinced that we were successful only because we were doing dry runs, so we decided to preheat the dies in external setup and actually try casting. We did feel somewhat uneasy about die height adjustments. Since dimensions had been made uniform to 500 ± 0.1, it was feared that at the time of injection the molten liquid might spatter. In fact, however, there were no leaks. What is more, with a machine precision tolerance of ± 0.1, we became confident that it would work. As *Figure 18-2* illustrates, die A was removed and die C was attached; the time it took until the first product was cast was three minutes and twenty-five seconds.

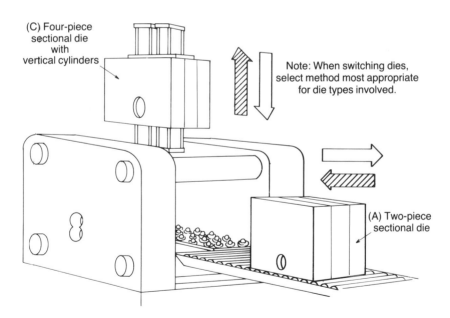

FIGURE 18-2. Example of a Die Changing Method

APPLICATIONS OF SMED

Die Standardization

Standardizing the dimensions of each die part for each type of machine made die bar dimension adjustments unnecessary. Also, centering and die clamping were simplified (*Figure 18-3*).

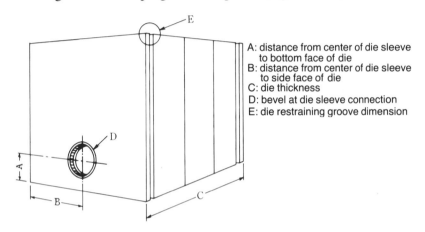

A: distance from center of die sleeve to bottom face of die
B: distance from center of die sleeve to side face of die
C: die thickness
D: bevel at die sleeve connection
E: die restraining groove dimension

FIGURE 18-3. **Standardization of Die Parts**

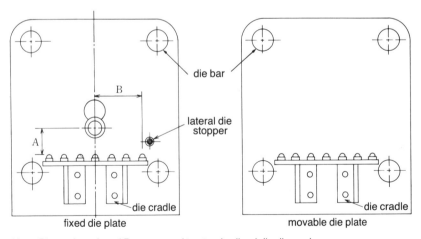

Note: Dimensions A and B correspond to standardized die dimensions.

FIGURE 18-4. **Die Positioning and Centering**

Die Positioning and Centering

Figure 18-4 shows the fixed and movable die plates with the stopper and respective die cradles attached. These made centering and positioning easy.

Die Movement and Locating Ring Engagement

The relationship between the horizontal die insertion rack and the die casting machine is shown in top and front views in *Figure 18-5*. Inserting and removing dies on rollers makes it possible to perform these operations easily by hand. Moreover, time previously spent waiting for a crane has been eliminated (*Figures 18-6, 18-7*, and *Plate 18-1*).

In addition, the locating ring can be engaged with the machine by linking the movable die and pressing it against the fixed element when intermediary jig (A) is inserted after the die is aligned (*Figure 18-7*).

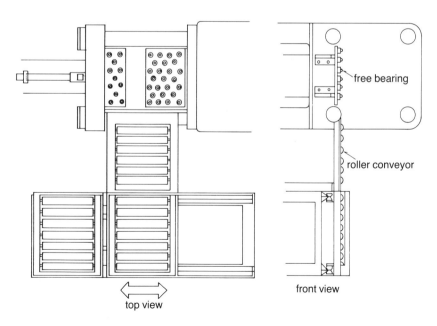

FIGURE 18-5. Die Insertion Rack and Die Casting Machine

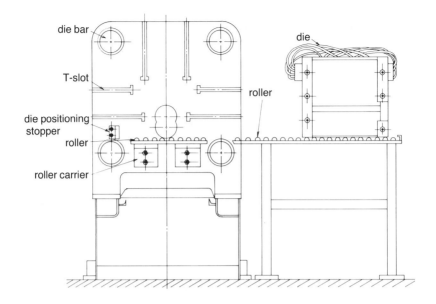

FIGURE 18-6. Die Movement (Horizontal Feed)

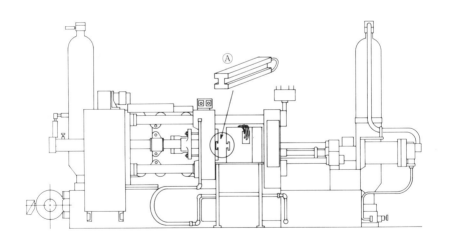

FIGURE 18-7. Locating Ring Engagement

A   B

PLATE 18-1. Die Movement

Improvement of Fixtures

It was possible to standardize clamping hardware because die clamping site thicknesses had all been made uniform. Screw-loosening operations were also made easier by fitting springs around bolts (*Figure 18-8*).

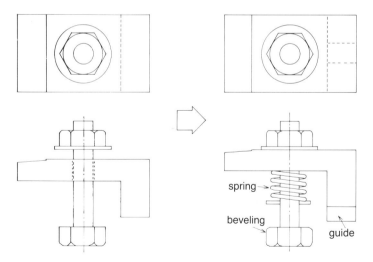

FIGURE 18-8. Improvement of Fixtures

Engagement of Fixed Die Sleeve and Plunger Sleeve

To make engagement of the fixed die sleeve and the plunger sleeve easier, bevels and R's were provided at the faces that came together. *Figure 18-9* shows the dimensions of the improved sections of the fixed die sleeve and the plunger sleeve.

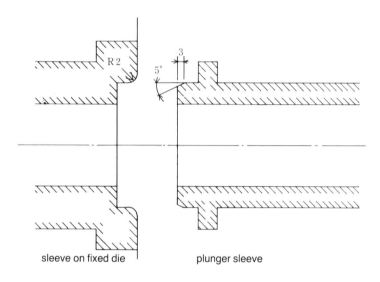

sleeve on fixed die   plunger sleeve

FIGURE 18-9. **Engagement of Fixed Die Sleeve and Plunger Sleeve**

Improved Method for Connecting Stripper Plates and Cylinder

Figure 18-10 shows an improved method for connecting stripper plates and a knockout cylinder. Before improvement, the connection had been made with screws and nuts. After improvement, it was sufficient to insert a knockout rod.

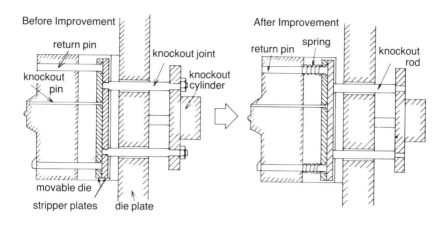

FIGURE 18-10. Improved Method for Connecting Stripper Plate and Cylinder

Improved Coolant Line Connections

We adopted a manifold-type method by which drainage lines could be attached as a group. *Figure 18-11* shows the arrangement of supply and drainage lines on the noncavity side of a movable die.

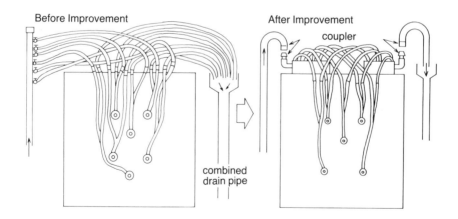

FIGURE 18-11. Improved Coolant Line Connections

Die Preheating

Figure 18-12 shows two methods of preheating with a burner. On the left, the burner flame enters through the sleeve hole. On the right, preheating is done from the bottom with an oblong burner.

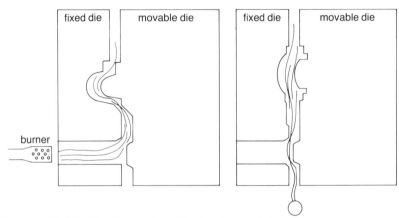

FIGURE 18-12. Two Examples of Preheating with Burners

Use of an Internal Spraying Device

Providing a spraying mechanism within the die eliminates the need to attach and adjust a device for spraying a die separation agent. This makes possible substantial setup time reductions. In addition, since spraying is done in parallel with die movement, the shot cycle is shortened and spraying direction becomes more accurate. It becomes

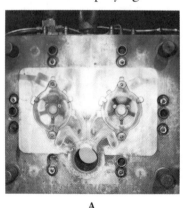

A   B

PLATE 18-2. Examples of Internal Spraying Device

possible, in effect, to coat the die with the die separation agent (*Figures 18-13, 18-14*, and *Plate 18-2*).

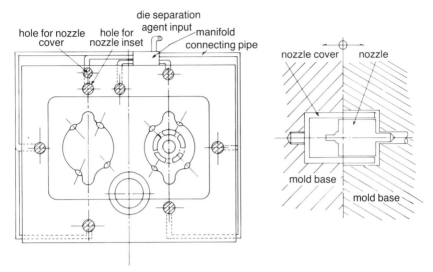

FIGURE 18-13. Internal Spray

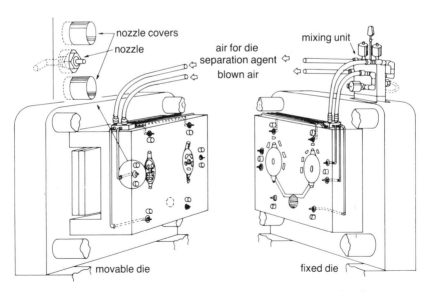

nozzle covers serve as covers for insert nozzles set into opposing die

FIGURE 18-14. Internal Spraying Mechanism

The Use of Figured Air Vents

Use of figured air vents (of the type shown in *Plate 18-3* and *Figure 18-15*) reduced baking of the vents, so die cleaning operations became easier.

PLATE 18-3. **Example of Figured Air Vent**

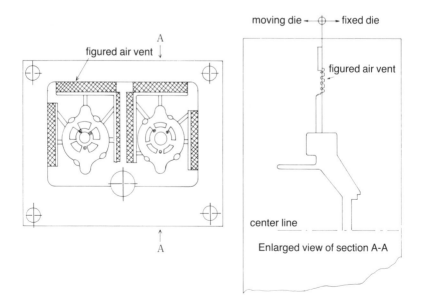

FIGURE 18-15. **Figured Air Vent**

Figured air vents were embedded symmetrically in multiple ob-
lique vent slots in both the fixed and movable dies, creating a thin
"figured weave-shaped" vent. This not only reduced the incidence of
baking, it also promoted air flow, so that flow defects and pin holes
showed up less frequently. Along with lowering the number of defects, this brought about an improvement in the shot cycle and made
low-pressure casting practical.

EFFECTS AND COSTS OF IMPROVEMENTS

To minimize costs accompanying the application of SMED to
die-casting die changes, we used leftover materials, constructed intermediary jigs, assembled roller conveyors, and made clamping
hardware. Costs for the purchase of springs, free bearings, and the in-
house repair of certain dies came to less than ¥ 30,000–¥ 50,000 per
die (about $124–$206). With SMED we were able to change dies in
an average of ten minutes. In terms of the die categories mentioned
earlier, setup times were as follows:

- Type A: within five minutes

- Type B: within seven minutes

- Type C: within nine minutes

In sum, with shortened setups, an average of three to four die
changes are carried out daily on each machine. Operating rates have
risen considerably. Where products used to be stocked for fifteen to
twenty days, they are now stocked for two days, a 90% reduction.
Operations have become easier since the space around machines has
become more orderly — this depends on layout, too — and work
clothes no longer get dirty during setups.

Using sprayers mounted inside dies to apply the die separation
agent has helped eliminate die adjustments. This helped us overcome
the problems inherent in applying SMED to automatic machines.
With one-touch engagement of the die and machine stripper plates,
SMED has become easier for dies requiring insertion.

— *(Reported by Ken'ichi Tamano)*

19

The Shingo One-Touch
Die Exchange System:
The Boltless Method

CONTRADICTIONS IN PAST DIE EXCHANGE METHODS

A Vague Sense of Objectives

I wonder if, when changing dies, you have ever called into question such issues as the following:

- Why must bolts be used?

- Why is it necessary to perform that final, teeth-clenching tightening?

- Why must dies be "fixed"?

- Why must upper and lower dies (in molding, fixed and movable dies) be bolted separately?

We repeat die changing operations unquestioningly, do we not, for one reason only: because they have always been done that way.

When we act without giving careful thought to our objectives, we frequently kick ourselves later for having done something stupid. With setup work, as with anything else, a closer look at our objectives often leads us to wonder why we are doing things the way we are.

The Purpose of Die Clamping

Dies are clamped for three reasons, whether for presses, plastic molding machines, or die casting machines:

- To make upper and lower dies (or fixed and movable dies) engage correctly all the time

- To prevent misalignment of rams and dies (on a press) or nozzles and dies (on a molding machine), due to wobble or some other similar cause

- To make it possible to open them

Problems with Past Methods

Past methods intended to respond to these objectives suffered from several shortcomings.

In the case of a molding machine or die casting machine, a die was like a mountain climber clinging to a sheer cliff, affixed in mid-air to the machine's die mounting plate only by the strength of bolts. If the grip of a bolt were in the least bit loose, then gravity and vibration would cause the die to fall. Newton's laws apply to more than just apples!

Even on a press, a die might appear to be safely secured because it sits on a bolster, but, as with a molding machine, there is a danger that vibration will cause lateral slippage.

If dies could be kept from slipping by some other means, then the need to fasten bolts tightly would nearly disappear.

Only two objectives remain, then:

- To open a die, the upper and lower die sections (fixed and movable dies) must be secured to the machine.

- Since guide pins and guide bushings will come off if a die is tilted too much, extreme die inclination should be prevented.

These two objectives, however, surely do not necessitate tightening bolts with one's teeth clenched.

Bolts must be turned many times with a wrench to tighten what could be taken care of in one second with a clamp or similar device. Laboriously climbing stairs is inefficient when we have elevators to whisk us upward.

Dies are equipped with guide pins and guide bushings that can correct misalignments to a certain extent. In that case, one might ask, is it not all right to allow a little bit of wiggle when tightening bolts as long as there is some guarantee that the die will not slip beyond a certain amount? It might even be, in fact, that securing a die to a machine is bad for the die.

One often hears that no matter how well the die is made, it cannot produce precision goods because the press is old and there is play in the ram. Perhaps, however, when play is intentionally created between the ram and die, precision goods can be produced on surprisingly old presses as long as the dies are in good shape. This will be explained in greater detail later on, where an example will be given.

THE BIRTH OF A NEW METHOD

The new method was conceived during a consulting visit to a plastic molding plant in Osaka. As I watched a die changing operation, I was suddenly moved to wonder, as a layman might, if there were not some slightly easier way to do things. From that point on, I considered the matter from various angles and worked my way back to questioning conventional methods as described above.

In the beginning, we limited ourselves to searching for a new method of changing dies for plastic molding machines. We investigated the problem through repeated trial and error. It was a plastics factory in the city of Otsu, in Shiga, that first tried out the new method for us. On this occasion, as shown in *Figure 19-1*, individual bolts — just in case — were set up on top of the holder and these bolts were gently turned once with a wrench during the first trial.

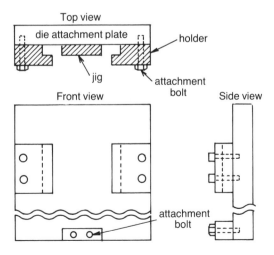

FIGURE 19-1. **The Boltless Method**

By no means, however, were these conventional attachment bolts. They played the role of spacers to prevent inclination of the die, and that is why a single turn was sufficient. Since the holder and jig protected against die slippage, no clamping bolts were required.

Next, we tried loosening the bolts we had used as spacers. We were somewhat apprehensive, for this was the first time this counterintuitive move had been made in Japan or anywhere else. No difficulties arose, however. Even after a month, no dies had been damaged and no defective goods had shown up. A new method had been born.

This was the genesis of the Shingo method of one-touch die exchange. I called this method the boltless method to describe the absence of not only clamping bolts, but also of any means of clamping to the machine (*Figures 19-1, 19-2*).

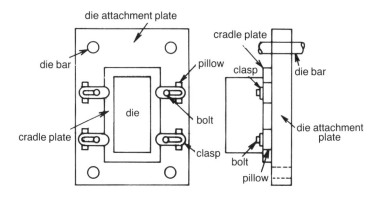

FIGURE 19-2. **Conventional Method**

Quick die change systems involving mechanisms to secure dies to machines by means of hydraulic clamps or the like are commercially available (*Figure 19-3*), but the boltless method, although similar in that the die is changed with a single movement, is entirely different in two respects:

- A number of die-handling advantages arise from the fact that the die is not clamped to the machine. (Details will be explained later.)

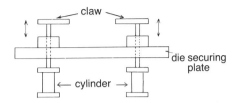

FIGURE 19-3. **Hydraulic Clamp Method**

- The boltless method is a low-cost technique because it is not dependent on devices. (It can be implemented with equipment costing only one-fourth that of the commercial systems referred to above — ¥ 100,000, or about $413, as opposed to ¥ 400,000).

HOW THE BOLTLESS METHOD IS USED

In situations where bolts are used for clamping, this new method can be applied either as is or with minor modifications. Examples of implementation of the method so far include:

- Setup changes for molding machine dies

- Setup changes for press dies (including trimming dies, bending dies, piercing dies, and drawing dies)

- Setup changes for the arms of a robot used for extracting products from a molding machine

- Setup changes for jigs for an automatic turntable-type machine

Since the boltless method constitutes a conceptual approach, it can be widely used in various situations, as long as a little ingenuity is put into applying it in forms appropriate to the conditions in specific plants. Indeed, to date, each firm that has used the boltless method has done things its own way. It will be helpful for you to think about how the method might be adapted to conditions in your company as you read the examples presented below.

The Boltless Method for Molding Dies

We will first discuss an application of the boltless method to plastic molding.

Preparation for Adoption

To prepare for adopting the method, several steps must be taken.

1. Standardize cradle plate dimensions for each molding machine. If standardization is rushed, however, large cradle plates will end up being used for small dies and this will be uneconomical.

In the past, standardization reached a dead end here, but this impasse can be overcome if, for each molding machine, similar sizes of dies are separated and permanent relationships are fixed (for example, between these five dies and machine 1 and those five dies and machine 2). This is, of course, what happens in principle. Standardization of cradle plate sizes is never uneconomical when the haphazard use of dies is abandoned.

Figure 19-4 indicates which cradle plate dimensions should be standardized, and *Figure 19-5* the relationships between molding machines and dies.

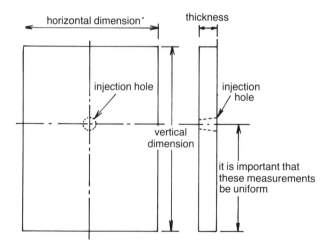

FIGURE 19-4. **Cradle Plate Standardization**

Die Use Chart			
Machine No.	OZ	Die Name	Die Dimensions
1	2OZ	X − 001	65 × 50 × 5
		X − 002	63 × 50 × 5
		X − 003	66 × 49 × 4
		X − 004	65 × 50 × 4
2	4OZ	Y − 001	30 × 60 × 5
		Y − 002	95 × 60 × 6

FIGURE 19-5. Die Use Chart

2. Select holders and jigs whose dimensions and materials match the dimensions, weights and materials of the dies.

3. Determine the appropriate clearance between holder and cradle plate. From the point of view of die insertion, it is desirable to have ample clearance between the holder and cradle plate. From the point of view of die positioning accuracy, on the other hand, it would be better to have no clearance at all. A compromise between these two extremes should be chosen. On the basis of our experience so far, 0.1–0.2 mm seems appropriate. The crucial thing is that insertion be easy and that there be no problems with accuracy. You should determine this for yourself (*Figure 19-6*).

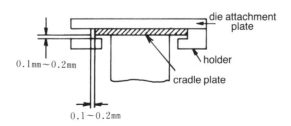

FIGURE 19-6. Clearance Setting

4. Standardize all new and active dies for the boltless method.
When standardizing, the usual approach is to begin by standardizing new dies, since a great deal of time and trouble goes into rebuilding the numerous dies already on hand. Even more trouble will be caused, however, unless all dies are standardized for the boltless method. Since we want to eliminate setup time losses immediately, the idea of starting from new dies is rather beside the point. We cannot afford to be so easygoing if we want to live through the cutthroat competition in the struggle for survival. On the other hand, standardizing dies that are not used at all amounts to waste.

While new dies may be ordered with standardized dimensions, existing dies may be classified as *active, dormant,* and *obsolete* (*Figure 19-7*). Giving priority to the standardization of active dies used daily will have an immediate economical effect. For dormant dies, it is less expensive to attach the existing dies in advance to extra, standard-dimension cradle plates, change them using the boltless method, and then, after they have been used, modify the standard-dimension cradle plates so they can be used for other dormant dies.

Category	Categorization Criteria	Proportion
active	dies used every day	1/3
dormant	dies used only once every three months or so	1/3
obsolete	dies no longer used	1/3

FIGURE 19-7. Active, Dormant, and Obsolete Dies

5. Use the boltless method for each machine. When active dies are apportioned to specific molding machines, there will normally be five or six — or at most ten — dies for each machine. Introducing the boltless method for each machine at this point will both give the quickest results and reduce confusion on the shop floor. A die use chart like that in *Figure 19-5* should be constructed first.

6. Eliminate the use of a locating ring. On conventional dies, a round protrusion called a locating ring is attached to the fixed die (*Figure 19-8*). In the past, this ring was fitted into a hole on the molding machine's die attachment plate and aligned with the nozzle. With

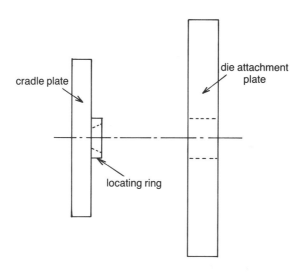

FIGURE 19-8. Locating Ring

the boltless method, however, die position is determined by the circumference of the cradle plate, so there is no need for a locating ring. With a locating ring attached, moreover, a die cannot be mounted merely by lowering it vertically. The numerous horizontal movements needed to fit the ring into the hole are uneconomical and complicate even the boltless method.

7. *Use measures to minimize problems caused by wobbling during die insertion.* When dies are being changed on molding machines, they are generally moved by cranes, lifts, or chain blocks. Yet a die that is wobbling back and forth has a hard time reaching its destination, especially when the 0.1–0.2 mm clearance between the die and holder is invisible to the naked eye. Without some means of dealing with this situation, die insertion will not be easy. Here, three measures are needed (*Figures 19-9, 19-10*):

- Taper the bottom of the cradle plate from every direction.
- Similarly taper the entrance of the holder.
- Attach an anti-wobble guide to the entrance of the holder, bring die into contact with guide, and lower.

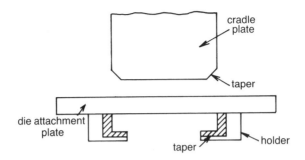

FIGURE 19-9. Tapered Sections

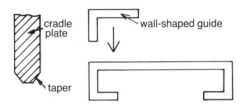

FIGURE 19-10. Anti-wobble Guide

8. Balance suspended dies. When inserting a die into a holder, it is important to suspend the die absolutely vertically, since it will stick to the holder and jam if suspended at an angle. In spite of this fact, suspension fixtures have in the past been attached with the attitude that everything is all right as long as the die hangs. This has led to problems with balance when dies are suspended. The question of balance should be looked into. Possible strategies for dealing with the problem are provided by methods of the kind shown in *Figure 19-11*.

9. Prepare die-moving devices in advance. Two devices for moving dies (cranes, hoists, chain blocks) should be prepared in advance. About three minutes before the die change, the next die should be suspended with one of these, raised just high enough to permit lateral movement. The other device should then be used to lift the old die (*Figure 19-12*).

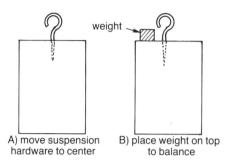

A) move suspension
hardware to center

B) place weight on top
to balance

FIGURE 19-11. Ways to Balance Dies

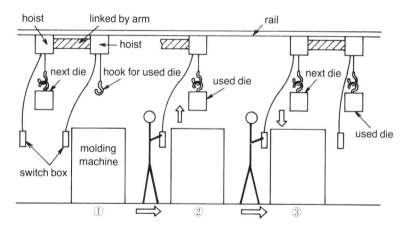

FIGURE 19-12. Operating Procedures for the Boltless Method

10. Standardize die thicknesses. Die insertion and extraction are greatly facilitated by standardizing die thicknesses (heights) and by making the interior of the molding machine uniform for die attachment and removal. This also makes it possible to eliminate stroke adjustments.

Operating Procedures for the Boltless Method

In this example, the preparatory phase of external setup consists of the following steps:

- Pull hoist near and hold ready.
- Suspend die with hoist just high enough to permit lateral movement.
- Prepare receptacle to receive product.
- Preheat die.

Internal setup consists of these tasks:

- Move cylinders back.
- Remove hoses.
- Lift old die with hoist.
- Move hoist sideways and deliver next die to set position.
- Lower next die and insert in holder.
- Detach hoist hook from suspension fixture.
- Connect hoses.
- Adjust conditions for molding.

External setup (after-adjustment) consists of the following:

- Transport old die sideways with hoist.
- Store old die on rack.
- Rearrange hoist.

Results of the Boltless Method for Molding Machines

Internal setup times will vary with the extent to which molding conditions are standardized. Results achieved so far are shown in *Table 19-1*.

The Boltless Method for Press Dies

Press dies can be positioned in much the same way as plastic molding machine dies, with a few minor differences:

- On a press die, dies are inserted from the front.

Name of Company	OZ	Before Improvement	After Improvement	Reduction Ratio
N Company	2	45 min.	1 min.	98%
B Company	4	60 min.	3 min.	95%
E Company	4	60 min.	5 min.	92%
T Company	10	90 min.	5 min.	94%

(Note 1) Post-improvement figures are for internal setup times.
(Note 2) Color changes excepted (for both pre- and post-improvement figures).

TABLE 19-1. **Results at Various Companies**

- Upper and lower die sections are kept together by means of a jig (die set) to integrate the two in advance.
- The raw material is in the form of either fixed lengths or of coil stock.

Presented below are the principal methods developed at various companies.

T-Slots (S Company)

As shown in *Figure 19-13*, fixing die position through the use of a T-slotted press bolster is an extremely inexpensive technique. This

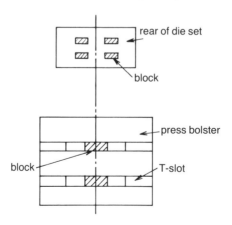

FIGURE 19-13. **Example from the S Company (T-Slots)**

example assumes that the die is incorporated into the die set, and the die functions without being influenced by the press ram. It is used, in other words, as a strike die.

Holders (S Company)

As shown in *Figure 19-14*, a holder and stopper are attached to the top of a bolster and the die is inserted from the front.

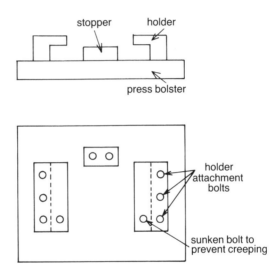

FIGURE 19-14. **Example from the S Company (Holders)**

The following points should be noted:

- The dimensions (horizontal, vertical, thickness) of the cradle plate (or the upper and lower bases of the die set in cases where a die set is used) should be standardized.

- There should be clearance of 0.1–0.2 mm between the holder and cradle plate.

- When the die is not used as a strike die, a holder and stopper should be attached to the ram as well as to the lower die section.

- When, using a die set, the die is used as a strike die and the upper die section is not pushed up by spring action, the die should be raised by the rising ram. A situation like this calls for the kind of strategy illustrated in *Figure 19-15*.

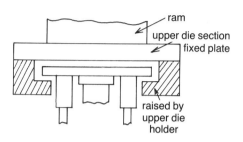

FIGURE 19-15. **Raising the Upper Die**

- As in other instances, standardizing die heights makes things easier by eliminating stroke adjustments for all but difficult bending dies.

- Some tactic is needed to prevent vibration from causing dies to creep forward (*Figures 19-16, 19-17, 19-18*).

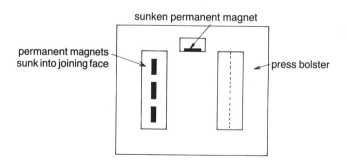

FIGURE 19-16. **Preventing Creeping Motion (with Magnets)**

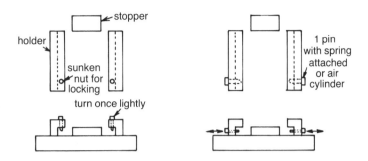

**FIGURE 19-17. The Use of
Sunken Bolts**

FIGURE 19-18. The Use of Pins

Roller Conveyors (A Company)

Dies for presses of up to 60 tons can be mounted and changed by hand; dies for presses of 80 tons and above are too heavy for manual changes. With such large machines, it is difficult to make changeovers in about three minutes without somehow dealing with the problem of die weights. One way to handle this problem is to use a forklift, but a simpler manual operation can be used.

As shown in *Figure 19-19,* when roller conveyors and die lifters are used to switch dies, even 500-kg dies for a 120-ton press can be manipulated relatively easily by human power.

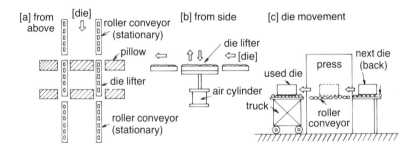

FIGURE 19-19. Die Handline with Roller Conveyors

The following points are important:

- Equipment is easier to use if dies are allowed to move only one way, either front-to-back or the reverse.

- One-way movement will not be feasible unless stoppers are of a movable variety. Up-and-down or slide systems may be used to make stoppers movable. The A Company used a slide system like the one shown in *Figure 19-20*, in which the operator has only to move the die as far as the stopper and the control circuit does the rest.

| pull die as far as stopper | → | die lifter descends and die rests on bolster | → | claws come out to prevent lower die from drifting | → | stopper withdraws |

FIGURE 19-20. **Outline of System**

- Because force is needed for both pushing and pulling, it helps if there are hand grips on the die. Attachment of a handle is surprisingly convenient (*Plate 19-1*).

PLATE 19-1. **Attaching a Handle**

- Mounting a roller conveyor on a cart for carrying dies is convenient because dies can be moved easily by hand when they are placed on or taken from the cart. This is dangerous, however, unless stoppers are attached to the cart (*Figure 19-21*).

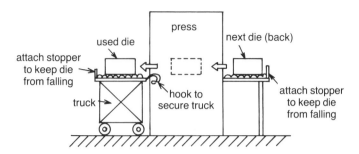

FIGURE 19-21. Cart Stoppers

Cassette Exchange System for Product Section Only (E Company)

Dies are categorized and separated into "mechanical sections" (for making identical strokes for upper and lower dies) and "product-forming sections." The E Company, in addition to using a die set, attaches the mechanical section, including the die set, permanently to the machine and changes only the product-forming section (*Plate 19-2*).

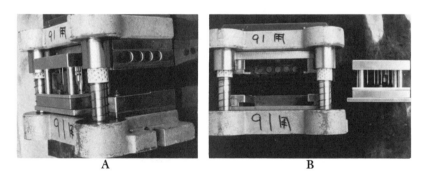

PLATE 19-2. Cassette Exchange System for Product Section Only

As a result, a mechanism that formerly weighed about 30 kg and required a cart to move it to the machine now weighs only 5 kg and can be delivered to the machine with one hand.

The following are points to note concerning this technique:

- Die sets are used.

- Upper and lower die sections to be exchanged are of double die set construction and are integrated by means of guide posts.

- As in the case of the A Company, handles are mounted on those sections of dies that are changed.

- Fit clearances are on the order of 0.1–0.2 mm.

- Permanent magnets are used to prevent creeping motion.

These measures seem to suffice for a 40-ton press. Although I have omitted detailed explanations of machine changes, *Table 19-2* shows examples of internal setup during such changes.
— *(Reported by Kiichi Shingo, Institute of Management Improvement)*

Name of Co.	Tonnage	Before Improvement	After Improvement	Reduction Ratio
A Company	20	45 min.	1 min.	98%
S Company	40	45 min.	1 min.	98%
S Company	60	60 min.	3 min.	95%
A Company	120	90 min.	5 min.	94%

TABLE 19-2. **Results of the Boltless Method as Applied to Presses**

Postscript

The term *setup* applies to much more than the preparation and after-adjustment of a processing operation; it also refers to inspection, transportation and waiting operations. Consequently, the approach — that is, the conceptual stages, corresponding methods, and specific techniques for improving setups — can be applied in precisely the same way to all operations.

In the past, the optimal solution with regard to setup improvement was thought to lie in the following steps:

- Acquire the skills required for setups.

- Conduct large-lot production.

- Control inventory produced as a result of large-lot production by taking economic lot sizes into consideration.

The unspoken assumption behind these steps was the view of resigned and apathetic managers that setups necessarily take a long time. These people, moreover, did not notice the mistaken equation of high-volume production with large-lot production.

Numerous applications of the SMED system have shown that setup time itself can be reduced overwhelmingly and that this, in turn, leads to drastic reductions in inventory. By this means we have moved from "anticipatory production" — a method of production by guesswork — to "confirmed production on the basis of confirmed orders," that is, production that responds to actual orders.

Furthermore, setup time reduction automatically leads us toward a flexible production system that responds to the actual state of demand. It is probably no exaggeration to say that it has given birth to a revolution in production methods. The Toyota Production System can be thought of as a pioneering step in this direction.

SMED was first used in an experiment on a 1,000-ton press at Toyota Motor Company, Ltd. in the fall of 1969. At that time it occurred to me that this approach could be applied not only to press operations, but to other operations as well.

In the fall of 1970, I brought together people from ten plants in M Electric's Television Operations Division. At the meeting, I explained the SMED concept and the results that could be expected from its application. With the idea in mind of applying it to a plastic molding machine, I requested a trial from the president of Dia Plastics, Mr. Tsukamoto, who was extremely enthusiastic about improvements. I told him I would visit his company the following day and explain concrete improvement methods.

When I arrived the next day, I was dumbfounded when I was told, "The single-minute setup is already finished. We did in eight minutes and thirty seconds what used to take one and a half hours to set up."

"But how on earth . . . ?" I asked.

"Well, actually, I rode back to work from M Electric with Mr. Araki, our Manufacturing Section chief, and on the way I said to him, 'How about it? Why don't we try it right away?'

"He had had some production technicians stay late and work on the single-minute setup from 6 P.M. straight through until 3:30 A.M. When they conducted a trial run, the experiment succeeded beautifully in under nine minutes.

"I never would have thought that a setup could be completed in less than ten minutes," President Tsukamoto finished, "but it really can be done."

Thus, SMED can be accomplished surprisingly easily and inexpensively if one makes a positive effort. In this particular case, the total cost was a mere ¥ 30,000 ($124) or so. As a result of further improvements, moreover, setups on the five-ounce molding machine in this example had been cut down to two minutes and fifteen seconds a year and a half later.

In July 1976, I spoke about SMED at a talk sponsored by the Japan Management Association. On that occasion, I began by saying:

"As I look at the list of participants now, I see that people from the same company have come here two and three times. More talk isn't going to help those people achieve SMED, however. Why don't those of you in that category go back right now and try putting it into practice?"

Ten months later, I received an unexpected letter from someone I did not know, the Manufacturing Division chief at Mitsubishi Heavy Industries, a Mr. Hitokuma:

> *I heard you speak on SMED last July. Actually, people from our firm had already attended your lectures, but they had not put anything into practice, so it really hit home when you said that just listening wouldn't get us anywhere.*
>
> *Our Production Technology Division chief and our Planning Division chief came with me, and we agreed that we had to do something, so we decided to experiment.*
>
> *We chose to work on a six-axis boring machine. Around the beginning of this year, setup on this machine took three days. At that point we read things you had written and, rearranging internal and external setup, we somehow shortened the time from twenty-four hours to eight. We never even considered lowering the time to the single-minute range, though.*
>
> *Hearing you speak in person this last time, however, I began to think it might be possible, so the day after the lecture I called the shop supervisor and told him I thought we should reduce setup time on the machine to within nine minutes. He was violently opposed to the idea.*
>
> *"That's absurd, sir. That takes eight hours now. There's no way we're going to do it within nine minutes."*
>
> *That's exactly what I had expected. I then explained to him the difference between internal and external setup and that when I said I wanted to shorten setup time, I meant internal setup time only. I asked him to take another look at the components of the setup and to clearly separate those that were internal from those that were external.*
>
> *The shop supervisor came to me the next day and said, "I've been thinking about it since yesterday, and as long as we're just*

talking about internal setup time, it looks as though we can *shorten it." With the help of technicians we made up a checklist. When the change was implemented a week afterwards, the time had been reduced to four hours and ten minutes.*

At that point I called in the foreman again and told him he had done a good job. But at your recent talk, you said that by performing parallel operations with several people working together at the same time, one can reduce internal setup time even when the number of setup man-hours remains the same. "How about giving parallel operations a try?" I suggested.

"Right," he replied. "The foreman will give me a hand and we'll run some experiments."

In an experiment a week later, the time had been shortened to one hour and fifteen minutes.

I explained next that the elimination of adjustments was most effective in shortening setup times and, with the cooperation of technicians, we made efforts to reduce adjustments significantly while preparing in advance, standardizing functions, introducing intermediary jigs, and so forth. Three weeks later, the time had been cut to twelve minutes and, with further improvement in a number of items, we were able roughly to halve that time, to six minutes and thirty-eight seconds.

At that time we had began a campaign designating the months of July and August as a "SMED Attainment Period." Amusingly enough, the employees secretly referred to this as the "No Way Movement." Since SMED had been achieved on the six-axis boring machine, however, we had the foreman tell about his hard work and the history of this success in front of everyone at a morning meeting early in October. We gathered together foremen from other posts and conducted a number of demonstration setups for them. As a result, the SMED concept spread throughout the plant. At that point we launched a sweeping campaign to shorten setup times. We even required everyone to make an individual report on his or her achievements, objectives, and deadlines.

I am writing you this letter, then, because of my great joy at having realized these epochal results.

I would be honored if you could come to my plant and see our situation for yourself.

Although I wanted to visit the plant and view the situation, I was unable to go at that time. When I finally visited in mid-December and was given a demonstration, the setup had been further improved so that it could be completed in two minutes and forty seconds.

In 1982, the following question came from an American who said he had read my book *Study of the Toyota Production System.*

"In your book it says that a setup that used to take twenty-four hours was reduced to two minutes and forty seconds, but can such things really be done? I wonder if they are not impossible, and I would like a more detailed explanation. . . ."

In my reply, I began by saying:

"That the setup of a six-axis boring machine has been accomplished in two minutes and forty seconds is a fact. I personally timed it with a stopwatch, so there is no mistake."

I then sent him the account given above.

Nonetheless, misconceptions and prejudices abound. One theory holds that SMED will be achieved naturally if thorough preventive maintenance is carried out. Yet SMED and preventive maintenance are entirely different, both in concept and in practical methods.

Another erroneous idea is advanced by some scholars who maintain: "Toyota Motors took thirty years to cut a three-hour setup down to three minutes, and we may hypothesize that during that time they must have had approximately 340,000 practice runs, which agrees entirely with calculations derived from skill engineering formulas."

This is entirely mistaken. When someone asks me to give an example of SMED, I am often not believed when I say merely that a setup that used to take one hour has been cut to three minutes. Because of this, I request a single hour of preparation time and go to the person's plant, where, for a relatively simple press of 100 tons or less, I give the following demonstration:

- I have two fairly similar dies brought out.

- I attach a block to the shorter die to make the die heights the same.

- For centering the dies, I mount a ruler on the far side of the bed to act as a reference plane. I then find the dimensions of the die and prepare two blocks to make up for the distance between the die center and the face of the ruler. At the left and right centers, I make registration marks on the bed and the center of the die with a magic marker.

- With gummed tape, I attach a block roughly 30 mm × 30 mm at the place where the die is bolted down, standardizing the thicknesses of the clamping points on the two dies.

- I have the press operation performed in parallel by two skilled workers, one handling operations on the left and the other on the right.

In this way, I show that the setup that used to take one hour will take three minutes or less.

Experiences like this are testimony that "seeing is believing" and "proof is better than discussion." Since a one-hour operation can be cut to less than three minutes with a single hour of preparation, as in this example, the issue is definitely not one of skill engineering.

The following statement appeared in a piece written by the economics correspondent of a certain newspaper:

> "The fact that, in an hour's time, a tooling setup that formerly took three hours was reduced to five minutes is proof of the extent to which needless operations used to be carried out and the extent to which people used to loaf on the job."

It does not matter how little this reporter may have known about factory conditions. Even his ignorance of SMED did not upset me. I remember my anger, however, at the contempt he showed for workers in the expression "loaf on the job."

Even though such views exist, I would like SMED to be understood correctly as something that is based on a scientific concept, sound methods, and concrete techniques.

As I have said before, the SMED system was born when I first became aware of the notions of internal and external setup(IED and OED) at Toyo Kogyo in 1950. It became a practical reality in 1969 when management at Toyota Motors demanded that I cut to three minutes a setup change that had already been shortened from four hours to an hour and a half. I think the inspiration to shift internal to external setup came to me then because of the great pressure under which I was working.

SMED would perhaps not have been born had it not been for this stringent demand. In this sense, I would like to express heartfelt thanks to Mr. Taiichi Ohno, consultant at Toyota Motors, who afforded me this opportunity. I am filled with admiration for the generous attitude of Mr. Ohno who, when he mentions SMED, always cites me as its creator.

Although it is of primary importance for you to understand the fundamental concepts involved, there is no doubt that knowledge of actual case examples is very effective as well. I wish to express my warm thanks to Mr. Kiichi Shingo, advocate of the boltless method in numerous plants, for his kindness in contributing excellent examples to this book.

I would also like to thank Mr. Kazuya Uchiyama of the Publications Department of the Japan Management Association and to Ms. Eiko Shinoda, who was directly responsible for the project.

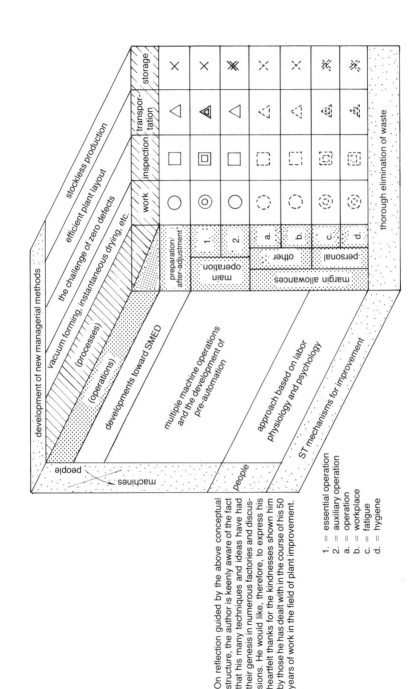

On reflection guided by the above conceptual structure, the author is keenly aware of the fact that his many techniques and ideas have had their genesis in numerous factories and discussions. He would like, therefore, to express his heartfelt thanks for the kindnesses shown him by those he has dealt with in the course of his 50 years of work in the field of plant improvement.

1. = essential operation
2. = auxiliary operation
a. = operation
b. = workplace
c. = fatigue
d. = hygiene

Relationship Between the Structure of Production and Various Improvement Techniques

About the Author

CAREER: 50 YEARS IN FACTORY IMPROVEMENT

First Period: Private Enterprise

1924 While studying at Saga Technical High School, reads and is deeply impressed by Toshiro Ikeda's *The Secret of Eliminating Unprofitable Efforts,* said to be a translation of Taylor's thesis.

1930 Graduates from Yamanashi Technical College; goes to work for the Taipei Railway Factory.

1931 While a technician in the casting shop at the Taipei Railway Factory, observes worker operations and feels the need for improvement. Reads accounts of the streamlining of operations at Japan National Railways plants and awakens to the need for rational plant management.

Reads Taylor's *The Principles of Scientific Management* and, greatly impressed, decides to make the study and practice of scientific management his life's work.

Reads and studies many books, including the works of Yoichi Ueno and texts published by the Japan Industrial Association.

1937 For two months beginning September 1, attends the First Long-Term Industrial Engineering Training Course, sponsored by the Japan Industrial Association. Is thoroughly instructed in the "motion mind" concept by Ken'ichi Horikome.

1943   Transfers to the Amano Manufacturing Plant (Yokohama) on orders from the Ministry of Munitions. As Manufacturing Section Chief, applies flow operations to the processing of depth mechanisms for air-launched torpedoes and raises productivity by 100%.

Second Period: The Japan Management Association

1945   On orders from the Ministry of Munitions, transfers to Ishii Precision Mfg. (Niigata), a maker of similar air-launched torpedo depth mechanisms, for the purpose of improving factory operations.

With the end of the war in August, accepts a post at Yasui Kogyo (Kita Kyushu) starting in April 1946 and moves to Takanabe-cho in Miyazaki Prefecture. Stops by Tokyo at this time and visits Isamu Fukuda at the Japan Management Association, where he is introduced to Chairman of the Board Morikawa. Is asked to participate temporarily in a plant survey to improve operations at Hitachi, Ltd.'s vehicle manufacturing facility at Kasado. Afterwards enters the service of the Japan Management Association.

1946   When asked by a survey team member during process analysis at the Hitachi plant how to treat times when goods are delayed while waiting for cranes, realizes that "processes" and "operations," which had previously been thought to be separate and parallel entities, form a "network of processes and operations" — a systematic, synthetic whole. Reports this finding at a Japan Management Association technical conference.

Invents a method of classifying like operations by counting non-interventions while studying the layout of a Hitachi, Ltd. woodworking plant.

1948 Elucidates the "true nature of skill" in *A Study of 'Peko' Can Operations* at Toyo Steel's Shitamatsu plant.

Between 1948 and 1954, takes charge of Production Technology Courses. Also runs production technology classes at companies.

At a production technology course held at Hitachi, Ltd.'s Fujita plant, begins to question the nature of plant layout. Studies and reflects on the problem.

1950 Perfects and implements a method for determining equipment layout based on a coefficient of ease of transport at Furukawa Electric's Copper Refinery in Nikko.

Analyzes work at a press at Toyo Kogyo and realizes that a setup operation is composed of "internal setup" (IED) and "external setup" (OED). This concept will become the first stage of SMED.

1954 Morita Masanobu from Toyota Motor Co., Ltd. participates in a production technology course at Toyoda Automatic Loom and achieves striking results when he returns to his company. This occasions a series of productivity technology courses inaugurated in 1955. By 1982, eighty-seven sessions of the course had been held, with approximately 2,000 participants.

1955 Observes multiple machine operations at the first production technology training course at Toyota Motor Corp. and is impressed by the separation of workers and machines.

1956 From 1956 to 1958 takes charge of a three-year study of Mitsubishi Shipbuilding's Nagasaki shipyards. Invents a new system for cutting supertanker assembly from four months to three and then to two. This system spreads to Japanese shipbuilding circles and contributes to the development of the shipbuilding industry.

1957 To raise the machining efficiency of an engine bed planer at

Mitsubishi Shipbuilding's Hiroshima shipyards, constructs a spare table, conducts advance setup operations on it and changes workpiece and table together. This doubles the work rate and foreshadows a crucially decisive conceptual element of SMED, that of shifting IED to OED.

Third Period: The Institute for Management Improvement (Domestic)

1959   Leaves the Japan Management Association to found the Institute of Management Improvement.

1960   Originates the "successive inspection system" for reducing defects and implements the system at Matsushita Electric's Moriguchi plant.

1964   From Matsushita Electric's insistence that no level of defects is tolerable, realizes that although selective inspection may be a rational procedure, it is not a rational means of assuring quality.

1965   Stimulated by Toyota Motor's "foolproof" production measures, eagerly seeks to eliminate defects entirely by systematically combining the concepts of successive inspection, independent inspection, and source inspection with "foolproof" techniques.

1966   Works as a business consultant to various Taiwanese firms, including Formosa Plastic Co., Matsushita Electric (Taiwan), and China Grinding Wheel Co. Consulted annually until 1981.

1969   Improves setup change for a 1,000-ton press at Toyota Motor's main plant from four hours to one and a half. Is soon afterward asked by management to cut setup time to three minutes and in a flash of insight thinks to shift IED to OED. With this, a systematic technique for achieving SMED is born.

Notices the difference between mechanization and automation when asked by Saga Ironworks' plant manager Yaya why automatic machines needed to be manned. This observation evolves into the concept of "preautomation" which, Shingo later realizes, is identical to Toyota Motor's "human automation."

1970 Is awarded the Yellow Ribbon Medal for contributions to streamlining operations in the shipbuilding industry, etc.

Fourth Period: The Institute for Management Improvement (International Expansion)

1971 Participates in observation tour of the European machine industry.

1973 Participates in observation tours of the machine industries in Europe and the United States.

1974 Lectures on SMED at die-cast industry associations in West Germany and Switzerland.

On this visit, observes vacuum die-casting methods at Daimler Benz in West Germany and Buehler in Switzerland and grows eager to implement vacuum molding in die-casting and plastic molding.

1975 Grows more enthusiastic about the "zero defects" concept on the basis of the achievement of zero defects in one month at the Shizuoka plant of Matsushita Electric's Washing Machine Operations Division.

Works for improvement based on fundamental approaches including high-speed plating, instantaneous drying, and the elimination of layout marking.

1976 Consults and lectures widely to promote SMED in Europe and the United States.

1977   Treats Toyota Motor's *kanban* system as essentially a scheme of "nonstock" production and develops systematic techniques for the system.

1978   Visits America's Federal-Mogul Corporation to provide on-site advice on SMED.

The sale by the Japan Management Association of an audio-visual set of slides on SMED and preautomation meets with considerable success.

1979   Further success is attained by the Japan Management Association's sale of "zero defects" slides.

Visits Federal-Mogul to give follow-up guidance on SMED.

The collected results of Shingo's experiences and ideas concerning improvement are published.

1981   Makes two trips, in the spring and fall, to provide plant guidance to the French automobile manufacturers Peugeot and Citrœn.

Travels to Australia to observe Toyota (Australia) and Borg-Warner.

1982   Makes follow-up consulting visits to Peugeot and Citrœn in France and is impressed by the considerable results achieved through the application of SMED and nonstock production.

Consults and lectures at the Siemens company in Germany.

Lectures on "The Toyota Production System — An Industrial Engineering Study" in Munich.

Gives lectures at Chalmers University in Sweden.

Lectures at the University of Chicago.

CONSULTING

Below is a list of companies where Shigeo Shingo has given a training course or lecture, or has consulted for productivity improvement.

Industry	Name of Company	
JAPAN		
Automobiles and Suppliers	Toyota Motor Car Co., Ltd. Toyota Auto Body Co., Ltd. Toyo Motor Car Co., Ltd. Honda Motor Co., Ltd. Mitsubishi Heavy Industries Co., Ltd. Daihatsu Motor Car Co., Ltd. Bridgestone Cycle Kogyo Co., Ltd.	Yamaha Motor Co., Ltd. Kanto Auto Works, Co., Ltd. Central Motor Car Co., Ltd. Arakawa Auto Body Co., Ltd. Koito Manufacturing Co., Ltd. (Car parts) Aishin Seiki Co., Ltd. (Parts of Motor Car, Diecast) Hosei Brake Co., Ltd.
Electric apparatus	Matsushita Electric Industrial Co., Ltd. Tokyo Shibaura Electric Co., Ltd. Sharp Electric Co., Ltd. Fuji Electric Co., Ltd. Nippon Columbia Co., Ltd. (Stereo Disk) Stanley Electric Co., Ltd. Matsushita Electric Works Co., Ltd. Matsushita Jutaku Setsubi Kiki Co., Ltd. (House equipment) Matsushita Denchi Kogyo Co., Ltd. (Lighting parts)	Hitachi Co., Ltd. Sony Electric Co., Ltd. Mitsubishi Electric Co., Ltd. Yasukawa Electric Mfg. Co., Ltd. Kyushu Matsushita Electric Co., Ltd. Asahi National Lighting Co., Ltd. Matsushita Denshi Buhin Co., Co., Ltd. (Electric parts) Sabsga Denki Co., Ltd. (Rectifier)
Precision machine	Nippon Optical Co., Ltd. Sankyo Seiki Mfg. Co., Ltd. (Music Box)	Olympus Optical Co., Ltd.
Steel, Non-ferrous Metals and Metal Products	Nippon Steel Co., Ltd. Toyo Steel Plate Co., Ltd. Mitsui Mining and Smelting Co., Ltd. Sumitomo Electric Industries, Ltd. Toyo Can Industry Co., Ltd. Nippon Spring Co., Ltd. Togo Seisakusho Co., Ltd. (Spring)	Nisshin Steel Co., Ltd. The Furukawa Electric Co., Ltd. The Fujikura Cable Works, Ltd. Hokkai Can Industry Co., Ltd. Chuo Spring Co., Ltd.
Machine	Amada Co., Ltd. (Metallic Press Machine) Iseki Agricultural Machinery Mfg. Co., Ltd.	Aida Engineering, Co., Ltd. (Metallic Press Machine) Toyota Automatic Loom Works, Ltd.

Industry	Name of Company	
	Kanzaki Kokyu Koki Co., Ltd. (Machine Tools)	Kubota Ltd. (Engine and Farming Machinery)
	Nippon Seiko Co., Ltd. (Bearings)	Daikin Kogyo Co., Ltd. (Coolers)
	Taiho Industry Co., Ltd. (Bearings)	Nach-Fujikoshi, Co., Ltd. (Bearings, Cutters, etc.)
	Asian Industry Co., Ltd. (Carburetor)	
Rubber	Bridgestone Tire Co., Ltd.	Toyota Gosei Co., Ltd.
	Nippon Rubber Co., Ltd.	Tsuki-Boshi Shoemaking Co., Ltd.
Glass	Asahi Glass Co., Ltd.	Nippon Sheet Glass Co., Ltd.
	Yamamura Glass Bottle Co., Ltd.	Onoda Cement Co., Ltd.
	Noritake China Co., Ltd.	
Marine products	Taiyo Fishery Co., Ltd.	
Mining	Mitsui Mining Co., Ltd.	Nippon Mining Co., Ltd.
	Dowa Mining Co., Ltd.	
Food	Morinage & Co., Ltd. (Confectionery)	Snow Brand Milk Products Co., Ltd.
	Hayashikane Sangyo Co., Ltd.	
Textile	Katakura Industries Co., Ltd.	Gunze Co., Ltd.
	Kanebo Co., Ltd.	Fuji Spinning Co., Ltd.
	Daiwa Spinning Co., Ltd.	Daido Worsted Mills Co., Ltd.
	Teikoku Jinken Co., Ltd.	Asahi Chemical Industry Co., Ltd.
Pulp and Paper	Jujyo Paper Co., Ltd.	Oji Paper Co., Ltd.
	Rengo Co., Ltd.	
Chemicals	Showa Denko Co., Ltd.	Nippon Soda Co., Ltd.
	Tokuyame Soda Co., Ltd.	Ube Industries Co., Ltd.
	Hitachi Chemical Co., Ltd.	Nippon Kayaku Co., Ltd.
	Shionogi Pharmaceutical Co., Ltd.	Fujisawa Pharmaceutical Co., Ltd.
	Shiseido Cosmetics Co., Ltd.	
Others	Nippon Gakki Co., Ltd. (Yamaha Piano)	The Sailor Pen Co., Ltd.
	Saga Tekkosho Co.,Ltd.	Nippon Baruka Kogyo Co., Ltd.
	Zojirushi Mahobin Co., Ltd.	Gihu Dai & Mold Engineering Co., Ltd.
	Iwao Jiki Kogyo Co., Ltd.	Dia Plastics Co., Ltd.
	Koga Kinzoku Kogyo Co., Ltd. (Metallic Press)	Yasutaki Industrial Co., Ltd. (Metallic Press)
	Sanei Metallic Col., Ltd. (Metallic Press)	

Industry	Name of Company	
U.S.A.	Federal-Mogul Corp. Omark Industries Storage Technology Corporation (Industrial products)	Livernois Automation Co., Ltd. Hewlett-Packard
FRANCE	Automobiles Peugeot	Automobiles Citrœn
WEST GERMANY	Daimler Benz Co., Ltd. Bayrisches Druckguss-verk Thurner KG Co., Ltd.	Verband Deutscher Druckgiesseien Co., Ltd. Beguform-Werke
SWITZERLAND	Gebr Buhler Co., Ltd. H-Weidmann Co., Ltd.	Bucher-guyer AC Co., Ltd.
TAIWAN	Formosa Plastic Co., Ltd. Co., Ltd. Formosa Chemicals and Fiber Co.,Ltd. China Grinding Wheel Co., Ltd. Matsushita Electric (Taiwan) Co.,Ltd. Chin Fong Machine Industrial Co., Ltd. (Metallic Press)	Nanya Plastic Fabrication Plywood and Lumber Co., Ltd. Sunrise Plywood Co., Ltd. Taiwan Fusungta Electric Co., Ltd. (Speakers) Super Metal Industry Co., Ltd.
NETHERLANDS	Philips	

PUBLICATIONS

Mr. Shingo's books have sold more than 40,000 copies worldwide. For convenience, all titles are given in English, although most were published in Japanese.

"Ten Strategies for Smashing Counterarguments," *Sakken to Kyoryoku* [*Practice and Cooperation*], 1938.

A General Introduction to Industrial Engineering. Japan Management Association, 1949.

Improving Production Control. Nihon Keizaisha, 1950.

Production Control Handbook (Process Control). Kawade Shobo, 1953.

Technology for Plant Improvement. Japan Management Association, 1955.

"Views and Thoughts on Plant Improvement," published serially in *Japan Management*, 1957. (Through the efforts of Mr. Gonta Tsunemasa, these essays were published together in a single volume by Nikkan Kogyo Shinbun.)

Plant Improvement Embodiments and Examples. Nikkan Kogyo Shinbunsha, 1957.

Don't Discard New Ideas. Hakuto Shobo, 1959.

Key Issues in Process Control Improvement. Nikkan Kogyo Shinbunsha, 1962.

Issues in Plant Improvement. Nikkan Kogyo Shinbun, 1964.

Techniques of Machine Layout Improvement. Nikkan Kogyo Shinbunsha, 1965.

Fundamental Approaches to Plant Improvement. Nikkan Kogyo Shinbunsha, 1976.

"The Toyota Production System — An Industrial Engineering Study," published serially in *Factory Management* (Nikkan Kogyo Shinbunsha), 1979.

A Systematic Philosophy of Plant Improvement. Nikkan Kogyo Shinbunsha, 1980.

The Toyota Production System — An Industrial Engineering Study. Nikkan Kogyo Shinbunsha, 1980. (Editions in English, French and Swedish have also been produced.)

The Single-Minute Setup—A Fundamental Approach. Japan Management Association, 1983.

"180 Proposals for Plant Improvement (Sayings of Shigeo Shingo)," published serially in *Factory Management* (Nikkan Kogyo Shinbunsha), 1980-83.

Index

BOOKS FROM PRODUCTIVITY PRESS

Productivity Press publishes books that empower individuals and companies to achieve excellence in quality, productivity, and the creative involvement of all employees. Through steadfast efforts to support the vision and strategy of continuous improvement, Productivity Press delivers today's leading-edge tools and techniques gathered directly from industry leaders around the world. Call toll-free 1-800-394-6868 for our free catalog.

5 Pillars of the Visual Workplace
The Sourcebook for 5S Implementation
Hiroyuki Hirano

In this important sourcebook recently published by Productivity Press, JIT expert Hiroyuki Hirano provides the most vital information available on the visual workplace. He describes the 5S's: seiri, seiton, seiso, seiketsu, shitsuke (which translate as organization, orderliness, cleanliness, standardized cleanup, and discipline). Hirano discusses how the 5S theory fosters efficiency, maintenance, and continuous improvement in all areas of the company, from the plant floor to the sales office. Presented in a thorough, detailed style, *5 Pillars of the Visual Workplace* explains why the 5S's are important and the who, what, where, and how of 5S implementation. This book includes numerous case studies, hundreds of graphic illustrations, and over forty 5S user forms and training materials.
ISBN 1-56327-047-1 / 353 pages, illustrated / $85.00 / Order FIVE-B180

REVISED!
20 Keys to Workplace Improvement
Iwao Kobayashi

The 20 Keys system does more than just bring together twenty of the world's top manufacturing improvement approaches—it integrates these individual methods into a closely interrelated system for revolutionizing every aspect of your manufacturing organization. This revised edition of Kobayashi's best-seller amplifies the synergistic power of raising the levels of all these critical areas simultaneously. The new edition presents upgraded criteria for the five-level scoring system in most of the 20 Keys, supporting your progress toward becoming not only best in your industry but best in the world. New material and an updated layout throughout assist managers in implementing this comprehensive approach. In addition, valuable case studies describe how Morioka Seiko (Japan) advanced in Key 18 (use of microprocessors) and how Windfall Products (Pennsylvania) adapted the 20 Keys to its situation with good results.
ISBN 1-56327-109-5/ 302 pages / $50.00 / Order 20KREV-B180

PRODUCTIVITY PRESS, DEPT. BK, P.O. BOX 13390, PORTLAND, OR 97213-0390
Telephone: 1-800-394-6868   Fax: 1-800-394-6286

Implementing TPM
The North American Experience
Charles J. Robinson and Andrew P. Ginder

The authors document an approach to TPM planning and deployment that modifies the JIPM 12-step process to accommodate the experiences of North American plants. They include details and advice on specific deployment steps, OEE calculation methodology, and autonomous maintenance deployment. This book shows how to make TPM work in unionized plants and how to position TPM to support and complement other strategic manufacturing improvement initiatives.
ISBN 1-56327-087-0 / 224 pages / $45.00 / Order IMPTPM-B180

JIT Factory Revolution
A Pictorial Guide to Factory Design of the Future
Hiroyuki Hirano

The first encyclopedic picture-book of Just-In-Time, using photos and diagrams to show exactly how JIT looks and functions in production and assembly plants. Unprecedented behind-the-scenes look at multi-process handling, cell technology, quick changeovers, kanban, andon, and other visual control systems. See why a picture is worth a thousand words.
ISBN 0-915299-44-5 / 218 pages / $50.00 / Order JITFAC-B180

Non-Stock Production
The Shingo System for Continuous Improvement
Shigeo Shingo

In the ideal production system, information flows from the customer backward through the manufacturing process and results in total elimination of non-value-adding wastes. That means no inventory, inspection, storage, or transportation. Shingo shows that a Non-Stock Production (NSP) system can become a reality for any manufacturer. Find out how, directly from the master himself.
ISBN 0-915299-30-5 / 479 pages / $85.00 / Order NON-B180

Poka-Yoke
Improving Product Quality by Preventing Defects
Nikkan Kogyo Shimbun Ltd. and Factory Magazine (ed.)

If your goal is 100 percent zero defects, here is the book for you—a completely illustrated guide to poka-yoke (mistake-proofing) for supervisors and shop-floor workers. Many poka-yoke devices come from line workers and are implemented with the help of engineering staff. The result is better product quality—and greater participation by workers in efforts to improve your processes, your products, and your company as a whole.
ISBN 0-915299-31-3 / 295 pages / $65.00 / Order IPOKA-B180

PRODUCTIVITY PRESS, DEPT. BK, P.O. BOX 13390, PORTLAND, OR 97213-0390
Telephone: 1-800-394-6868   Fax: 1-800-394-6286

Manufacturing Strategy
How to Formulate and Implement a Winning Plan
John Miltenburg

This book offers a step-by-step method for creating a strategic manufacturing plan. The key tool is a multidimensional worksheet that links the competitive analysis to manufacturing outputs, the seven basic production systems, the levels of capability and the levers for moving to a higher level. The author presents each element of the worksheet and shows you how to link them to create an integrated strategy and implementation plan. By identifying the appropriate production system for your business, you can determine what output you can expect from manufacturing, how to improve outputs, and how to change to more optimal production systems as your business needs changes. This is a valuable book for general managers, operations managers, engineering managers, marketing managers, comptrollers, consultants, and corporate staff in any manufacturing company
ISBN 1-56327-071-4 / 391 pages / $45.00 / Order MANST-B180

P-M Analysis
An Advanced Step in TPM Implementation
Kunio Shirose, Yoshifumi Kimura, and Mitsugu Kaneda

P-M analysis is an effective methodology for finding and controlling the causes of equipment-related chronic losses. Chronic loss stems from complex and interrelated causes, and in most cases it is very difficult to know how any single cause impacts the overall problem. P-M Analysis is meant to overcome the weaknesses of traditional improvement activities in addressing this type of loss. This book provides a disciplined step-by-step approach to identifying and eliminating causes of chronic equipment-related loss, thorough discussion with good illustrations, and case studies of implementation.
ISBN 1-56327-035-8/ 198 pages / $85.00 / Order PMA-B180

The Sayings of Shigeo Shingo
Key Strategies for Plant Improvement
Shigeo Shingo

Quality Digest calls Shigeo Shingo "an unquestioned genius—the Thomas Edison of Japan." Shingo "offers new ways to discover the root causes of manufacturing problems. These discoveries can set in motion the chain of cause and effect, leading to greatly increased productivity." Hundreds of examples illustrate ways to identify, analyze and solve workplace problems.
ISBN 0-915299-15-1 / 207 pages / $45.00 / Order SAY-B180

PRODUCTIVITY PRESS, DEPT. BK, P.O. BOX 13390, PORTLAND, OR 97213-0390
Telephone: 1-800-394-6868   Fax: 1-800-394-6286

The Shingo Production Management System
Improving Process Functions
Shigeo Shingo

In his final book, Dr. Shingo gives us a comprehensive system for the improvement of production functions, encompassing such diverse topics as value engineering, CAD/CAM, and information management. A handy overview of his brilliant concepts.
ISBN 0-915299-52-6 / 238 pages / $50.00 / Order SHPMS-B180

A Study of the Toyota Production System from an Industrial Engineering Viewpoint
Shigeo Shingo

Here is Dr. Shingo's classic industrial engineering rationale for the priority of process-based over operational improvements for manufacturing. He explains the basic mechanisms of the Toyota production system in a practical and simple way so that you can apply them in your own plant. This book clarifies the fundamental principles of JIT including levelling, standard work procedures, multi-machine handling, and more.
ISBN 0-915299-17-8 / 291 pages / $50.00 / Order STREV-B180

Toyota Production System
Beyond Large-Scale Production
Taiichi Ohno

Here's the first information ever published in Japan on the Toyota production system (known as Just-In-Time manufacturing). Here Ohno, who created JIT for Toyota, reveals the origins, daring innovations, and ceaseless evolution of the Toyota system into a full management system. You'll learn how to manage JIT from the man who invented it, and to create a winning JIT environment in your own manufacturing operation.
ISBN 0-915299-14-3 / 162 pages / $45.00 / Order OTPS-B180

The Visual Factory
Building Participation Through Shared Information
Michel Greif

If you're aware of the tremendous improvements achieved in productivity and quality as a result of employee involvement, then you'll appreciate the great value of creating a visual factory. This book shows how visual management can make the factory a place where workers and supervisors freely communicate and take improvement action. It details how to develop meeting and communication areas, communicate work standards and instructions, use visual production controls such as kanban, and make goals and progress visible. Includes more than 200 diagrams and photos.
ISBN 0-915299-67-4 / 305 pages / $55.00 / Order VFAC-B180

PRODUCTIVITY PRESS, DEPT. BK, P.O. BOX 13390, PORTLAND, OR 97213-0390
Telephone: 1-800-394-6868   Fax: 1-800-394-6286

TPM Team Guide
Kunio Shirose (ed.)

This book makes TPM team activities understandable to everyone in the company. *TPM Team Guide* gives simple explanations of basic TPM concepts like the 6 big losses, and emphasizes the integration of TPM activities with production management. Chapters describe the team-based improvement process step by step, from goal setting to standardization of the improved operations. Team leaders will learn how to hold effective meetings and work with the human issues that are a big part of success. The tools for team problem solving and the steps for preparing a good presentation of results are detailed here as well. Written in straightforward, easy to digest language, with abundant illustrations and cartoon examples. Frontline supervisors, operators, facilitators, and trainers in manufacturing companies will want to use this practical guide to improve company performance and build a satisfying workplace for employees.
ISBN 1-56327-079-X/175 pages / $25.00 / Order TGUIDE-B180

Zero Quality Control
Source Inspection and the Poka-Yoke System
Shigeo Shingo

Dr. Shingo reveals his unique defect prevention system, which combines source inspection and poka-yoke (mistake-proofing) devices that provide instant feedback on errors before they can become defects. The result: 100 percent inspection that eliminates the need for SQC and produces defect-free products without fail. Includes 112 examples, most costing under $100. Two-part video program also available; call for details.
ISBN 0-915299-07-0 / 328 pages / $75.00 / Order ZQC-B180

Implementing a Lean Management System
Thomas L. Jackson with Karen R. Jones

Does your company think and act ahead of technological change, ahead of the customer, and ahead of the competition? Thinking strategically requires a com-pany to face these questions with a clear future image of itself. *Implementing a Lean Management System* lays out a comprehensive management system for aligning the firm's vision of the future with market realities. Based on hoshin management, the Japanese strategic planning method used by top managers for driving TQM throughout an organization, Lean Management is about deploying vision, strategy, and policy to all levels of daily activity. It is an eminently practical methodology emerging out of the implementation of continuous improvement methods and employee involvement. The key tools of this book builds on the knowledge of the worker, multiskilling, and an understanding of the role and responsibilities of the new lean manufacturer.
ISBN 1-56327-085-4 / 182 pages / $65.00 / Order ILMS-B251

PRODUCTIVITY PRESS, DEPT. BK, P.O. BOX 13390, PORTLAND, OR 97213-0390
Telephone: 1-800-394-6868   Fax: 1-800-394-6286

Corporate Diagnosis
Meeting Global Standards for Excellence
Thomas L. Jackson with Constance E. Dyer

All too often, strategic planning neglects an essential first step- and final step-diagnosis of the organization's current state. What's required is a systematic review of the critical factors in organizational learning and growth, factors that require monitoring, measurement, and management to ensure that your company competes successfully. This executive workbook provides a step-by-step method for diagnosing an organization's strategic health and measuring its overall competitiveness against world class standards. With checklists, charts, and detailed explanations, *Corporate Diagnosis* is a practical instruction manual. The pillars of Jackson's diagnostic system are strategy, structure, and capability. Detailed diagnostic questions in each area are provided as guidelines for developing your own self-assessment survey.
ISBN 1-56327-086-2 / 115 pages / $65.00 / Order CDIAG-B251

TO ORDER: Write, phone, or fax Productivity Press, Dept. BK, P.O. Box 13390, Portland, OR 97213-0390, phone 1-800-394-6868, fax 1-800-394-6286. Send check or charge to your credit card (American Express, Visa, MasterCard accepted).

U.S. ORDERS: Add $5 shipping for first book, $2 each additional for UPS surface delivery. Add $5 for each AV program containing 1 or 2 tapes; add $12 for each AV program containing 3 or more tapes. We offer attractive quantity discounts for bulk purchases of individual titles; call for more information.

ORDER BY E-MAIL: Order 24 hours a day from anywhere in the world. Use either address:
　　To order: *service@ppress.com*
　　To view the online catalog and/or order: *http://www.ppress.com*

QUANTITY DISCOUNTS: For information on quantity discounts, please contact our sales department.

INTERNATIONAL ORDERS: Write, phone, or fax for quote and indicate shipping method desired. For international callers, telephone number is 503-235-0600 and fax number is 503-235-0909. Prepayment in U.S. dollars must accompany your order (checks must be drawn on U.S. banks). When quote is returned with payment, your order will be shipped promptly by the method requested.

Note: Prices are in U.S. dollars and are subject to change without notice.

PRODUCTIVITY PRESS, DEPT. BK, P.O. BOX 13390, PORTLAND, OR 97213-0390
Telephone: 1-800-394-6868　Fax: 1-800-394-6286